Question Time 6

150 More Questions and Answers on the Catholic Faith

QuestionTime6

150 Questions and Answers on the Catholic Faith

FR JOHN FLADER

Foreword by Cardinal George Pell

Published in 2024 by Connor Court Publishing Pty Ltd

Copyright © John Flader 2024

ALL RIGHTS RESERVED. Not to be reproduced without the permission of the copyright holder. This book contains material protected under International and Federal Copyright Laws and Treaties. Any unauthorised reprint or use of this material is prohibited. No part of this book may be reproduced or transmitted in any form or by any means, electronic or mechanical, including photocopying, recording, or by any information storage and retrieval system without express written permission from the publisher.

Connor court Publishing Pty Ltd
PO Box 7257
Redland Bay QLD 4165
sales@connorcourt.com
www.connorcourt.com

Nihil obstat: Rev. Peter Joseph, STD
Imprimatur: +Most Reverend Anthony Fisher OP, Archbishop of Sydney
Date: 19 December 2023

The *Nihil obstat* and *Imprimatur* are a declaration that a book or pamphlet is considered to be free from doctrinal or moral error. It is not necessarily implied that those who have granted them agree with the contents, opinions or statements expressed.

ISBN: 9781922815965

Scripture quotations are from the Revised Standard Version, Second Catholic Edition, Ignatius Edition, of the Bible, copyrighted 2006, by the Division of Christian Education of the National Council of Churches in the United States of America, and are used by permission. All rights reserved.

Cover design by Ian James

Printed in Australia

*In memory of St Josemaría Escrivá
who taught me love for the Church*

CONTENTS

Foreword to *Question Time 1* xv

Introduction to *Question Time 5* xvii

Abbreviations xix

I. CATHOLIC DOCTRINE 1

Sacred Scripture 1
   751 The inspiration of Scripture 1
   752 The truthfulness of Scripture 3
   753 The interpretation of Scripture 5
   754 Literary forms in the Bible 7
   755 Discrepancies in the Gospels 9
   756 New translations of the Bible 11
   757 Who is a prophet in the Bible? 13
   758 Cutting off our hand? 15
   759 Does Christ bring peace? 17

Jesus Christ 20
   760 Christ the Messiah 20
   761 Christ the suffering servant 22
   762 Christ's death and our Redemption 24
   763 The Scarlet Thread 26
   764 The Title of the Cross 28
   766 The seamless garment of Jesus 30
   767 The Sudarium of Jesus 32
   768 The chalice of the Last Supper 38

CONTENTS

The Church 39
   769 Blood in Judaism 39
   770 Jewish laws and Christian laws 41
   771 The conversion of Jews 43
   772 Jewish Christians 45
   773 The Jewish Temple 47
   774 Parts of the Jewish Temple 49
   775 The Jewish Synagogue 51
   776 King Herod the Great 53
   777 Herod Archelaus 55
   778 Herod Antipas 57
   779 Herod Agrippa 59
   780 Philip the Tetrarch 61
   781 Hellenists and Hebrews in the Bible 63
   782 Why were Jews and Samaritans not on good terms? 65
   783 The tomb of St Peter 67
   784 The Confession in St Peter's Basilica 70
   785 The Chair of St Peter 72
   786 The ministry of catechist 74
   787 Nazism and the Church 76
   788 Planned Parenthood, eugenics, Nazism and the Church ... 78
   789 Freemasons and the Church 80
   790 Christadelphians 82
   791 Who are the Mormons? 84
   792 Reflections on Cardinal Pell 87

The angels 90
   793 Hierarchy of the angels 88
   794 Knowledge of the angels 92
   795 Questions on the guardian angels 94

CONTENTS

Our Lady and St Joseph 97
   796 Baptism in the early Church 97
   797 The wedding of Mary and Joseph 99
   798 The wedding of Mary and Joseph 101
   799 The Assumption of Our Lady into Heaven 103
   800 The place of Mary's Assumption 105
   801 Was St Joseph assumed into heaven? 107

The Last Things 110
   802 The dead were raised 110
   803 Christ's Ascension and souls going to heaven 112

II. THE SACRAMENTS 115

Baptism 116
   804 Changing the formula for Baptism 116
   805 Consequences of invalid Baptism 118

The Eucharist 121
   806 The Mass as sacrifice 121
   807 Offering the Mass 123
   808 Mass intentions 125
   809 The Mass as centre of all activity 127
   810 The priest in the Mass 129
   811 Care in the Mass 131
   812 Fragments of the host in Mass 133
   813 Changing the words of the Consecration 135
   814 The Supper of the Lamb 137
   815 Masses on-line 139
   816 Women Acolytes and Lectors 141

817 New Latin Mass restrictions 143
818 Regulations on the traditional Latin Mass 145
819 Martin Luther on the Mass 147
820 Luther on the Real Presence 149
821 The age for First Communion 152
822 Communion under both species 154
823 More about Communion under both species 156
824 Communion for Protestants 158
825 Communion for the divorced 160
826 Communion for the mentally impaired 162
827 President Biden and Holy Communion 164
828 Spiritual Communion 166
829 The Eucharistic miracle of Legnica 168

Penance and Holy Orders 171

830 Repentance and absolution 171
831 The Third Rite of Reconciliation for Australia 173
832 Women Deacons? 175

III. MORAL LIFE IN CHRIST 179

General Moral Issues 180

833 The call to holiness 180
834 Discerning a vocation 182
835 Learning to forgive 184
836 How to grow in patience 186
837 Abortion and Excommunication 188
838 Kinesiology and the faith 190
839 Children with same-sex attraction 192

840 Pope Francis and civil unions 194
841 *Amoris Laetitia* and the Year of the Family 196
842 Parental rights in education 198
843 Using human remains as compost 200

Gender issues 203
844 Treating gender dysphoria 203
845 The Church and gender variance 205
846 Assisting transgender children 207
847 Conversion therapy legislation 209
848 A conversion therapy testimony 211
849 Gender terminology 213

Covid-19 and vaccinations 216
850 The morality of Covid-19 vaccinations 216
851 Should vaccination be mandatory? 218
852 Life with Covid-19 restrictions 220
853 The bright side of isolation 222

Euthanasia 224
854 The value of life 224
855 Attending the dying 226
856 Why the call for euthanasia 228
857 Is euthanasia legal in many countries? 230
858 Medical care at the end of life 232
859 Sharing the suffering of others 234
860 Finding meaning in suffering 236
861 Euthanasia and financial pressure 238
862 Cooperation in euthanasia 240
863 Advanced directives and euthanasia 242
864 Pastoral care of the dying 244

IV. CHRISTIAN PRAYER 247

Prayer and Devotions 248

865 Holy Hour before the Blessed Sacrament 248
866 Priests and the Holy Hour 250
867 Promises of the rosary 252
868 The Memorare 254
869 The "Hymn of the Three Young Men" 257
870 Devotion to the angels 259
871 The Seven Sundays of St Joseph 261
872 A crucifix and an icon of Our Lady 263

Our Lady and the Saints 266

873 Our Lady of the Snows 266
874 The Desert Fathers 268
875 St Corona 270
876 St Tarcisius, patron saint of alter servers 272
877 St Januarius 274
878 St Lydwine of Schiedam 275
879 Thomas à Kempis 277
880 St Nicholas of Flüe 279
881 St Camillus de Lellis 282
882 St Philip Neri 284
883 St Joseph Calasanz 286
884 St Peter Claver 288
885 St Joseph of Cupertino 290
886 St Kateri Tekakwitha 292
887 St Elizabeth Ann Seton 294
888 Blessed Anne Catherine Emmerich 296
889 St Dominic Savio 298

- 890 St Maria Goretti 301
- 891 Pope St Paul VI 303
- 892 Blessed Alexandrina da Costa 305
- 893 Blessed Franz Jägerstätter 307
- 894 Venerable Jérôme Lejeune 309
- 895 Blessed Carlo Acutis 311
- 896 St José Sánchez del Rio 313
- 897 Saints Francisco and Jacinta Marto 315
- 898 A new pathway to canonisation 317

Apparitions of Our Lady 320
- 899 Apparitions of Mary in the Ukraine 320
- 900 A recent apparition of Mary in the Ukraine 322

INDEX 325

Foreword to *Question Time 1*

Contrary to some stereotypes in our society, the life of the Christian is one of constant reflection and questioning. The more we learn about God, the more we read the Bible, the more we puzzle over problems in our daily lives and in our societies which seem to challenge Christian beliefs and Catholic teachings, the more questions we have. Praying and meditating regularly also gives rise to many questions as we ponder God's mercy and love, his promises to us, and the evil and suffering that frequently confront us in our daily lives.

Father John Flader's book *Question Time 1 - 150 Questions and Answers on the Catholic Faith* is a wonderful resource for every Catholic who has ever had questions about the faith or about our life together with God. This book brings together answers from Fr Flader's popular column in *The Catholic Weekly* and reflects the timelessness and fascination that different questions have for Christians of all ages and across all generations. The ground covered in this book is nothing if not wide ranging. Can we hurt God? What does the Church think about Evolution? Did the children of Adam and Eve commit incest? Is everyone saved? What does infallibility mean? Does limbo exist? What is an indulgence?

Fr Flader also covers important questions about the life and teaching of Jesus, the sacraments of the Church, the Mass, Mary, and prayer. Moral problems such as suicide, the death penalty, homosexuality, and gambling are also discussed.

Question Time 1 will be a much referenced resource for everyone who uses it. Different questions at different times of the year and at different times in our lives will bring readers back to it again and again. In its succinct and elegant explanations of Catholic teaching and belief, Catholics will find information, encouragement, reassurance, and clarity. They will probably also find some new questions to ask.

Fr Flader has done us all an enormous service in collating his columns and in bringing them to print in this book. I have enjoyed reading it and learnt much from it and I hope you do too.

+George Cardinal Pell
ARCHBISHOP OF SYDNEY
7 March, 2008

Introduction to *Question Time 5*

Now that fifteen years have passed since I began writing the *Question Time* column for *The Catholic Weekly* and this fifth volume of questions and answers sees the light of day, it is time to write a new Introduction.

How did this whole project begin? It started in 2004 when I was Director of the Catholic Adult Education Centre of the Archdiocese of Sydney and was receiving occasional questions about the Catholic faith. I duly answered them and filed the answers in a folder on my office computer. In December of that year I was sitting with the editor of *The Catholic Weekly* at a lunch and offered to use this material to write a question-and-answer column for the paper. His eyes lit up because the Archbishop had asked him to find someone to write such a column and now here was someone offering to do so.

I began writing the column in January 2005 and have done so every week since then. Soon I was receiving reports of people who were cutting out the columns and pasting them on paper for future reference, or photocopying them for others. Over those first years numerous people asked if there was any plan to publish the columns as a book.

Although I hadn't thought of doing so, it seemed more and more appropriate to satisfy the desires of those people. Thus was born *Question Time 1*, the first 150 columns, published by Connor Court in 2008. To be honest, the first volume was simply titled *Question Time,* since it was not certain there would be a second or subsequent volumes.

That first book came to be published in Spanish and Indonesian, and there was another English edition published in the Philippines. Also, the column was soon being used by Catholic newspapers in Perth and Brisbane.

As regards the structure of the book, it seemed appropriate to arrange the questions and answers systematically by topic, following the general structure of the *Catechism of the Catholic Church*. Thus, in all the volumes Chapter 1 deals with matters of Catholic doctrine, Chapter 2 with questions relating to the sacraments and the liturgy in general, Chapter 3 with matters of morals and Chapter 4 with questions relating to prayer and Christian devotions.

People sometimes ask if I am running out of questions. The answer is an emphatic no. I receive an envelope from *The Catholic Weekly* from time to time containing questions sent in by readers and from that source alone I have more questions than I can answer. But questions also come directly by email from around the country, and even from abroad, and many others come from personal conversations and from classes I give. So there is no shortage of questions.

How long can I keep this up? God only knows. I continue to write the column and all the new ones go into a folder on my computer titled *Question Time 6*. So my intention at present is to write long enough at least to bring that book to light. After that, we shall see.

I want to pay special tribute and a note of heartfelt thanks to Anthony Cappello of Connor Court Publishing, who courageously undertook the risk of publishing the first volume and has continued to publish all the others.

And to Fr Peter Joseph, who appears as the censor of all the books but who, in reality, is much more than that. He makes numerous helpful suggestions to add to the text itself and he points out editorial corrections to be made. His help has been invaluable.

I pray that *Question Time 5* will help those who read it to understand their faith better and to come to a deeper love for Jesus Christ, Our Lady and the Church.

Deo omnis gloria!

Fr John Flader

Abbreviations

AM	Pope Francis, Motu Proprio *Antiquum ministerium* (2021)
Can.	Canon
CCC	*Catechism of the Catholic Church*
CV	Pope Francis, Apostolic Exhortation *Christus vivit* (2019)
D	Denziger, *Sources of Catholic Doctrine* (1954)
DD	Pope Francis, Apostolic Letter *Desiderio desideravi* (2022)
DS	Denziger-Schönmetzer, *Sources of Catholic Doctrine* (1963)
DV	Second Vatican Council, Dogmatic Constitution on Divine Revelation *Dei Verbum*
Enc.	Encyclical
EV	Pope St John Paul II, Encyclical *Evangelium vitae* (1995)
GE	Second Vatican Council, Declaration on Chtistian Education *Gravissimum educationis*
ibid	In the same place
SC	Second Vatican Council, Constitution on the Sacred Liturgy *Sacrosanctum Concilium*
STh	St Thomas Aquinas, *Summa Theologiae*

I. CATHOLIC DOCTRINE

Sacred Scripture

751 The inspiration of Scripture

I know that the Bible is truthful in everything it says because it is inspired by the Holy Spirit. But how exactly does the Holy Spirit inspire the writer to keep him in the truth?

The teaching of the Church is that the whole of Sacred Scripture, although written by different authors, is inspired by the Holy Spirit. In the words of the Catechism, quoting the Second Vatican Council's Dogmatic Constitution on Divine Revelation, *Dei verbum*, "The divinely revealed realities, which are contained and presented in the text of Sacred Scripture, have been written down under the inspiration of the Holy Spirit. For Holy Mother Church, relying on the faith of the apostolic age, accepts as sacred and canonical the books of the Old and the New Testaments, whole and entire, with all their parts, on the grounds that, written under the inspiration of the Holy Spirit, they have God as their author and have been handed on as such to the Church herself" (*CCC* 105; *DV* 11).

How does the Holy Spirit inspire the sacred writer? Again, we read in the Catechism, quoting *Dei verbum*, "To compose the sacred books, God chose certain men who, all the while he employed them in this task, made full use of their own faculties and powers so that, though he acted in them and by them, it was as true authors that they consigned to writing whatever he wanted written, and no more" (*CCC* 106; *DV* 11).

The interplay between the Holy Spirit and the sacred writer is in some way mysterious. It does not depend on the personal qualities of the writer, for a prophet like Amos was a shepherd, while Isaias was very learned and from a distinguished family. The Holy Spirit takes the writer, as he is, and disposes him to write what God wants him to write.

This divine help is gratuitous, freely given by God to a particular person. It is not merited in any way. And it is passing, transient, moving the writer first to decide to write and then to guide him while he is writing. Inspiration is not in the writer in a permanent, stable, way, as are, for example, sanctifying grace and the infused virtues in the soul.

In his Encyclical *Providentissimus Deus* (1893), Pope Leo XIII wrote of inspiration: "For with his supernatural power, God so stimulated and moved men to write and so assisted them in their writing that they properly understood and willed to write faithfully and express suitably with infallible truthfulness all that he ordered, but nothing more. Otherwise, God would not be the author of Sacred Scripture in its entirety" (D 1952).

The Holy Spirit acts in both the intellect and the will of the writer. Pope Benedict XV wrote in his Encyclical *Spiritus Paraclitus* (1920): "With his grace God brings light to the mind of the writer in order to propose to men the truth in the name of God; furthermore, he moves his will and urges him to write; finally he assists him in a special and continual manner until he finishes the book" (*DS* 3651).

In assisting the sacred writer in the composition of the book, the Holy Spirit acts not only in the intellect and will but in all the other faculties: memory, imagination, external senses, muscles, the hand for writing or the mouth for dictating, etc. The assistance is not only negative, in the sense of protecting the work from deficiencies or errors, but positive, influencing the faculties to be an instrument of God during the writing. It is commonly accepted too that when another person intervenes in the work, for example in writing down what the sacred writer dictates, the Holy Spirit assists him or her too in the measure that may be necessary.

In all this process, God respects the freedom of the writer and his individual traits, so that each one writes with his own style, choice of words and phrases, etc. It is probably the case that the writer was not aware of the action of the Holy Spirit in deciding to write and in determining what to write. An obvious exception is St John when writing the book of Revelation. He begins: "The revelation of Jesus Christ, which God gave him to show to his servants what must soon take place; and he made it known by sending his angel to his servant John, who bore witness to the word of God and to the testimony of Jesus Christ, even to all that he saw" (*Rev* 1:1-2).

752 The inspiration of Scripture

I was recently at a class in which the teacher said that the Bible was truthful only in spiritual matters, not in historical, scientific or other ones. Is this right?

The teaching of the Church, and indeed of common sense, is that the Bible is truthful in everything it teaches. It has to be that way, since the Bible, all of it, is the word of God. God is the author of Scripture, even though the different books were written by different writers. The Catechism of the Catholic Church, quoting the Second Vatican Council teaches: "God is the author of Sacred Scripture. 'The divinely revealed realities, which are contained and presented in the text of Sacred Scripture, have been written down under the inspiration of the Holy Spirit'" (*CCC* 105; *DV* 11).

If God is the author of all the books of the Bible, the Bible cannot contain error, since God, who is the Truth, would not pass on to man anything erroneous. God can neither deceive nor be deceived.

Again quoting the Second Vatican Council, the Catechism teaches: "The inspired books teach the truth. 'Since therefore all that the inspired authors or sacred writers affirm should be regarded as affirmed by the Holy Spirit, we much acknowledge that the books of Scripture firmly, faithfully, and without error teach that truth which God, for the sake of our salvation, wished to see confided to the Sacred Scriptures'" (*CCC* 107; *DV* 11).

In order to avoid the possible interpretation of this text to mean that only those truths that refer to our salvation are without error, the Council placed commas before and after "for the sake of our salvation".

This was the teaching of the Church from the beginning. Jesus himself argues from the truthfulness of Scripture to defend his own claim to be God: "Is it not written in your law, 'I said, you are gods? If he called them gods to whom the word of God came (and Scripture cannot be nullified), do you say of him whom the Father consecrated and sent into the world, 'You are blaspheming,' because I said, 'I am the Son of God?'" (*Jn* 10:34-36). The phrase "and Scripture cannot be nullified" means that it cannot be in error. The phrase "It is written" is used numerous times in the New Testament when asserting a truth, to mean that whatever is written in the Old Testament scriptures is considered definitive and beyond appeal.

St Jerome was very clear: "The Scripture cannot lie" (*In Jer.*, 31, 55). So too, St Augustine writes in a letter to St Jerome: "I confess to your charity that I have learned to accord to those books of Scripture alone which are nowadays called canonical such reverence and honour, as to believe most firmly that none of their authors committed any error in writing them. And if I find anything in those writings which seems contrary to the truth, I shall merely feel sure that either the manuscript is incorrect, or that the translator has not grasped what was said, or that I myself have not understood" (*Ep.*, 82, 1-3).

In the thirteenth century St Thomas Aquinas wrote: "Whatever is contained in Sacred Scripture is true," and "He who thinks the contrary is a heretic" (*Quodlibet, XII, q. 17, ad 1*).

Alluding expressly to the writings of St and St Thomas Aquinas, Pope Leo XIII wrote in his encyclical *Providentissimus Deus* (1893): "It is utterly impossible for the least error to be divinely inspired. In fact, by its very nature inspiration not only excludes all error, but makes its presence as utterly impossible as it is for God, the supreme truth, to be the author of any error whatever" (*D* 1951).

Although the truthfulness of Scripture has not been formally defined as a dogma of faith, the Pontifical Biblical Commission in 1934 went so far as to speak of the "Catholic dogma of the inspiration and inerrancy of the Sacred Scriptures" (*Decree on the work of Friedrich Schmidtke*, 27 February 1934). There is no doubt that, because of its intimate connection with the defined dogma of the inspiration of the Scriptures, inerrancy, or truthfulness, can be considered an implicitly defined truth of faith.

753 The interpretation of Scripture

In a recent column you wrote that the Bible is truthful in everything it says, and I am happy to accept that. But when there seem to be problems in some books, for example in describing aspects of nature, how can we say that it is always truthful?.

The answer to your question lies in the interpretation of Scripture, in how we understand each passage. This is obviously a matter for the experts, the exegetes, as we call them, who help us understand the meaning of the texts. And it is also a matter for the Holy See, which intervenes when particular questions of interpretation are put to it. Nonetheless, there are some general principles of interpretation, which can help us understand the Scriptures better ourselves. Pope Leo XIII, in his encyclical *Providentissimus Deus*, On the Study of Holy Scripture (1893), gives us some of these principles.

A first principle is that in Sacred Scripture natural phenomena are spoken of not directly and intentionally, but only insofar as they are useful for the teaching of religious truths. In light of this, St Augustine teaches that "the Holy Spirit didn't intend to teach men things which would in no way be useful for salvation", and also that God did not promise the Holy Spirit in order to instruct men about the course of the sun and the moon, because he wanted to make them Christians and not mathematicians (*Gen. ad litteram*, 2, 9, 20; cf. *De actis cum Felice Manich.*,1, 10). Thus, it is not the intention of Sacred Scripture to teach us about the inner workings of nature, as this is not necessary for salvation, but rather to teach us that all of creation is the work of God.

A second principle is that the Scriptures do not intend to explain the intimate essence and constitution of natural phenomena. Pope Leo

XIII says: "As to the equity of this rule let us consider, first, that the sacred writers or more truly the Spirit of God, who spoke through them, did not wish to teach men these things (namely, the innermost constitution of the visible universe) as being of no profit to salvation; that, therefore they do not carry an explanation of nature scientifically, but rather sometimes describe and treat the facts themselves, as today in many matters of daily life is true among most learned men themselves. Moreover, when these things which fall under the senses, are set forth first and properly, the sacred writer (and the Angelic Doctor also advised it) describes what is obvious to the senses, or what God himself, when addressing men, signified in a human way, according to their capacity". In view of this, we can understand that the Scriptures describe natural phenomena by their outward appearances, as we do too, when saying, for example, that the sun rises and sets.

Thirdly, *Providentissimus Deus* makes clear that sometimes the Scriptures describe natural phenomena using figurative language, which is not meant to be interpreted literally. For example, "He who sends forth the light, and it goes, called it, and it obeyed him in fear; the stars shone in their watches, and were glad" (*Bar* 3:33-34). In passages like this, nature is, as it were, personified. This does not mean that nature can think or have emotions like fear or gladness. The Scriptures here are using figurative language to express the reality that all of nature is subject to God's almighty power.

Fourth, since there cannot be error in the Bible, which would be a lack of conformity between the judgment of the sacred writer and the reality he is describing, we must understand, as the writer inspired by the Holy Spirit does, that the object of the description is not the inner nature of the phenomenon, but its outward appearance.

The Pontifical Biblical Commission sometimes gives an authentic interpretation of the Bible too. For example, in answer to the question of whether the six days of creation mentioned in Genesis must be understood in the sense of six natural days, the Commission answered on 30 June 1909 that they may be understood equally as a certain space of time.

In that same decree, the Commission stated that, provided the literal and historical sense of the first three chapters of Genesis is presupposed, in the light of the teaching of the Fathers and of the Church itself, certain passages may be interpreted in an allegorical and prophetic sense

754 Literary forms in the Bible

In a recent discussion in our Bible study group about the interpretation of the scriptures, someone mentioned that we have to take into account the different literary forms that are used. I hadn't heard of them. What are they?

In order to interpret the biblical texts correctly it is important to know what particular literary form, or genre, each text has. A literary form is a type of writing used in a particular age or region and regulated by customary norms in order to express one's ideas. Among these forms are the historical, juridical, prophetic, poetic, sapiential, evangelical, epistolary and apocalyptic.

An important official teaching on the matter comes from the Second Vatican Council's Dogmatic Constitution on Divine Revelation *Dei Verbum*: "To search out the intention of the sacred writers, attention should be given, among other things, to 'literary forms'. For truth is set forth and expressed differently in texts which are variously historical, prophetic, poetic, or of other forms of discourse. The interpreter must investigate what meaning the sacred writer intended to express and actually expressed in particular circumstances by using contemporary literary forms in accordance with the situation of his own time and culture. For the correct understanding of what the sacred author wanted to assert, due attention must be paid to the customary and characteristic styles of feeling, speaking and narrating which prevailed at the time of the sacred writer, and to the patterns men normally employed at that period in their everyday dealings with one another" (*DV* 12; cf. Pius XII, Enc. *Divino afflante Spiritu*).

Recognition of these different types of literature goes back to the early centuries, where the Fathers and Doctors of the Church mentioned and classified them. St Thomas Aquinas, for example, teaches that in the Bible "multiple forms or modes are found" (*In Psalmos, proem.*). He distinguishes the narrative form used in the historical books; the deprecative, exhortative and preceptive forms in the Pentateuch, prophets and wisdom books; the disputative form in the book of Job and the letters of St Paul; the laudative or deprecative form in the psalms, etc. He also mentions parables, metaphors and allegories, which he usually groups under the heading of metaphors (cf. *STh* I, q. 1, a. 10, ad 3).

Towards the end of the nineteenth century, scripture scholars were moved to develop further the concept of literary forms in order to defend the truthfulness of Scripture. Among those scholars were Marie-Joseph Lagrange, F. Prat, A. Poels and F. von Hummelauer, who made a systematic exposition of the literary forms. In his encyclical *Divino afflante Spiritu* in 1943, Pope Pius XII accepted and recommended the study of literary forms, and the Second Vatican Council's document *Dei verbum* made reference to that encyclical.

The Church over the years has given us principles for the correct use and understanding of literary forms. First, in Sacred Scripture there is room for any literary form as long as it is not repugnant to the truthfulness and holiness of God. For example, the form of legend, understood as a deformed or mythical account of a supposed historical event, cannot be found in the Bible.

Second, God made use of our human ways of writing and speaking in communicating his revelation, and we should understand the biblical texts in this light.

Third, the truth is not identical in the different literary forms, but rather conforms to the proper nature of each form. For example, the truth in an historical narrative is not the same as in a parable, where truth lies not in the facts narrated but in the message conveyed by the parable. Similarly, the truth in the primitive form of history used in the book of Genesis is different from that in the Gospels, in relating the life of Christ.

Fourth, which literary form is used in each text must be established only after careful study, based on solid scientific foundations.

In all of this, biblical fundamentalism, in which each text is to be interpreted literally regardless of the literary form employed, is, of course, unacceptable. The Pontifical Biblical Commission's document *The interpretation of the Bible in the Church*, 1 F (1993) is very clear on this.

755 Discrepancies in the Gospels

In reading the Gospels I come across different accounts of the same event, and sometimes there are discrepancies between them. Can we trust the truthfulness of the Gospels when such obvious differences appear?

The discrepancies, rather than being proof that the Gospels are not faithful to the events as they occurred, are rather evidence for their authenticity and truthfulness. But let me explain.

If the accounts of the same event were all identical to each other, it could be questioned whether the writers had conspired among themselves in writing them. This in turn could cast doubts about whether the events were reported truthfully, or whether they were possibly fabricated. Alternatively, it could be thought that there was really only one eye-witness to the events, which were written down by one evangelist and copied by the others. If, however, there are slight differences in them, it is what one would expect when different people witness the same event and record later what they remembered. We see this often when a group of people who have witnessed the same event get together to relate what they saw. They all agree on the basic facts, but they remember different details and they may disagree on some of them.

In any case, while there are some differences among the Gospel accounts, usually in minor details, what is remarkable is that there is substantial agreement among them in all the important matters. Let us look at some examples.

We can begin with the account of the healing of the servant of a centurion. Matthew relates that it was the centurion himself who begged Jesus to heal his servant (cf. *Mt* 8:5-13), whereas Luke says that the centurion sent elders of the Jews to ask for the healing (cf. *Lk* 7:1-10). This is a very small detail and the explanation is simple. In both cases it was the centurion who asked Jesus to do the healing. Whether he did it in person or through others, he was the one who asked for it. What is more, both Gospels agree on other significant details: that the request was made in Capernaum, that the centurion said that he was unworthy for Jesus to come under his roof, that Jesus said that not even in Israel had he found such faith, etc.

Another example is the casting of demons into a herd of swine. Matthew says the event took place in the country of the Gadarenes (cf. *Mt* 8:28-34) while Mark and Luke say it happened in the country of the Gerasenes (cf. *Mk* 5:1-20, *Lk* 8:26-39). What is important is that the towns of Gadara and Gerasa were close to one another in the Decapolis region to the East of the Sea of Galilee. The people of that area were not Jews and hence could raise pigs, a meat not eaten by the Jews. Since the miracle did not take place in the town itself but in the countryside, where the swine were feeding, that two of the evangelists called the area that of the Gerasenes and the other that of the Gadarenes is a very small matter.

Another discrepancy in this same account is that Matthew says there were two demoniacs, while Mark and Luke say there was only one. All three, however, agree that there were many demons in the man, or men, that they were fierce and powerful, and that the demons were cast into a large herd of pigs, which rushed down the steep bank into the sea. These were the important details. As regards whether there was one demoniac or two, we should take into account that it is most likely that Matthew, being an apostle, was an eye-witness to the event, while Mark and Luke may have heard of it later from the apostles.

An important discrepancy comes in the genealogies of Christ in the Gospels of Matthew and Luke (cf. *Mt* 1:1-17, *Lk* 3:23-38). There are many differences in the names, especially from King David on. A number of explanations have been given, a very plausible one being that one genealogy traces Jesus' family tree through Mary's line and the other through that of Joseph. I dealt with this matter in my book *Question Time* 4, q. 459.

Finally, another significant difference among the Gospels regards whether the Last Supper was held in the celebration of the Passover, as Matthew, Mark and Luke attest, or whether it was done the night before the Passover, as John writes. This question too I have discussed, in *Question Time* 3, q. 34.

756 New translations of the Bible

I read with interest your article about gender ideology applied to language. Here in Ireland the Church has decided to use the Revised New Jerusalem Bible for the lectionary, citing its use of inclusive language. In that Bible I don't like the absence of pronouns and the use of the passive voice to accommodate inclusive language. Can you comment?

You, like many other women, see no need to do away with "masculine" words like "man" and "he" in order to accommodate women's sensitivities. After all, we have been using these words in common speech and, ever since the English translation of the Bible in the Douay-Rheims version in the sixteenth century, in the Bible itself for centuries. It is especially the rise of feminism in the twentieth century, with all its good points in the promotion of women in society, that has led to what many regard as an overreaction when it comes to the use of inclusive, or gender-neutral, language.

This overreaction leads to cumbersome constructions in the Bible you mention in familiar passages like the following: "If one of you hears me calling and opens the door, I will come in to share a meal with that person and that person with me" (*Rev* 3:20). Or to constructions which lack the clarity and precision of the original, like: "Whoever wants to save life will lose it, and whoever loses life will save it" (*Mt* 15:25).

The effort to avoid common words like "man" or "men" when they mean simply "human beings" to distinguish humans from God or animals, gives rise to: "I will make you fishers of people" (*Mt* 4:19). And even words like "brother", which in the context refers to both brothers and sisters, becomes expanded so that St Peter now asks Our Lord: "How often must I forgive my brother or sister who wrongs me?" (*Mt* 18:21).

Another strange translation comes in the passage where St Paul asks us to "Put off the old man that belongs to your former manner of life… and be renewed in the spirit of your minds, and put on the new man, created after the likeness of God in true righteousness and holiness" (*Eph* 4:22-24). In the *Revised New Jerusalem Bible* this becomes putting off "the old self" and putting on "the New Man". Why this difference? Everyone understands that "man" in this context refers to our fallen and restored nature, which is inclusive of men and women.

In the letter to the Colossians, this same "old man – new man" expression is rendered "old personality" and "new personality", which means something totally different from the original of St Paul.

In ordinary speech, too, some people are now adopting inclusive terminology so that, for example, the Holy Spirit becomes "it", man becomes "humankind", and even God is not to be called "he". I have even heard the expression "Godself" in order to avoid "himself", thus inventing an altogether new term.

What we are dealing with is what I believe to be a passing fad in the evolution of culture, responding to the need to be expressly inclusive of women in our language, to a political correctness which has become normative, but which will inevitably pass away like so many other fads, only to be looked upon later as quaintly curious, however well intentioned.

After all, the English language has been with us for many centuries and words like "man", "he" and "brother" have always been understood in an inclusive sense. Many women, like you, see no need to resort to awkward expressions like the ones we have mentioned in order to feel validated. And where will it all end? After all, even words like "woman" and "human" have "man" imbedded in them. Must these too be discarded?

The language of the liturgy has always been in some way timeless, independent of passing trends, and the average person understands that and is happy with it. The decision to leave the wording of the Lord's Prayer in the Mass in its traditional rendering of "Our Father who art in heaven, hallowed be thy name" was, and continues to be, generally accepted. To change the readings in the lectionary or the language of the missal to something more politically correct but circumstantial and passing is both unnecessary and contrary to basic liturgical principles.

757 Who is a prophet in the Bible?

I always thought a prophet in the Bible was someone who wrote one of the prophecies. But now I have heard that people like Moses, Samuel and John the Baptist were also regarded as prophets. Can you please clarify this for me?

First, let us look at how we understand the word "prophet" in general. In everyday speech we usually understand the word to mean someone who predicts the future. So if someone says something that later came to be true, we say that his statement was "truly prophetic". In the Bible, a prophet may sometimes predict a future reality but this is not his essential role.

The word "prophet" comes from the Greek *pro-phetes*, meaning to speak on behalf of someone, especially a divinity. It has nothing to do with predicting the future, an activity described in Greek as *mantis*. The Hebrew word for prophet is *nabî*, meaning someone chosen by God to speak in his name. The prophet is thus a spokesman for God, an intermediary between God and the people.

The prophet's role is indicated in these words spoken by God to Moses in the book of Deuteronomy: "I will raise up for them a prophet like you from among their brethren; and I will put my words in his mouth and he shall speak to them all that I command him" (*Deut* 18:18). So important is it for the prophet to be faithful to what God has commanded him that God goes on to say: "But the prophet who presumes to speak a word in my name which I have not commanded him to speak, or who speaks in the name of other gods, that same prophet shall die" (*Deut* 18:20).

The Letter to the Hebrews too speaks of the prophet in this sense: "In many and various ways God spoke of old to our fathers by the prophets" (*Heb* 1:1). In the Nicene Creed we express this idea when we say that the Holy Spirit "has spoken through the prophets".

Moses is often regarded as the greatest prophet of the Old Testament: "And there has not arisen a prophet since in Israel like Moses, whom the Lord knew face to face" (*Deut* 34:10). Yet Moses did not write any of the books which we call prophecies. As is commonly taught, he did write the first five books of the Bible: Genesis, Exodus, Leviticus, Numbers and Deuteronomy.

As an institution, prophecy is considered to have begun during the early times of the monarchy, at the shrines to which the Israelites went for answers to their questions and to learn what God was asking of them. In this sense Samuel, who anointed King Saul and King David and was a prophet at the temple of Shiloh (cf. *1 Sam* 3:19-21), is considered to have been the earliest of the prophets (*1 Sam* 3:20). St Peter calls Samuel the first of the prophets to speak of the Messiah: "And all the prophets who have spoken, from Samuel and those who came afterwards, also proclaimed these days" (*Acts* 3:24). In addition to Shiloh, prophecy was an established ministry also at the shrines of Jericho, Gilgal and Bethel.

Others who did not write any prophetic works and whom the Bible itself calls prophets are Abraham (*Gen* 20:7), Miriam, the sister of Moses and Aaron (*Ex* 15:20), the seventy elders of the people (*Num* 11:25-29), and Deborah (*Judg* 4:4).

Still others who performed a prophetic role on occasion were Balaam, Gad, Nathan, Micaiah and Abijah. And, of course, figures like Elijah and his successor Elisha are regarded as important and very influential prophets.

St John the Baptist is regarded as the last of the prophets. Jesus himself said of John: "Why then did you go out? To see a prophet? Yes, I tell you, and more than a prophet. This is he of whom it is written, 'Behold, I send my messenger before your face, who shall prepare your way before you'" (*Mt* 11:9-10). Naturally, Jesus himself, the very Word of God, is the greatest prophet, the one who would come after Moses, who passes on God's message by everything he says and does.

As regards the prophets who wrote what is called the "prophetical literature" or "prophetical books", they too spoke on behalf of God but recorded their message in writing. They are traditionally divided, based especially on the length of their books, into the four "major prophets" – Isaiah, Jeremiah, Ezekiel and Daniel – and the twelve "minor prophets – Baruch, Hosea, Joel, Amos, Obadiah, Jonah, Micah, Nahum, Habakkuk, Zephaniah, Haggai and Malachi.

758 Cutting off our hand?

In the Gospel in a recent Mass Our Lord says we must be prepared to cut out our eye or cut off our hand if it is an occasion of sin for us. How are we to understand these hard words?

The passage to which you refer is from the Sermon on the Mount, where Our Lord says that "every one who looks at a woman lustfully has already committed adultery with her in his heart. If your right eye causes you to sin, pluck it out and throw it away; it is better that you lose one of your members than that your whole body be thrown into hell. And if your right hand causes you to sin, cut it off and throw it away; it is better that you lose one of your members than that your whole body go into hell" (*Mt* 5:28-30).

These are indeed hard words. What Our Lord is saying is that eternal damnation in hell is so dire that it is worth doing whatever it takes, anything at all, to avoid it, even to the point of cutting off a limb or cutting out an eye. Naturally, there is no circumstance in which these drastic measures would be necessary. But it is vital to take other strong measures to avoid going to hell.

There is an analogy to this in the area of our bodily life. The Principle of Totality in surgery says that if amputating a limb or cutting out an organ is necessary to save the life of a person, this may be done. That is, the part may be sacrificed for the sake of the whole. For example, if someone has gangrene in a leg or cancer in a kidney and they will die without surgery, the surgery may be performed. Anyone would prefer to lose a leg or a kidney and continue to live rather than die from their condition without the surgery.

All the more, we should be prepared to resort to strong measures to avoid committing serious sins which might imperil our eternal salvation. After all, our eternal salvation is far more important than our bodily health. To be separated from God forever while suffering grievous torments in hell would be the greatest possible misfortune, the frustration of the very reason we exist: to know, love and serve God on earth in order to be happy with him forever in heaven.

Well known are the examples of saints who have done just this. St Francis of Assisi, when faced with a strong temptation, took off his habit and rolled in the snow to overcome the temptation. St Benedict threw himself into a thorn bush and St Bernard of Clairvaux plunged into a freezing pond.

St Josémaría Escrivá, the founder of Opus Dei, who relates these examples in his book *The Way* (n. 143) in the chapter on purity, himself took drastic measures to avoid an occasion of sin. It happened during the Spanish Civil War (1936-1939), in which over six thousand priests were killed in hatred of the faith. One day early in October, 1936, when he was moving from house to house in Madrid to find safe refuge, he learned that two of his closest priest friends had been assassinated. Shortly afterwards he met a friend in the street who offered him the key to a flat, whose owners were away, where he could take refuge. When he asked what he would do, living there on his own, if someone came to the door or called on the telephone, the friend answered that there was a maid there who was trustworthy and would look after him.

Fr Josémaría then asked how old she was and the answer was twenty-two or twenty-three. He then explained to his friend that in the perilous circumstances of the war, when nerves were frayed and he was a priest, he did not want to be alone with a young woman day and night. He said his commitment to God came ahead of everything else and he would rather die than offend God by breaking his commitment of love. He then took the key and threw it into a sewer.

We too should be prepared to take strong measures to avoid putting ourselves into the occasion of serious sin and to overcome strong temptations. In the area of chastity, for example, we should avoid reading certain books, watching films or accessing internet sites which we know contain offensive material. We might have to break off certain friendships if they could lead us into sin. And since the internet offers indecent material in abundance, many have blocked certain sites, put filters on their phone, or left their phone outside their bedroom to reduce the temptations. We don't have to pluck out our eye or cut off our hand, but we should be prepared to take other drastic action. Missing out on heaven is too important.

759 Does Christ bring peace?

In the Gospel of a recent weekday Mass Jesus said he had come not to bring peace but a sword, and to set parents against their children. I have never understood this passage. Can you enlighten me?

The passage to which you refer is in the Gospel of Matthew: "Do not think that I have come to bring peace on earth; I have not come to bring peace, but a sword. For I have come to set a man against his father, and a daughter against her mother, and a daughter-in-law against her mother-in-law; and a man's foes will be those of his own household" (*Mt* 10:34-36).

These words are indeed disturbing and difficult to understand. If this were the only time Christ spoke of peace, we would be understandably troubled and inclined not to follow him at all. How are we meant to interpret these words?

The first thing to remember is that a troublesome passage like this must interpreted not on its own, but in light of the whole of Scripture.

Quoting the Second Vatican Council, the Catechism of the Catholic Church gives this as one of three principles for interpreting the Bible: "Be especially attentive 'to the content and unity of the whole Scripture.' Different as the books which comprise it may be, Scripture is a unity by reason of the unity of God's plan, of which Christ Jesus is the centre and heart, open since his Passover" (cf. *DV* 12 §4; *CCC* 112).

We should begin then by looking for other passages in which Christ speaks of peace. Fortunately, there are a good number. For example, he says: "Peace I leave with you; my peace I give to you; not as the world gives do I give to you" (*Jn* 14:27). "I have said this to you, that in me you may have peace" (*Jn* 16:33). "Blessed are the peacemakers, for they shall be called sons of God" (*Mt* 5:9).

Besides Christ himself, others too say that he came to bring peace. At his birth the angels praise God and say, "Glory to God in the highest, and on earth peace among men with whom he is pleased!" (*Lk* 2:14). St Paul too says that Christ came to bring peace: "Therefore, since we are justified by faith, we have peace with God through our Lord Jesus Christ" (*Rom* 5:1). He also says that Christ "is our peace" and that "he came and preached peace to you who were far off and peace to those who were near" (*Eph* 2:14, 17).

So, it is clear from the whole of the New Testament that Christ indeed came to bring peace. This is an example of what a scripture scholar friend of mine likes to say: "If you take the text out of the context, all you are left with is a con."

Then why does Christ say he has come not to bring peace, but a sword? We see a glimpse of the answer in the Gospel of Luke, where Christ says he has come to bring "division" (cf. *Lk* 12:51). He goes on to say in the Gospel passage we have quoted above, as in the other synoptic Gospels, that he has come to set a man against his father, a daughter against her mother and that a man's foes will be those of his own household (cf. *Mt* 10:35-36).

He does not want division, but he knows that it may result when one member of a family takes his word seriously and others do not. For example, a son may tell his father that he wants to follow God's call to the priesthood or the religious life, and his father rejects him because he wanted him to take over the family business. Or a Muslim girl tells her parents that she is becoming a Christian and the family rejects her and may even threaten to kill her.

These are not outcomes Christ wants but he knows they may result when someone follows him rather than following the wishes of his or her parents. For this reason he goes on to say: "He who loves father or mother more than me is not worthy of me; and he who loves son or daughter more than me is not worthy of me, and he who does not take his cross and follow me is not worthy of me" (*Mt* 10:37-38).

The apostles followed this exhortation when they were threatened by the Jewish council and told not to preach in the name of Christ anymore. They replied: "We must obey God rather than men" (*Acts* 5:29). We too must be prepared to incur the anger or rejection of our family or friends if God is calling us to follow him more closely.

Jesus Christ

760 Christ the Messiah

I have a very good friend who is Jewish and we sometimes talk about religious issues. How can I show her that the Messiah promised in the Old Testament is in fact Jesus Christ?

A good answer to your question comes from a former Jew, Roy Schoeman, in his book *Salvation is from the Jews*. He has a long chapter on Jesus as the one who fulfilled the Old Testament prophecies about the Messiah. Here I will mention just a few of the obvious prophecies, leaving the ones about the Messiah's suffering and death for my next column.

The Messiah will be a descendant of Jesse, the father of King David: "There shall come forth a shoot from the stump of Jesse, and a branch shall grow out of his roots. And the Spirit of the Lord shall rest upon him" (*Is* 11:1-3). That Jesus is descended from Jesse is seen in the genealogies of Matthew (*Mt* 1:6) and Luke (*Lk* 3:32).

The Messiah will be a descendant of King David, to whom God says: "When your days are fulfilled and you lie down with your fathers, I will raise up your offspring after you, who shall come forth from your body, and I will establish his kingdom... and I will establish the throne of his kingdom for ever" (*2 Sam* 7:12-13). The angel Gabriel speaks to Mary about Jesus: "He will be great, and will be called the Son of the Most High; and the Lord God will give to him the throne of his father David, and he will reign over the house of Jacob for ever; and of his kingdom there will be no end" (*Lk* 1:32-33).

The Messiah will be born in Bethlehem: "But you, O Bethlehem Ephrathah, who are little to be among the clans of Judah, from you shall come forth for me one who is to be ruler in Israel, whose origin is from of old, from ancient days" (*Mic* 5:2). When the wise men asked Herod where the king of the Jews was to be born, he consulted the chief priests and scribes, who answered: "In Bethlehem of Judea", and they quoted the passage from the prophet Micah (*Mt* 2:5-6).

The Messiah will be born of a virgin: "Behold, a virgin shall conceive and bear a son, and shall call his name Immanuel" (*Is* 7:14). Jesus was born of the virgin Mary. St Matthew, referring to the conception of Jesus by the Holy Spirit, says: "All this took place to fulfil what the Lord had spoken by the prophet: 'Behold, a virgin shall conceive and bear a son, and his name shall be called Emmanuel' (which means, God with us)" (*Mt* 1:22-23).

Kings will come, bearing gifts for the Messiah: "Give the king your justice, O God, and your righteousness to the royal son!... May the kings of Tarshish and of the isles render him tribute, may the kings of Sheba and Seba bring gifts! May all kings fall down before him, all nations serve him" (*Ps* 72:1, 10-11). The wise men came from the East, bringing gifts to Jesus.

The Messiah's way will be prepared by a precursor: "A voice cries: 'In the wilderness prepare the way of the Lord, make straight in the desert a highway for our God'" (*Is* 40:3). St Matthew applies this passage to St John the Baptist: "In those days came John the Baptist, preaching in the wilderness of Judea, 'Repent, for the kingdom of heaven is at hand.' For this is he who was spoken of by the prophet Isaiah when he said, 'The voice of one crying in the wilderness: Prepare the way of the Lord, make his paths straight'" (*Mt* 3:1-3).

The Messiah will heal the sick: "Behold, your God will come with vengeance, with the recompense of God. He will come and save you. Then the eyes of the blind shall be opened, and the ears of the deaf unstopped; then shall the lame man leap like a deer, and the tongue of the mute sing for joy" *(Is* 35:4-6). Jesus in fact healed many blind, deaf, mute and lame people.

The Messiah will live in the land of Zebulun and Naphtali. Isaiah writes: "In the former time he brought into contempt the land of Zebulun and the land of Naphtali, but in the latter time he will make glorious the way of the sea, the land beyond the Jordan, Galilee of the nations. The people who walked in darkness have seen a great light ..." (*Is* 9:1-2). This prophecy was fulfilled when Jesus lived for a time in Capernaum. St Matthew says of Jesus: "... and leaving Nazareth he went and dwelt in Capernaum by the sea, in the territory of Zebulun and Naphtali, that what was spoken by the prophet Isaiah might be fulfilled: 'The land of Zebulun and the land of Naphtali, toward the sea, across the Jordan, Galilee of the Gentiles – the people who sat in darkness have seen a great light" (*Mt* 4:13-16).

761 Christ, the suffering servant

You said you were going to relate some of the Old Testament prophecies that speak of the suffering of the Messiah, prophecies that were fulfilled by Christ. What are they?

There are many Old Testament passages which speak of the suffering the Messiah was to undergo.

The Messiah will enter Jerusalem in triumph riding on a donkey. Zechariah writes: "Shout aloud, O daughter of Jerusalem! Behold, your king comes to you; triumphant and victorious is he, humble and riding on a donkey" (*Zech* 9:9). St John, relating Christ's entry into Jerusalem on Palm Sunday, says: "And Jesus found a young donkey and sat upon it; as it is written, 'Fear not, daughter of Zion; behold your king is coming, sitting on a donkey's colt'" (*Jn* 12:14-15).

Another prophecy of Zechariah predicts the scourging of the Messiah: "And if one asks him, 'What are these wounds on your back?' he will say, 'The wounds I received in the house of my friends'" (*Zech* 13:6). Isaiah elaborates on the scourging, saying it was for our sins: "But he was wounded for our transgressions, he was bruised for our iniquities; upon him was the chastisement that made us whole, and with his stripes we are healed" (*Is* 53: 5).

Chapter 53 of Isaiah has a detailed description of the suffering of the Messiah, many aspects of which were fulfilled by Christ in his passion. This chapter, known as the "Suffering servant", has been used for centuries to demonstrate that Jesus is the promised Messiah.

Among these prophecies is the fact that the Messiah would be disfigured by his suffering: "... he had no form or comeliness that we should look at him, and no beauty that we should desire him" (*Is* 53:2). This was fulfilled with the beating, scourging and crowning with thorns that Christ suffered.

The Messiah would be silent before his accusers: "He was oppressed, and he was afflicted, yet he opened not his mouth" (*Is* 53:7). St Matthew relates: "And the high priest stood up and said, 'Have you no answer to make?'... but Jesus was silent" (*Mt* 26:62-63).

The Messiah would be numbered among transgressors: "...he poured out his soul to death, and was numbered with the transgressors; yet he bore the sin of many, and made intercession for the transgressors" (*Is* 53:12). Mark explicitly applies this verse to Christ: "And with him they crucified two robbers, one on his right and one on his left. And the Scripture was fulfilled which says, 'He was reckoned with the transgressors'" (*Mk* 15:27-28).

Another important prophecy of the suffering of Christ is Psalm 22, the whole of which describes the Messiah's suffering. Jesus himself quoted the first verse of the psalm from the cross: "My God, my God, why have you forsaken me?" (*Ps* 2:1; cf. *Mt* 27:46).

Verse 16 of the psalm reads: "They have pierced my hands and my feet." This was borne out when nails were driven through Christ's hands and feet in the crucifixion. Zechariah says of the piercing that "when they look on him whom they have pierced, they shall mourn for him, as one mourns for an only child, and weep bitterly over him, as one weeps over a first-born" (*Zech* 12:10). St John applies this passage to Christ: "And again, another Scripture says, 'They shall look on him whom they have pierced'" (*Jn* 19:37).

Verse 18 says that "they divide my garments among them, and for my clothing they cast lots". This is a very specific prophecy which was made a reality on Mt Calvary: "When the soldiers had crucified Jesus they took his garments and made four parts, one for each soldier; also his tunic. But the tunic was without seam, woven from top to bottom; so they said to one another, 'Let us not tear it but cast lots for it to see whose it shall be.' This was to fulfil the Scripture, 'They parted my garments among them, and for my clothing they cast lots'" (*Jn* 19:23-24).

Psalm 34 contains another specific prophecy of Christ's death: "He keeps all his bones; not one of them is broken" (*Ps* 34: 20). When the soldiers broke the legs of the two thieves to hasten their death, they saw that Christ was already dead, and "they did not break his legs. But one of the soldiers pierced his side with a spear... For these things took place that the Scripture might be fulfilled, 'Not a bone of him shall be broken'" (*Jn* 19:33-37).

762 Christ's death and our Redemption

Why did Christ choose to die on the cross in order to redeem us? Couldn't he have redeemed us in some other less painful way?

I was very happy when you, a primary school girl, asked me this question. It reveals an understanding of the need for redemption and also a love for Christ, in not wanting him to have had to suffer for our sake.

The answer to your question is simple. No, Christ did not need to die in order to redeem us. But we did need to be redeemed. As a result of the original sin of Adam and Eve, mankind had incurred, so to speak, a debt before God and man alone could never have repaid the debt. God had to cancel it. Mankind had offended God by original sin, and only God could forgive it.

But God could have cancelled the debt in many ways. It was up to him. He could have sent a legion of angels, with the blaring of trumpets and flashing of lights, to declare mankind redeemed of sin and the debt cancelled. St Thomas Aquinas in his *Summa Theologiae*, in answer to the question of whether it was necessary for Christ to suffer for the deliverance of the human race, says that there are several meanings of the word "necessary": "In one way it means anything which of its nature cannot be otherwise; and in this way it is evident that it was not necessary either on the part of God or on the part of man for

Christ to suffer". A little later in that same article St Thomas goes on to say that neither was there any necessity of compulsion for Christ to die on the cross for our redemption: "It was not necessary, then, for Christ to suffer from necessity of compulsion, either on God's part, who ruled that Christ should suffer, or on Christ's own part, who suffered voluntarily" (*STh* III, q. 46, art. 1).

In the following article St Thomas raises the question of whether there was any other possible way of human deliverance besides the Passion of Christ. He answers by quoting St Augustine: "We assert that the way whereby God deigned to deliver us by the man Jesus Christ, who is mediator between God and man, is both good and befitting the divine dignity; but let us also show that other possible means were not lacking on God's part, to whose power all things are equally subordinate" (St Augustine, *De Trin.* xiii; *STh* III, q. 46, art. 2). St Thomas comments that "speaking simply and absolutely, it was possible for God to deliver mankind otherwise than by the Passion of Christ, because 'no word shall be impossible with God'" (*Lk* 1, 37; *STh* III, q. 46, art. 2). St Thomas also says: "God could have liberated mankind solely by his Divine will" (*STh* III, q. 46, art. 3).

If then it was not necessary for Christ to undergo his Passion, why did God choose this way to redeem us? St Thomas explains that it was fitting that it be this way: "That man should be delivered by Christ's Passion was in keeping with both his mercy and his justice. With his justice, because by his Passion Christ made satisfaction for the sin of the human race, and so man was set free by Christ's justice; and with his mercy, for since man of himself could not satisfy for the sin of all human nature, as was said above, God gave him his Son to satisfy for him" (*STh* III, q. 46, art. 1).

St Thomas goes on to explain that in Christ's death on the Cross, many other things besides deliverance from sin resulted for our salvation: "In the first place, man knows thereby how much God loves him, and is thereby stirred to love him in return ... Secondly, because thereby he set us an example of obedience, humility, constancy, justice, and the other virtues displayed in the Passion, which are requisite for man's salvation... Thirdly, because Christ by his Passion not only delivered man from sin, but also merited justifying grace for him and the glory of bliss ... Fourthly, because by this man is all the more bound to refrain from sin ... Fifthly, because it redounded to man's greater dignity, that as man was overcome and deceived by the devil, so also it should be a man that should overthrow the devil; and as man deserved death, so a man by dying should vanquish death" (*STh* III, q. 46, art. 3).

In summary, while it was not strictly necessary for Christ to die on the Cross in order to redeem us, many great blessings came from his death and for that we should be very grateful.

763 The Scarlet Thread

A Jewish friend told me a curious story about a thread which changed colour if the sacrifice for atonement offered in the Temple in Jerusalem was accepted by God, and it stopped changing colour around the year when Christ died on the cross. Is this true?

Roy Schoeman, a brilliant Jewish convert to the Catholic faith, relates the story in his book *Salvation is from the Jews* and it is based on early Jewish writings.

From the time of Moses, animal sacrifices were offered daily, first in the Tabernacle or Tent of Meeting, and then in the Temple in Jerusalem. These sacrifices could not atone adequately for the sins of mankind. But when Christ, the Son of God, died on the cross, his sacrifice, offered once and for all, did atone adequately. The Letter to the Hebrews explains that "the priests go continually into the outer tent, performing their ritual duties; but into the second only the high priest goes, and he but once a year; and not without taking blood which he offers for himself and for the errors of the people... According to this arrangement, gifts and sacrifices are offered which cannot perfect the conscience of the worshipper ... But when Christ appeared as a high priest of the good things that have come, then through the greater and more perfect tent (not made with hands, that is, not of this creation) he entered once for all into the Holy Place, taking not the blood of goats and calves but his own blood, thus securing an eternal redemption" (*Heb* 9:6-11).

Two early Jewish documents, the Talmud, a collection of writings compiled between the third and sixth centuries AD that cover the full gamut of Jewish law and tradition, and the Zohar, an early mystical commentary on the Torah, the first five books of the Old Testament, relate the account of the scarlet thread. They explain how the High Priest would enter the Holy of Holies in the Temple once a year on the Day of Atonement (Yom Kippur) to offer sacrifice for the atonement of the sins of all Israel, and that a scarlet thread would miraculously turn white as a sign that God had accepted the sacrifice. The Zohar records that the people "used to know by a certain thread of scarlet if the priest had been successful ... [I]t was known by the thread changing its colour to white, when there was rejoicing above and below. If it did not, however, all were distressed, knowing that their prayer had not been accepted". This custom reflected the words of Isaiah: "Though your sins are like scarlet, they shall be as white as snow" (*Is* 1:18).

The Talmud relates that forty years before the Temple was destroyed, by Titus in the year 70 AD, the miracle of the thread changing colour stopped happening: "Originally they used to fasten the thread of scarlet on the door of the [Temple] court on the outside. If it turned white the people used to rejoice, and if it did not turn white they were sad... For forty years before the destruction of the Temple the thread of scarlet never turned white but it remained red" (*Rosh Hashanah* 31b).

Christ's death on Mount Calvary took place around the year 30 AD, or forty years before the destruction of the Temple. His death was the means of atonement for the sins of all mankind, and it was totally acceptable to God. With his death the need for daily sacrifices of animals in the Temple, and the yearly sacrifice of atonement on Yom Kippur, came to an end, replaced by the one and only sacrifice of Christ, which is made present in the Mass.

We should remember too that at the moment of Christ's death on Mount Calvary, the curtain in the Temple at the entrance to the Holy of Holies was torn in two from top to bottom, symbolising the end of the Old Covenant, with its sacrifices of animals, and the beginning of the New Covenant, with the sacrifice of Christ (cf. *Mt* 27:51).

One can also see in the tearing of the curtain the opening of heaven, represented by the Holy of Holies. Heaven had been closed ever since the original sin of Adam and Eve, and now it was opened for all who deserved to go there.

It is interesting to note too that Christ's final words on the Cross, "It is finished", or Kalah in Aramaic, (cf. *Jn* 19:30) were the same words that the High Priest would say when the priests had finished slaughtering the last lamb for the Passover to be celebrated that evening. With those words, the Old Covenant was finished and the New had begun.

764 The true Cross of Christ

I understand there are numerous pieces of the true Cross of Christ around the world. Is it known how they were found and came to be in those various places?

The finding of the true Cross is well documented. First, though, we should go back to some events preceding the finding by St Helena in the fourth century.

After the destruction of Jerusalem by the Roman general Titus in 70 AD, following an uprising by the Jews, the Romans regarded Judaism and Christianity as insurrectionary and they did all they could to destroy their influence.

Emperor Hadrian, who reigned from 117 to 138, made Jerusalem a new capital with the name Aelia Capitolina, and he forbade Jews to enter it. To eradicate the influence of Christianity he levelled the top of Mount Calvary and erected on it a temple to the pagan goddess Venus. He also levelled the hillside where Jesus' tomb had been and built there a temple to the god Jupiter Capitolinus.

In 312 Constantine became emperor and the following year he legalised Christianity with the Edict of Milan. At about this time his mother St Helena converted to Christianity. Around the year 324, with the authority of her son, she went to Palestine to search for the sacred sites. In the following years she had churches built to mark significant events in Christ's life, among them the Annunciation to Our Lady in Nazareth and Christ's birthplace in Bethlehem.

Around 326 she ordered the temple of Jupiter to be demolished and excavations under it to be carried out. They discovered the remains of Our Lord's tomb and St Helena had a shrine built over it, the present church of the Holy Sepulchre. They also demolished the temple of Venus, exposing the site where Christ was crucified.

Emperor Constantine wrote to Macarius, bishop of Jerusalem, ordering him to help in the search for the Cross of Christ. A learned Jew named Jude helped in the search and they found just East of Calvary a rock cistern containing three crosses, some nails, and the titulus, or plaque, with the words Jesus of Nazareth, King of the Jews, in Latin, Greek and Hebrew, as described in the Gospels.

But which of the three crosses was the true Cross of Christ? Although the accounts given by St John Chrysostom, St Ambrose and several early historians vary somewhat, it seems that a woman dying from a terminal disease was brought to the site and she touched the crosses one by one. After touching one of them she was cured, identifying it as the true Cross of Christ.

In a letter to Constantine's son and successor, St Cyril of Jerusalem wrote: "The saving wood of the Cross was found at Jerusalem in the time of Constantine." In one of his Catecheses he said: "He was truly crucified for our sins. For if you would deny it, the place refutes you visibly, this blessed Golgotha, in which we are now assembled for the sake of him who was here crucified; and the whole world has since been filled with pieces of the wood of the Cross."

St Helena took part of the true Cross and the nails back to Constantinople, and she had another part placed in a reliquary covered with silver which she entrusted to Macarius. In the 380s a nun named

Egeria visited Jerusalem and described in her diary a ceremony conducted by the bishop in which the Cross, kept in a silver-gilt casket, was venerated.

St Helena took another piece of the Cross to Rome, where she had a church built for the benefit of those who could not travel to Jerusalem. The church was built within a Roman villa which St Helena chose as a residence. She had taken some soil from Jerusalem for the floor of the church and hence it was called the Church of the Holy Cross in Jerusalem. It is located near the Lateran Basilica. Among the items still on display in that church are part of the true Cross, a nail thought to be used in the crucifixion and part of the title of execution, written in the three languages.

Many other pieces of the Cross are distributed throughout the world, most of them coming from the Cross in Constantinople.

765 The Title of the Cross

I have heard that the original tablet that Pilate had fastened to the Cross of Christ, with the INRI words, is on display in a church in Rome. Is this true and, if so, do we know if it is authentic?

As you say, the tablet that Pilate asked to be fastened to Christ's Cross, or at least a replica of it, is indeed on display in a church in Rome. The tablet, whose proper Latin name is Titulus Crucis, or Title of the Cross, is in the Church of the Holy Cross in Jerusalem in Rome. The tradition is that St Helena, the mother of Emperor Constantine, found the Title along with the true Cross and other relics associated with the crucifixion around the year 326 AD.

According to St John, the words Pilate ordered to be put on the Title were "Jesus of Nazareth, the King of the Jews", and the words were written "in Hebrew, in Latin and in Greek" (*Jn* 19:19-20). The first letter of each of the Latin words, *Iesus Nazarenus Rex Iudaeorum*, give us the familiar INRI, which we sometimes see on crucifixes as an abbreviation.

As regards when the Title arrived in Rome, the pilgrim Egeria reported in 383 AD that in a visit to Jerusalem she had been present at a ceremony where "both the wood of the Cross and the Title are placed upon the table" and then venerated by the faithful. If the Title was still in Jerusalem in 383 it was not St Helena, who died around 328 AD, who took it to Rome.

Moreover, in the year 570 Antonio de Piacenza described having venerated both the Cross and the Title in the Basilica built by Constantine in Jerusalem. He said the Title was made of walnut wood and had the words, as recorded by St Luke, "This is the King of the Jews" (Lk 23:38). Italian Professor Maria Rigato believes the Title may have been taken to Rome by Pope Gregory the Great around the end of the sixth century.

The Title on display in Rome is made of walnut wood and is 25 centimetres long by 14 centimetres wide, with a thickness of 2.6 centimetres. It is written in the three languages, with Hebrew first, then Greek and Latin. Since the Hebrew language is written right to left, the other two languages are also written in this way, with not only the words but each letter written in reverse. The top of the tablet with the first line, in Hebrew, is almost destroyed but the other two lines are intact and quite legible.

Among the recorded events associated with the Title is the renovation of the Church of the Holy Cross by Cardinal Gherardo Caccianemici early in the twelfth century. He was made Cardinal Priest of the church in 1124 and he had the church renovated and the Title deposited in a lead box bearing his seal as Cardinal sometime before he was elected Pope in 1144.

Three centuries later, when workers were restoring a mosaic in the church on 1 February 1492, they discovered the box hidden behind a brick bearing the inscription *Titulus Crucis*. The Spanish Cardinal Priest of the church at the time, Pedro González de Mendoza, then encouraged veneration of the rediscovered relic.

Can we be sure that the Title in Rome is the original one from the Cross of Christ? In 1997 the German historian and author Michael Hesemann showed the inscription of the Title to seven experts in Hebrew, Greek and Latin palaeography, all of whom were associated with universities and other historical institutes in Israel. According to Hesemann, none of the experts found any indication of forgery and they all dated the Title to between the first and fourth centuries AD. A majority preferred, and no one excluded, the first century. Hesemann's conclusion was that it was quite likely that the Titulus was indeed the original one on the Cross of Christ.

Nonetheless, in 2002 the Roma Tre University carried out radiocarbon dating on the Title, which showed that it was made sometime between 980 and 1146 AD. This obviously casts doubts on the belief that the Title is the original from the Cross of Christ. Professor Maria Rigato has proposed the possibility that the Title is a copy of the original, which would now be lost. In the absence of any explanation as to why the carbon dating might be mistaken, the Title is most probably at least a copy of, or very similar to, the original.

766 The seamless garment of Jesus

A friend told me that the seamless garment that Jesus wore on his way to Mt Calvary is still in existence. I had never heard this before. Is it true? If so, where is the garment now and how sure is it that this is in fact Christ's garment?

As regards the scriptural reference to the garment, St John tells us: "When the soldiers had crucified Jesus they took his garments and made four parts, one for each soldier; also his tunic. But the tunic was without seam, woven from top to bottom; so they said to one another, 'Let us not tear it, but cast lots for it to see whose it shall be.' This was to fulfil the Scripture, 'They parted my garments among them, and for my clothing they cast lots'" (*Ps* 22:18; *Jn* 19:23-24).

Since the soldiers regarded the garment so highly that they cast lots for it, it is only natural that the soldier who acquired it would have taken it home and it would never have been seen again in public. But as the tradition that the garment is still in existence is so strong, a possible explanation is that the centurion who said, "Truly this was the Son of God" (*Mt* 27:54) might have been the one who acquired it and gave it to one of Jesus' followers.

What then, do we know about the history of the garment, often known now as the Holy Robe? According to the tradition, St Helena, mother of the Emperor Constantine the Great, discovered the garment in Jerusalem, where she found other objects, including the cross on which Jesus died and other objects associated with the Passion. One tradition has it that she then sent the robe to the city of Trier, Germany, where Constantine had lived for some years before becoming emperor.

The history of the garment is certain at least from the end of the twelfth century. On 1 May 1196, the Archbishop of Trier, Johann I, consecrated an altar in which the seamless garment was kept. Sections of taffeta and silk have been added over the years, and the robe was dipped in a rubber solution in the nineteenth century to preserve the fabric. The few remaining original sections are not suitable for carbon dating. Of interest is the fact that the German mystic and stigmatist Therese Neumann (1898-1962) declared the Trier garment to be authentic.

Testimony to the belief that the garment is genuine is the postage stamp issued by the German government for the exhibition of the Holy Robe in 1959.

The garment is normally kept folded in a reliquary where it cannot be viewed directly by the public. In 1512, Emperor Maximilian I asked to see it and the Archbishop arranged the opening of the altar where the garment was enshrined and he exhibited it. The people of Trier heard about it and asked to see it too. Since then, pilgrimages to view it have been held periodically. The 1996 exhibition was seen by over a million pilgrims, and since then the Archdiocese has held an annual ten-day festival known as the "Days of the Holy Robe".

There are two other places which claim to have the Holy Robe, although their claims are less certain. One is Argenteuil, a present-day suburb of Paris, where a convent was built in the seventh century and later a Benedictine monastery, which was destroyed during the French Revolution. According to this tradition, the Empress Irene made a gift of the seamless robe to Charlemagne around the year 800. Charlemagne in turn gave it to his daughter Theocrate, abbess of Argenteuil, and it was preserved in the monastery. In 1793, the parish priest, fearing that the robe would be desecrated in the French Revolution, cut it into pieces and hid them in separate places. Only four pieces remain, which were moved to the church of Argenteuil in 1895. The earliest document referring to the robe dates from 1156. It was written by Archbishop Hugh of Rouen, who described the robe, however, as one worn by the child Jesus.

Another tradition has it that the robe was given to the Georgian Orthodox Church. According to this tradition, a Jewish rabbi from Georgia, who was present in Jerusalem at the time of the crucifixion, bought the robe from the soldier who had acquired it and took it back to his native town of Mtskheta, where it was preserved in the Patriarchal Cathedral. Later two portions of the robe were taken to St Petersburg and one to Moscow, where it is venerated annually on July 10 in the Cathedral of the Dormition.

767 The Sudarium of Jesus

I understand it is claimed that the cloth which was wrapped around Jesus' head after he died is now in the cathedral of Oviedo in Spain. Is there any evidence for this?

There is substantial evidence that the so-called Sudarium, literally sweat cloth or face cloth, in Oviedo is the one that was wrapped around Jesus' head when he died. St John records how on Easter Sunday morning when St Peter entered the tomb he saw "the linen cloths lying, and the napkin, which had been on his head, not lying with the linen cloths but rolled up in a place by itself" (Jn 20:6-7). That napkin would be the Sudarium now in Oviedo.

The history of the cloth is well documented, especially by the twelfth-century bishop of Oviedo, Pelayo. According to this history, the Sudarium was in Palestine until shortly before the year 614, when Chosroes II, king of Persia, attacked and conquered Jerusalem. It was taken in a chest with other relics first to Alexandria, Egypt, by the presbyter Philip, and then across the north of Africa to Spain, where it was given to Leandro, bishop of Seville. When St Isidore became bishop of Seville he entrusted the chest with the relics to St Ildefonso, who had been appointed bishop of Toledo. The chest stayed in Toledo until the year 718, when it was taken further north to avoid capture by the Moors, who were advancing through the Iberian peninsula. It was first kept in a cave, now called Monsacro, near Oviedo and then taken to a special chapel in the cathedral of Oviedo. There it was opened on 14 March 1075 in the presence of King Alfonso VI. A list was made of all the relics, including the Sudarium, and the chest was covered with silver plating with an inscription inviting Christians to venerate the relics. It has remained there ever since.

The Sudarium is a piece of cloth measuring 84 by 53 centimetres. It has no image but only numerous stains made by blood and other substances. The reason for the Sudarium is that Jewish tradition demanded that if the face of a dead person was in any way disfigured, as was that of Jesus, it should be covered with a cloth so as not to be seen. Recent tests carried out on the cloth by scientists from the Spanish Centre for Sindonology have yielded some remarkable results.

First, it is evident that the man whose face was covered by the cloth died in an upright position, consistent with crucifixion. The stains consist of one part blood and six parts oedema fluid, which collects in the lungs when a crucified person dies of asphyxiation. If the body suffers jolting movements, the fluid can come out through the nostrils. The oedema stains near the nose are superimposed on each other, in such a way that the earlier stains had already dried when the later ones were formed. The marks of the fingers that held the cloth to the nose are visible.

The cloth was most likely placed on the head when the body was still on the cross. The second stains were made about an hour later, when the body was taken down from the cross and laid on the ground. The third stains came some forty-five minutes after this, when the body was lifted from the ground and taken for burial. The Sudarium was most likely removed before the person was buried, explaining why it was found wrapped up by itself.

In addition to the main stains there are smaller bloodstains all over the head made by small sharp objects, like thorns. There is pollen on the cloth, as found in Oviedo, Toledo, North Africa and Jerusalem, confirming the route taken by the cloth. And there are residues most probably of myrrh and aloes, as described in the Gospel (cf. *Jn* 19:39-40). The person covered by the cloth had typically Jewish features, including a prominent nose and pronounced cheekbones.

There are remarkable similarities between the Sudarium and the Shroud of Turin. The nose is exactly the same length, about eight centimetres. The blood type is the same, the rare AB type. If the face on the Shroud of Turin is placed over the stains on the Sudarium, there is an exact correspondence of the stains with the beard on the face. Likewise, the thorn stains on the nape of the neck coincide perfectly with those on the Shroud. In fact, there are a total of seventy points of coincidence with the stains on the front of the Shroud and fifty on the back.

The conclusion is that the Sudarium of Oviedo covered the same face as the Shroud of Turin, most likely that of Jesus of Nazareth. The very fact that the cloth was kept at all and was so well documented points to its authenticity, since in itself it has no artistic or monetary value.

768 The chalice of the Last Supper

I read somewhere that the chalice Christ used in the Last Supper is still in existence, supposedly in Valencia, Spain. I find that hard to believe. Is it true?

St Matthew relates that in the Last Supper, Our Lord "took a chalice, and when he had given thanks he gave it to them, saying, 'Drink of it, all of you; for this is my blood of the covenant, which is poured out for many for the forgiveness of sins" (*Mt* 26:27-28). There is a strong tradition that the chalice he used is kept in the cathedral of Valencia.

The pilgrim Antoninus of Piacenza related in his account of the holy places he visited in Jerusalem in 570 AD that he saw, among the relics displayed at the Basilica of the Holy Sepulchre built by Constantine, "the cup of onyx, which Our Lord blessed at the Last Supper." In the seventh century, Arculf, an Anglo-Saxon pilgrim, also mentioned having venerated the holy chalice there.

The chalice on display in the cathedral of Valencia has a cup of dark red agate, mounted by means of a knobbed stem and two curved handles on a base made from an inverted cup of chalcedony. Only the upper cup is of ancient origin, the rest having been added centuries later. Apparently, the agate from which it is made is found only in the Holy Land. It is thought to have been made in a Palestinian or Egyptian workshop between the fourth century BC and the first century AD.

The chalice is kept along with an inventory on vellum, said to date from 262 AD, which accompanied a lost letter which detailed the persecution of the Church by the Roman emperor Valerian. According to the tradition, in 258 AD, when the emperor asked that all the Church's relics be handed over, Pope Sixtus II gave the chalice to his deacon St Lawrence, who in turn passed it on to a Spanish soldier, Proselius, with instructions to take it for safekeeping to Lawrence's home country of Spain.

The inventory describes the physical properties of the chalice and says that it was used to celebrate Mass by the early Popes following St Peter. According to this tradition, which obviously conflicts with the accounts of the veneration of the chalice in Jerusalem in the sixth and seventh centuries, St Peter himself took the chalice to Rome in the first century.

Another explicit reference to the Valencia chalice is found in an inventory in the tenth-century monastery of San Juan de la Peña, located near the town of Jaca, in the province of Huesca, in the north of Spain. Drawn up on 14 December 1134, it states: "In an ivory chest is the Chalice in which Christ Our Lord consecrated his Blood, sent by

St Lawrence to his homeland, Huesca." A further reference was made in 1399, when the chalice was given by the monastery to King Martin I of Aragon in exchange for a gold cup.

Janice Bennett, in her book *Saint Lawrence and the Holy Grail* (2004), argues for the authenticity of the chalice, tracing its history from St Peter taking the chalice to Rome, through Pope Sixtus II and St Lawrence, to the Monastery of San Juan de la Peña, and then to King Martin I. She presents as evidence a seventeenth-century Spanish text entitled Life and Martyrdom of the Glorious Spaniard St Lawrence found in a monastery in Valencia. It is supposedly a translation of a sixth-century life of Saint Lawrence written in Latin by Donato, an Augustinian monk who founded a monastery near Valencia. It contains circumstantial details of the life of St Lawrence and of the transfer of the chalice to Spain.

Bennett argues that St Juan de Ribera (1532-1611), the Archbishop of Valencia, allowed the veneration only of relics whose authenticity could be verified with certainty, and that he encouraged veneration of the holy chalice.

The Spanish art historian Ana Mafé Garcia, in her doctoral dissertation on the chalice, writes that there is a 99.9 per cent chance of the chalice being the one used by Christ. Based on the form and measurements of the chalice, as well as on other details, she concludes that it is of ancient Jewish heritage, of the time of King Herod the Great.

Of interest is the fact that Pope St John Paul II celebrated Mass with the chalice on a visit to Valencia in November 1982, and Pope Benedict XVI did likewise at the closing Mass of the Fifth World Meeting of Families in July 2006.

The Church

769 Blood in Judaism

It is clear in the Bible that Jews were forbidden to eat meat with the blood in it. Why was that and what consequences did it have?

You are correct in what you say, and there are a number of important consequences. The basis of the Jewish outlook is that blood was regarded as the life of the being. For example, in the book of Leviticus we read: "If any man of the house of Israel or of the strangers that sojourn among them eats any blood, I will set my face against that person who eats blood, and will cut him off from among his people… For the life of every creature is the blood of it" (*Lev* 17:10, 14).

Because of this, there was an absolute prohibition on the consumption of blood, so meat could not be eaten with the blood still in it. The blood had to be drained from the animal or bird before the flesh was eaten, following the kosher regulations still in force today. We see this too in the New Testament, when the apostles and elders met in Jerusalem and decided to tell the Christians in Antioch that among the few things to be demanded of Gentile converts was that they were to "abstain from what has been sacrificed to idols and from blood and from what is strangled" (*Acts* 15:29). Naturally, the prohibition of eating blood was only for that particular time, as blood was not forbidden for Christians in later times.

In view of this absolute prohibition among the Jews, we can understand better why, when Jesus told the people in the synagogue of Capernaum that they should eat his flesh and drink his blood, they were horrified. St John relates: "The Jews then disputed among themselves, saying, "How can this man give us his flesh to eat?"" (*Jn* 6:52). It was not only that the Jews interpreted Jesus literally, thinking that he expected them to be cannibals and eat his flesh, but also, and perhaps especially, that they would never think for an instant of drinking blood.

For the Jews, blood was shed in sacrifices for the atonement of sin. God tells the Israelites in the Old Testament: "For the life of the flesh is in the blood; and I have given it for you upon the altar to make atonement for your souls; for it is the blood that makes atonement, by reason of the life" (*Lev* 17:11). The Jews at that time had a variety of sacrifices of animals, one of which was offered for the atonement of sins. We can see here how those atonement sacrifices prefigured Christ's shedding of blood on the Cross for the atonement of the sins of mankind.

When Moses had received the Ten Commandments from God, he read them out as the terms of the covenant between God and the people. When the people agreed to abide by the Commandments, Moses sprinkled the blood of oxen first on the altar and then on the people, saying, "Behold the blood of the covenant which the Lord has made with you in accordance with all these words" (*Ex* 24:3-8). These words prefigure the words of Christ in instituting the Eucharist in the Last Supper: "This chalice which is poured out for you is the new covenant in my blood" (*Lk* 22:20).

Blood was also used in the rite of purification of a leper who had been cured of the disease. A live bird was dipped in the blood of a bird that had been killed and the blood was then sprinkled seven times on the one who had been cured (cf. *Lev* 14:1-9). On the eighth day the blood of a male lamb that had been killed as a sin offering was daubed on various parts of the person's body (cf. *Lev* 14:10-20).

Apart from the use of blood in these ritual ceremonies, Jews were forbidden to touch blood in many ways. For example, a man would become ritually impure if he engaged in sexual acts with a woman during her period of menstruation or after she had given birth (cf. *Lev* 18:19, 12:2). He would also become impure if he touched a corpse (cf. *Num* 19:11). This may explain why, in the parable of the Good Samaritan, when a man had been beaten and left half dead, a priest and a Levite passed by on the other side of the road, and only a Samaritan attended to him. The priest and Levite put their possible ritual impurity before the duty of charity, while the Samaritan, who was not a Jew and would not incur ritual impurity, looked after the man (cf. *Lk* 10:30-37).

770 Jewish laws and Christian laws

Jesus said that not one jot or one tittle of the law would pass away, yet it seems that many Jewish laws were no longer observed with the coming of Christ. How do we explain this?

The passage to which you refer is in Jesus' Sermon on the Mount: "Do not think that I have come to abolish the law and the prophets; I have come not to abolish them but to fulfil them. For truly, I say to you, till heaven and earth pass away, not an iota, not a dot, will pass from the law until all is accomplished" (*Mt* 5:17-18). An iota, or jot, is the smallest letter in the Hebrew alphabet, and a dot, or tittle, is an even smaller stroke to distinguish one letter from another. Jesus said that not even these would pass away.

Yet, as you say, many Jewish laws were not observed by Christians. For example, the requirement of circumcision for males to enter the Church, the prohibition of eating certain foods like the flesh of the pig or anything with blood in it, the prohibition of certain works on the Sabbath, etc. How do we explain this?

The Old Testament laws given by God to the Jews were of three types: moral, judicial and ceremonial. Among the moral laws were the Ten Commandments. These are based on the natural law, the law of nature common to all human beings, and so they continue to oblige down the ages. They are valid always and everywhere, and they oblige not only Jews and Christians but all human beings. Jesus came to fulfil them and he even made some of them more demanding.

For example, in the Sermon on the Mount he said: "You have heard that it was said to the men of old, 'You shall not kill; and whoever kills shall be liable to judgment.' But I say to you that every one who is angry with his brother shall be liable to judgment" (*Mt* 5:21-22). And "You have heard that it was said, 'You shall not commit adultery.' But I say to you that every one who looks at a woman lustfully has already committed adultery with her in his heart" (*Mt* 5:27-28).

Even on the question of divorce, which had been permitted by Moses in the Old Law, Jesus went back to the beginning and declared that it was no longer permitted: "For your hardness of heart Moses allowed you to divorce your wives, but from the beginning it was not so. And I say to you: whoever divorces his wife, except for unchastity, and marries another, commits adultery; and he who marries a divorced woman, commits adultery" (*Mt* 19:8-9).

The second type were what can be called judicial laws. The books of Leviticus and Deuteronomy are full of them. They relate especially to the various crimes and other offences against the law of God, and the punishments to be meted out for them. These were laws given to the Jews in the Old Testament and were intended by God for a specific stage of salvation history. By observing them, the Jews showed their obedience and reverence for the God who had delivered them from slavery in Egypt and who looked after them throughout the following centuries until the coming of Jesus Christ, the Messiah. St Thomas Aquinas, in his *Summa Theologiae*, says of these laws: "The judicial precepts did not bind for ever, but were annulled by the coming of Christ" (*STh* I-II, q. 104, art. 3).

The third type were ceremonial, or liturgical, laws. Among these were laws concerning the vestments to be worn by priests, the purifications upon entering a sacred place, the ceremony of ordination of priests, the various feast days and how they were to be celebrated, the different types of sacrifices to be offered, the requirement of circumcision, the purification of women after the birth of a child, the treatment of lepers, etc. These laws laid down how God was to be worshipped in the Old Testament until the coming of Christ. The Old Testament worship foreshadowed and was brought to fulfilment in the worship established by Jesus himself in the seven Sacraments and the sacrifice of the Mass. Thus, circumcision is fulfilled in Baptism, the bread of the manna is fulfilled in the Eucharist, the various sacrifices are fulfilled in the sacrifice of the Mass, etc.

St Thomas Aquinas sums it up: "The Old Law is said to be for ever simply and absolutely, as regards its moral precepts; but as regards the ceremonial precepts it lasts for ever in respect of the reality which those ceremonies foreshadowed" (*STh* 1-II, q. 103, art. 3, ad 1).

771 The conversion of Jews

I work with a Jewish man who shows great interest in the Catholic faith, but at the same time feels attached to his Jewish heritage and all it means for him. Is there some way I can show him that becoming a Catholic respects his Jewish heritage?

As I have written before in this column, one of principal articles of Jewish belief is the expectation of the Messiah who was to come. It is a belief that runs through the Old Testament Jewish scriptures. Today's Jews are still awaiting the coming of the Messiah. But, as we Catholics and other Christians know, the Messiah has already come and he is Jesus Christ.

In view of this, a Jew who comes to believe that Jesus Christ is truly the Messiah is not abandoning his Jewish heritage but rather bringing it to fulfilment. The first Christians, including the apostles, were practically all Jews who believed that Jesus was the promised Messiah. And the preaching of the apostles, beginning with St Peter's discourse on the day of Pentecost, was aimed at showing the Jews that the Old Testament prophecies were fulfilled by Jesus (cf. *Acts* 2:14-36; 3:12-26).

Roy Schoeman, in his book *Salvation is from the Jews*, shows how many contemporary, and older, Jewish converts to the Catholic faith saw their conversion precisely in this way. He quotes, for example, Rosalind Moss, a contemporary Jewish-Catholic evangelist, who says that becoming Catholic is "the most Jewish thing a person can do" (p. 323).

A prominent convert from Judaism was Cardinal Jean-Marie Lustiger, who was born into a family of Polish-Jewish immigrants, became a Catholic, was ordained a priest and later a bishop, and was Archbishop of Paris from 1981 to 2005. He said: "I explained [to my father] that baptism would not make me abandon my Jewish condition – quite the contrary, it would lead me to find it, to receive the plenitude of its meaning. I did not have the feeling that I was betraying my heritage, or camouflaging myself or abandoning anything whatsoever. Just the opposite: I felt that I was going to find the import, the meaning of what I had received at birth" (*ibid.*, pp. 323-24).

Schoeman, himself a Jewish convert, writes: "This same perception, that a Jew in becoming Catholic is not changing his religion at all but rather coming into the fullness of its truth, is shared by virtually all Jews who have entered the Church. It is in fact the fundamental reason for Jewish conversion" (*ibid.*, p. 326).

One of the best known and most surprising conversions of Jews in recent times was that of Rabbi Israel Zolli, the former Chief Rabbi of Rome. Zolli was born in 1881 in Galacia, on the border between Poland and Austria, the youngest of five children of a wealthy, cultured Jewish family. His mother came from a line of over two centuries of learned Rabbis. Zolli pursued Jewish studies and at the age of only thirty-seven was made chief Rabbi of Trieste, one of the most important Jewish centres in Europe at the time.

He became Chief Rabbi of Rome in 1939, and when the Nazis took control of the city in 1943, he did all he could to protect the Jewish community. At one point the Nazis demanded a ransom of fifty kilograms of gold to spare the Jews. Zolli, after collecting all the gold he could, found himself still fifteen kilograms short. He then went to Pope Pius XII, who generously gave him the remainder.

Zolli's conversion took place when he was celebrating Yom Kippur, the most solemn Jewish feast of Atonement, in Rome in 1944. During the ceremony he somehow saw Jesus Christ in a meadow and felt a great interior peace. He heard the words, "You are here for the last time", to which he responded that so it should be. That evening, during dinner, his wife said that during the ceremony she had seen Jesus blessing him. His daughter Miriam, who was in another room, called out and said she had been dreaming of Jesus. A few days later Zolli resigned his post and a few weeks later was baptised in the Catholic Church. In gratitude for all Pope Pius XII had done during the war to save Jews, he took as his baptismal name the Pope's name, Eugenio.

When he was asked why he had given up the Synagogue for the Church, Zolli replied, "But I have not given it up. Christianity is the integration, completion or crown of the Synagogue. For the Synagogue was a promise, and Christianity is the fulfilment of that promise" (p. 341).

772 Jewish Christians

I was delighted to read your column on the conversion of Jews, including in our own day. Are there many Jews becoming Christians these days?

Roy Schoeman, in his book *Salvation is from the Jews*, explains that in recent decades there have been many Jews becoming Christians, seeing their conversion as the fulfilment of their Jewish faith. Schoeman's book was published in 2003, so twenty more years have passed and the number has increased substantially since then.

The effort of Jewish converts to bring other Jews into the Church has a long history, going back to the very beginning of the Church. We should remember that Jesus himself was a Jew, having been circumcised eight days after his birth, presented in the temple forty days after his birth, taken to Jerusalem to celebrate the Passover every year by his parents, and going to the synagogue on Saturdays. But he was also the Son of God and the long-awaited Messiah, whose mission was to bring Judaism to its fulfilment in Christianity.

In the prophecy of Jeremiah, God says: "My people have been lost sheep; their shepherds have led them astray (*Jer* 50:6). The Jews understood that the Messiah would come to gather those lost sheep and lead them to good pasture. Jesus, who fulfilled the prophecy, called himself the good shepherd and he said to the Canaanite woman: "I was sent only to the lost sheep of the house of Israel" (*Mt* 15:24). That is, his first mission was to preach the Gospel to the Jews.

Jesus instructed his apostles too to "go rather to the lost sheep of the house of Israel. And preach as you go, saying, 'The kingdom of heaven is at hand'" (*Mt* 10:6-7). The apostles were of course Jews who discovered that Jesus was the Messiah and they spent their lives preaching that truth, first to their fellow Jews. On the very day of Pentecost, St Peter preached to the thousands of Jews gathered in Jerusalem for the feast, telling them that "whoever calls on the name of the Lord shall be saved" (*Acts* 2:21). That very day three thousand were converted and baptised, and a few days later the number had risen to five thousand (cf. *Acts* 2:37-41; 4:4).

St Paul, at first a fervent Jew and Pharisee, wrote to the Romans that he would be willing to give up his own relationship with Christ in order to convert his fellow Jews: "I could wish that I myself were accursed and cut off from Christ for the sake of my brethren, my kinsmen according to the flesh. They are Israelites, and to them belong the sonship, the glory, the covenants, the giving of the law, the worship, and the promises; to them belong the patriarchs, and of their race, according to the flesh, is the Christ, who is God over all, blessed for ever" (*Rom* 9:2-5).

In the sixteenth century, when the printing press was invented, Jewish converts translated the New Testament into their native languages of Hebrew and Yiddish to help other Jews discover the Christian faith. In 1808 Joseph Frey founded the London Society for Promoting Christianity among Jews. In 1824, Rabbi Michael Alexander became the Anglican Bishop of Jerusalem and he established a training centre for Jewish Christian missionaries. In 1893, in Britain, David Baron founded the missionary organisation Hebrew Christian Testimony to Israel.

In more recent times, in 1913 Arthur Kuldell founded the Hebrew Christian Alliance of America, and twenty years later Leon Levison founded the International Hebrew Christian Alliance. In 1965 Carmelite Jewish convert Fr Elias Friedman began what would become the Association of Hebrew Catholics and in 1976 Redemptorist convert Father Arthur Klyber founded a community of Jewish Catholics called the Remnant of Israel. In the Protestant denominations converts in similar groups are known as Messianic Jews.

Roy Schoeman estimates that before 1967 there were only a few thousand Jewish Christians in the U.S., but by the mid-1970s *Time* magazine put the number at over 50,000. In 1993 the number had grown to 160,000, with some 350,000 worldwide. In 2013 a survey conducted by the Pew Research Center found there were about 1.6 million adult Jewish Christians in the U.S., most of them Protestant. This is a very significant number, especially compared with the approximately 7.5 million Jews in the country at that time.

So yes, the number of Jews converting to Christianity is large. And growing.

773 The Jewish Temple

I know that Jesus was presented in the Temple forty days after his birth and that he often went there during his public life. Can you tell me something of the history of the Temple?

The Temple was the centre of Jewish worship of God. It was there that they offered daily sacrifices, that they had the Holy of Holies with the Ark of the Covenant and other holy items, that boys were made over to God on the fortieth day after their birth, and so much more.

The forerunner of the Temple was the Tabernacle, or tent, that the Israelites made following God's instructions at the time of Moses in the thirteenth century BC. There God would be especially present in the midst of his people. It contained the Ark of the Covenant with the stone tablets of the ten commandments, a table for the Bread of the Presence, a lampstand made of pure gold, and an altar of sacrifice (cf. *Exodus*, 25-27). The Israelites kept this Tabernacle throughout their forty years in the desert and they took it with them when the crossed the Jordan into the Promised Land under Joshua. They kept it until the first Temple was built by King Solomon.

Solomon built the first Temple in the tenth century BC. King David,

Solomon's father, had wanted to build the Temple but God told him he was not to do so because he had shed much blood and waged many wars, and that Solomon would be the one to build it (cf. *1 Chron.* 22:7-10). The Temple was built on a threshing floor King David had purchased on Mount Moriah, where the patriarch Abraham had brought his son Isaac for sacrifice (cf. *Gen* 22:14). The mount is also known as Mount Zion. King David had gathered all the best materials and workmen to do the building.

The building of the Temple is described in the Second Book of Chronicles, chapters 3 and 4. Its length was sixty cubits and its width twenty cubits, or about thirty metres by ten metres. The inside of the building was overlaid with pure gold throughout. An inner sanctuary, where there were two cherubim of wood overlaid with gold, occupied one third of the length of the Temple. It was separated from the rest of the Temple by a veil of fine fabrics. The Temple had a golden altar, tables for the Bread of the Presence, and lampstands with lamps of pure gold to burn before the inner sanctuary. There were two tall pillars in front of the Temple.

When the Temple was finished, Solomon had the Ark of the Covenant brought in with great ceremony and placed in the inner sanctuary, beneath the wings of the cherubim. Meanwhile many sheep and oxen were sacrificed (cf. *2 Chron* 5).

This first Temple lasted until about 587 BC, when the Babylonian King Nebuchadnezzar II destroyed Jerusalem and its Temple and took many of the Jews into exile in Babylon. After the fall of the Babylonian Empire to the Persians in 539 BC, King Cyrus the Great allowed the Jews to return to Israel and he ordered them to rebuild the Temple, sending with them the sacred vessels which Nebuchadnezzar had taken. Construction began around the year 537 BC and it took some twenty years to complete. The Book of Ezra relates the rebuilding and dedication of the Temple under the Jewish governor Zerubbabel. The Temple was dedicated with great ceremony, including the sacrifice of hundreds of animals (cf. *Ezra* 6:3-17).

This second Temple was desecrated in the second century BC by the Seleucid ruler Antiochus IV Epiphanes, as related in the Books of Maccabees. Antiochus forbade the observance of the Sabbath and circumcision, ordered pigs to be sacrificed and their flesh eaten, which was forbidden under Jewish law, and he erected a statue of Zeus in the Temple. After many battles, the Maccabees regained their freedom and their leader, Judas the Maccabean, rededicated the Temple in 165 BC (cf. *2 Mac* 10:1-8). The Jews to this day celebrate the rededication as the feast of Hanukkah.

Around 20 BC, King Herod the Great renovated and enlarged the Temple and it was this Temple that Jesus often visited. The Roman general and later emperor, Titus, destroyed the Temple in 70 AD and it was never rebuilt. A Muslim shrine, known as the Dome of the Rock, and the Al-Aqsa mosque, built in the eighth century, now occupy the site.

774 Parts of the Jewish Temple

In the Bible we see many references to the Temple in Jerusalem and its various parts. Could you please explain the main parts of the Temple, to give me a better understanding of it?

At the time of Our Lord the Temple, which had been enlarged by King Herod the Great beginning around 20 BC, had three main parts, surrounded by a high wall.

The outermost area was called the Court of the Gentiles because it could be entered by all people, including non-Jews. It comprised all the area inside the outer wall and outside the Temple proper and was, by far, the largest of all the courts. It was accessed by way of Solomon's Porch, a covered area on either side of the Court's eastern entrance. This was the only entrance through the outer wall to the Temple. This court was frequented by Jerusalem's sick and the poor seeking help (cf. *Acts* 3:11, 5:12, 15).

Access to the Temple from the Court of the Gentiles was gained through the Soreg, a fence surrounding the Temple, with many gates.

Gentiles, or non-Jews, and ritually unclean Jews were forbidden, on pain of death, to pass through these gates to the Temple proper. The Jews were so zealous in keeping the purity of the Temple area that they placed stones along the Soreg fence, written in Greek, which threatened death to any Gentile who would dare enter. St Paul refers to this fence in his letter to the Ephesians. He tells them that they were once Gentiles but now Christ "has broken down the dividing wall of hostility" (*Eph* 2:14).

The main entrance from the Court of the Gentiles to the Temple proper was through the Beautiful Gate, just inside Solomon's Porch. It was called beautiful because it was made with Corinthian brass and was richly ornamented. It is mentioned in the Bible (cf. *Acts* 3:2, 10). Inside this gate was the second main part of the Temple, the Court of Women, or Outer Court. Women could worship God there and they could not go beyond it unless they were bringing a sacrifice.

In this court was the market where sacrificial animals, doves and pigeons were bought and foreign currency was exchanged for Temple money, and where Christ drove out the money changers and others (cf. *Jn* 2:13-16, *Mt* 21:12). Within the Court of Women were various chambers where oil and wine were kept, wood for burnt sacrifices was stored, lepers who had been healed stayed until they were declared clean, and those who had taken a vow of Nazarite cooked their peace offerings and burned their cut hair. Also in this court was the treasury where people could place their monetary offerings (cf. *Mk* 12:41, *Lk* 21:1).

From the Court of Women, one passed through the Nicanor Gate to the Inner Court, the principal part of the Temple. Just inside this gate was the Hall of Israel, where Israelites waited in silence while their sacrifices to God were burned. From this hall three steps, called the Dukan, led to the Hall of Priests, where priests blessed the people. Further on was the brazen altar, or altar of burnt offerings, where daily sacrifices were offered. On either side of the altar were areas where the animals to be sacrificed were killed and washed. Also burned on the altar were grain-based and liquid offerings.

Behind the altar, twelve steps led up to an enclosed area comprising the Holy Place and the Holy of Holies. In the Holy Place were a seven-branched candlestick, a golden altar on which incense was burned and a table on which showbread was placed. It also had five tables along the sides. It was here that the priest Zechariah, Elizabeth's husband, was burning incense when an angel appeared to him and announced the birth of John the Baptist (cf. *Lk* 1:5-13).

Behind this, separated by a beautiful curtain, was the most sacred part of the Temple, the Holy of Holies. In Solomon's Temple it contained the Ark of the Covenant, inside of which were the stone tablets of the commandments. The Letter to the Hebrews says that it also contained an urn with manna and Aaron's budded rod (cf. *2 Chron* 5:10, *Heb* 9:4). In Herod's Temple at the time of Christ, the Holy of Holies was empty. A slightly raised part of the floor indicated where the Ark of the Covenant had once stood. Here only the high priest entered, once a year on the Day of Atonement, Yom Kippur, to sprinkle the blood of sacrificed animals. He would also burn incense on the golden altar in the Holy Place.

775 The Jewish Synagogue

We know that Jesus often preached in the synagogue in different cities. I have some questions. What exactly was a synagogue and what activities took place there? When did synagogues come into existence, and what were the principal parts of a synagogue?

The word synagogue is Greek and it means "place of assembly". It is a literal translation of the Hebrew term *Beit K'nesset*, meaning House of Assembly. The Yiddish term is shul, which is derived from the German word *schule*, meaning school, and it emphasises the synagogue's role as a place of learning. The synagogue was, and still is, the centre of the life of the Jewish community. It is a place of prayer, learning, social and charitable work, as well as being a social centre.

When did synagogues first appear? It is clear in the Old Testament that they did not exist in the first centuries after the Exodus, when the tabernacle, or tent of meeting, containing the Ark of the Covenant, was the focus of God's dwelling among his people. The tabernacle was replaced by the Temple, built by Solomon in the tenth century BC. It seems that synagogues first appeared when the Temple was destroyed by Nebuchadnezzar II in the sixth century BC, and private homes were used temporarily for public worship and religious instruction. Synagogues were then built in the principal cities throughout Israel, and Our Lord preached in several of them.

The synagogue had a number of features which are obvious forerunners of features in a Catholic church. At the front of the synagogue was the *sanctuary*, where the prayer services were performed. Catholic churches always have a sanctuary, indicated by a raised platform or a different floor covering, where Mass is celebrated on the altar. In some synagogues today, the sanctuary is located in the part closest to Jerusalem, so that the people face Jerusalem when praying. In the early days of the Church, the sanctuary with its altar was often located in the Eastern part of the church, so that the people faced East, *ad orientem*, the direction of the rising sun, a symbol of Christ, the Sun of Justice.

Within the sanctuary of the synagogue was its most important feature, the Ark, an acrostic of the Hebrew words *Aron Kodesh*, meaning "holy cabinet". The Ark was a cabinet embedded in the wall, and it contained the scrolls of the Torah, or Pentateuch, the first five books of the Bible. It is easy to see how the Ark containing God's word became a Catholic church's tabernacle, containing the very Word made flesh. Moreover, inside the Ark was a curtain, imitating the curtain in the Temple which separated the Holy of Holies from the rest of the Temple. Many tabernacles in Catholic churches today have a curtain inside the door, behind which is the ciborium containing the hosts of the Body of Christ.

In front of the Ark and slightly above it was the *ner tamid*, the Eternal Lamp, which God ordered to be placed in the tent of meeting and to be kept burning constantly: "And you shall command the sons of Israel that they bring to you pure beaten olive oil for the light, that a lamp may be set up to burn continually" (*Ex* 27:20). Here we see a forerunner of the sanctuary lamp in all Catholic churches, which is burning before the tabernacle whenever the Blessed Sacrament is present.

Another feature of the synagogue was the *menorah*, a six or eight-branched candelabrum with its candles lit during services. While the *menorah* in the Temple had seven branches, it was considered improper to make an exact duplication of any item in the Temple. The Catholic church today has candles lit on or beside the altar during the celebration of Mass or other ceremonies.

The synagogue also had a raised platform called the *bimah*, on which the scrolls of the Torah were placed when they were read. Some synagogues also have a lower lectern called an amud. Here we see the lectern, or pulpit, a feature of all Catholic churches where the readings are proclaimed and the homily is preached.

At the entrance to some synagogues was the *mikvah*, a bath for the restoration of ritual purity. A vestige of this bath may be found in the holy water font at the entrance to churches, so that those entering can bless themselves with the water.

Since the destruction of the Temple in Jerusalem by Titus in 70AD, synagogues have been the only place for Jewish worship. Some Jews believe the Temple will be rebuilt when the Messiah comes, and others say it will never be rebuilt.

776 King Herod the Great

In the account of the Passion, Pilate sent Jesus to Herod. Is this the same Herod who wanted to kill Jesus after he was born?

No, this is not the same Herod but rather his son, Herod Antipas. There are various Herods in the New Testament, all related to each other. Here I will write about the Herod the Great, who was king when Jesus was born, and later about the others.

Herod the Great, or Herod I, was born around 74-73 BC and died in 4 BC. Obviously, being the one who wanted to kill Jesus, the year of Jesus' birth must be placed at 4 BC or earlier (see my book *Question Time 3*, q. 317).

Herod was born in Idumea, south of Judea, the second son of Antipater, an Idumaean, and Cypros, a Nabatean. His father's ancestors had converted to Judaism and hence Herod was raised as a Jew. His rise to power was due largely to his father's good relationship with Julius Caesar, who had entrusted Antipater with the public affairs of Judea.

Herod himself was appointed provincial governor of Galilee around 47 BC, when he was in his late twenties. During that time he came to have a good relationship with Sextus Caesar, the acting Roman governor of Syria, who appointed him general of Coelesyria and Samaria, expanding his sphere of influence. He enjoyed the backing of Rome but his brutality was condemned by the Jewish council, the Sanhedrin.

In 41 BC Herod and his brother Phasael were named tetrarchs by the Roman leader Mark Antony, in order to support Hyrcanus II, the ruler of Judea. When Hyrcanus was overthrown by his nephew Antigonus, Herod went to Rome where he pleaded with the Romans to restore Hyrcanus to power. To his surprise, the Senate appointed Herod himself King of the Jews in 37 BC. It is to be noted that the title King of the Jews was a civil title granted by the Romans, not a spiritual one granted by the Jews.

Herod then returned to Judea where, in a war lasting three years, he won back the kingship from Antigonus. He married Hyrcanus's granddaughter Mariamne in an attempt to secure his claim to the throne and to gain favour with the Jews. Since he was already married to Doris, with whom he had a young son named Antipater, he chose to banish Doris and her son. Herod remained king of Judea until his death. He was, in a sense, a vassal of the Roman Empire and was expected to support the interests of the Romans. Over the years he had ten wives.

Herod suffered from paranoia and had several high-ranking people put to death who posed a threat to his reign. Among those executed were several members of his own family, including his wife Mariamne I and her son Antipater, her mother Alexandra, his brother-in-law Kostobar, and his own sons Alexander and Aristobulus. To protect himself he had a personal bodyguard of 2000 soldiers. In view of his deep-seated fear of being overthrown and his cruelty, it is not surprising that when the three Wise Men said they wanted to worship Jesus, the King of the Jews (cf. *Mt* 2:1-2), Herod sought to kill Jesus too (cf. *Mt* 2:16).

Although he publicly identified himself as a Jew, the authenticity of his faith was questioned by many and his decadent lifestyle and cruelty only added to the antipathy of observant Jews. He made attempts to conform to the traditional Jewish laws and customs, but there were more instances where he was insensitive. For example, he introduced foreign forms of entertainment and erected over the entrance of the temple a golden eagle, which was considered a pagan idolatrous symbol.

Herod was renowned as a great builder. He rebuilt the temple in Jerusalem along with such other projects as the harbour at Caesarea Maritima, the fortresses of Masada and Herodium, and the pagan city of Sebaste.

Before his death Herod provided for his succession by dividing his kingdom among three of his sons. Herod Archelaus was made ruler of Judea, Herod Antipas tetrarch of Galilee and Peraea, and Philip tetrarch of territories north and east of the Jordan. Since he did not confirm his will, none of them received the title of king.

777 Herod Archelaus

In the Gospel of Matthew we read that God sent an angel to warn St Joseph not to go to Judea after the time in Egypt because Archelaus, the son of Herod, reigned there. What sort of person was Archelaus? Was he too someone to be feared like his father?

Before King Herod died in 4 BC, he provided for three of his sons to be put in charge of different parts of his kingdom. Archelaus was to rule over Judea, Samaria and Idumea. This was half of his father's kingdom.

Archelaus was born in 23 BC, so when he assumed power he was only 19 years of age. He reigned for nine years, until 6 AD, when he was removed by Caesar Augustus.

Archelaus was in fact not much different from his father. Shortly after assuming power he had to contend with the fact that his father King Herod, just before his death, had ordered the execution of two teachers and forty youths who had removed the golden eagle he had erected over the entrance to the temple. Many considered the eagle to be a blasphemous symbol and so they chopped it down with axes. King Herod had also ordered the killing of all male lineal descendants of his predecessors, the Hasmoneans.

According to the account given by Jewish historian Flavius Josephus, when Archelaus began his reign, just before Passover in 4 BC, he ascended a golden throne, dressed in white and showed kindness to the people in Jerusalem in order to satisfy their desires for lower taxes and an end to the political imprisonment of Herod's enemies. At some point the crowd began to call for the punishment of those who had ordered the death of the two teachers and the forty youths. They also demanded the replacement of the high priest appointed by King Herod with one of greater piety and purity.

Archelaus acceded to these requests, although he became ever more angry with the presumptuousness of the crowd. He asked for moderation and told the people that all would be well if they would calm down and wait until Caesar Augustus confirmed him as king. He then went off to feast with his friends.

It was evening, and soon mourning and wailing for the teachers and youths began in the temple area, with the crowd becoming ever more threatening, recruiting others to their cause. Archelaus then sent a general, some others and finally a tribune in command of a cohort to convince the seditionists to stop their rioting and to wait until Archelaus could go to Rome and return with his mandate from Caesar Augustus.

The crowd stoned those sent by Archelaus, killing many of them. Those who had done the stoning then returned to their sacrifices in the temple as if nothing had happened. It was now after midnight. Archelaus responded by sending his whole army to the temple, where they began killing all who confronted them. Josephus records the death toll as 3000. Archelaus then sent heralds throughout the city to announce the cancellation of Passover.

Archelaus sailed to Rome to see Augustus but he was met there by a group who opposed him – his own family. Antipas, his younger brother, who had been removed from his father's will a short time before, argued that Archelaus merely feigned grief for his father and that his actions, which resulted in the death of the 3000 in the temple, amounted to a threat to Caesar himself, since Archelaus had acted in every way like a king before he had been given that title by Caesar.

At this point Nicolaus of Damascus, who had been King Herod's confidant for years, defended Archelaus before Caesar, arguing that Herod's last will, which named Archelaus as king instead of his brother Antipas, should be considered valid. Archelaus then fell at Caesar's feet and Caesar raised him up, declaring that he was worthy to succeed his father, and named him ethnarch over Judea and the other territories.

When Archelaus later violated the law of Moses by marrying a woman whose husband was still alive, and he continued his cruelty, the Jews complained to Augustus, who deposed him in the tenth year of his reign and banished him to Gaul. In view of all this, it is understandable that God sent an angel to warn Joseph and Mary not to return to Judea, where Archelaus reigned (cf. *Mt* 2:19-23).

778 Herod Antipas

You have written that the Herod who appeared at the end of Jesus' life was not the Herod who wanted to kill him after he was born. Who was this second Herod, what was his relationship with the first Herod and what sort of person was he?

The Herod at the end of Jesus' life was the son of King Herod the Great, who had tried to kill Jesus by having all the boys under the age of two put to death. His official name was Antipater but he is more commonly known as Herod Antipas, or simply Herod. He was born sometime before 20 BC and died after 39 AD. He was the brother of Archelaus, who ruled Judea after their father's death in 4 BC.

After the death of Herod the Great, the emperor Augustus recognised Herod Antipas as ruler of Galilee, in the north of Israel, and of Peraea, to the east of the Jordan River. He had the title of tetrarch, meaning one of four rulers at the time. In the New Testament he is called both "Herod the tetrarch" (*Mt* 14:1) and "King Herod" (Mk 6:14-29) although he never had the title of king. It is he who imprisoned John the Baptist and consented to his beheading at the request of his wife Herodias' daughter (cf. *Mk* 6:14-29).

Herod the Great had originally designated Antipas to succeed him as ruler of Judea, but shortly before he died he changed his will, naming instead Antipas' brother Archelaus as his successor. In the end, Augustus accepted King Herod's will and named Archelaus ethnarch of Judea and Antipas tetrarch of Galilee and Peraea. Antipas governed until 39 AD.

Like his father, King Herod, Antipas was known as a builder. One of his greatest achievements was the building of his capital, Tiberias, on the western shore of the Sea of Galilee, named after his patron, the emperor Tiberius, who succeeded Augustus in 14 AD.

At first, observant Jews refused to live in Tiberias because it was built on top of a graveyard, resulting in ritual impurity for them. Antipas had to resort to bringing in a mixture of foreigners, forced migrants, poor people and slaves to populate the city. Another of Antipas' projects was the rebuilding and fortifying of Sepphoris, which had been destroyed by fire.

Early in his reign Herod Antipas married Phasaelis, the daughter of King Aretas IV of Nabatea, which bordered on Peraea. But on a visit to Rome he stayed with his half-brother Philip, also known as Herod II, and fell in love with Philip's wife Herodias, the granddaughter of Herod the Great, and Antipas' niece. They agreed to marry after Herod divorced Phasaelis. John the Baptist condemned Herod for this marriage, moving Herod to have him arrested and later beheaded.

Phasaelis came to know of the planned marriage and she travelled back to her father Aretas, who later waged war on Herod, defeating his forces. Emperor Tiberius ordered a Roman counter-offensive against Aretas but it was abandoned on the death of Tiberius in 37 AD.

It was in Herod Antipas' territory of Galilee that Jesus grew up and began his public ministry. When he heard of Jesus' teaching and miracles, Herod feared that Jesus might be John the Baptist risen from the dead and he sought to see him (cf. *Lk* 9:7-9). Later some Pharisees told Jesus to leave Galilee because Herod wanted to kill him, prompting Jesus to call Herod a "fox" and to imply that he would not fall victim to Herod because "it cannot be that a prophet should perish away from Jerusalem" (*Lk* 13:31-32).

When Jesus was later arrested in Jerusalem, Pilate, hearing that Jesus was a Galilean and therefore belonged to Herod's jurisdiction, sent him to Herod, who was in Jerusalem at the time. Herod was very happy to see Jesus because he had heard about him and hoped to see him perform a miracle. He questioned him at length, but because Jesus did not answer him, he sent him back to Pilate. Herod and Pilate, who had been at enmity with each other, became friends that day (cf. *Lk* 23:6-12).

In 39 AD Herod was accused by his nephew Agrippa I of conspiracy against the new Roman emperor Caligula, who sent him into exile in Spain. Herod's wife Herodias chose to join him and he died there sometime after 39 AD.

779 Herod Agrippa

In the Acts of the Apostles, King Herod killed the apostle James and imprisoned Peter. Is this the same Herod, before whom Jesus appeared when Pilate sentenced him to death?

This is not the same Herod, but his nephew Herod Agrippa I. Lest we get hopelessly confused, let us recall that it was King Herod the Great who sought to kill Jesus after he was born by having all the boys under the age of two slaughtered. Herod the Great died in 4 BC, leaving his son Archelaus to reign over Judea and another son Antipas, to be tetrarch of Galilee. In 39 AD Antipas was accused by his nephew Agrippa I of conspiracy against the new Roman emperor Caligula, who sent him into exile in Spain, where he died. So, thus far we have seen three Herods. There are two more, both named Agrippa.

The first is Agrippa I, whom we have just mentioned. A grandson of Herod the Great, he was born to King Herod's son Aristobulus IV and Bernice around 10 BC and he died in 44 AD. After Herod the Great executed Agrippa's father Aristobulus, Herod sent Agrippa to the imperial court in Rome, where the emperor Tiberius took a great liking to him and had him educated alongside his son Drusus. There Agrippa also befriended the future emperor Caligula.

Upon the death of Drusus, Agrippa, deeply in debt, fled Rome and went to Idumea, south of Judea, where he married Cypros. Through the mediation of Cypros and his sister Herodias, the wife of Herod Antipas, he was given money by Antipas and was allowed to live in Tiberias. After a quarrel with Antipas, he fled to different cities and finally ended up back in Rome, where the emperor Tiberius received him warmly and entrusted him with the education of his grandson Tiberius Gemellus. After the death of Tiberius in 37, the new emperor Caligula made Agrippa king of the territories of Gaulanitis, Auranitis, Batanaea and Trachonitis, formerly held by his uncle Philip the Tetrarch, along with the territory of Abila.

In 39 Agrippa returned to Rome and brought about the banishment of his uncle Antipas, after which Caligula gave him Antipas' territories of Galilee and Peraea. Following the assassination of Caligula in 41, the new emperor Claudius gave Agrippa dominion over Judea and Samaria, so that his domain was virtually the whole of Israel, approximately equal to that of his grandfather Herod the Great.

Herod Agrippa appears in the Acts of the Apostles, where he killed James, the brother of John, and arrested Peter, who was led out of prison by an angel (cf. *Acts* 12:1-11). Later, when the people acclaimed Herod as a god, "an angel of the Lord struck him, because he did not give God the glory; and he was eaten by worms and died" (Acts 12:23). The year was 44 AD.

Agrippa and his wife Cypros had a son, Agrippa II, who was born around 27 AD, and three daughters: Bernice, Mariamne and Drusilla, who would go on to marry Antonius Felix, the governor of Judea. Agrippa II had been sent to Rome by his father, where he was raised and educated at the imperial court. Because he was only 17 when his father died in 44, the emperor Claudius returned Judea to the status of a province. In 48 Agrippa II received authority over the temple affairs in Jerusalem and two years later he was made king of Chalcis in southern Lebanon. In 53 he exchanged this land for Philip the Tetrarch's former territory, over which his father had reigned. In 54 the emperor Nero added territory near the Sea of Galilee.

Like his father Agrippa I, King Agrippa II was an ardent collaborator with Rome and he did all in his power to prevent the rupture between Rome and the Jews, but to no avail. In 67 the Roman commander Vespasian arrived in Judea and Agrippa assisted him, as he did in 70 when Vespasian's son Titus conquered Jerusalem. Agrippa died in 93 AD.

In chapter 24 of the Acts of the Apostles St Paul is brought before governor Felix, married to Herod's sister Drusilla (cf. *Acts* 24:24). Two years later, when Felix has been succeeded by Porcius Festus, Herod and his sister Bernice arrive in Caesarea and Festus invites Herod to hear the case against Paul. At the end, Herod tells Festus that if Paul had not appealed to Caesar he could have been set free (cf. Acts 26:32). So, thus far, we have seen five Herods who are mentioned in the New Testament.

780 Philip the Tetrarch

If, as the gospels relate, Herod Antipas married his brother Philip's wife Herodias, Philip too must have been a Herod. Is this the case?

It is indeed the case, although there is a question about whether it was this Philip whose wife was Herodias. When we say someone was a Herod, we mean he was part of the extended family of King Herod the Great. If the person became a ruler, he was considered to be one of the rulers of the Herodian dynasty, which ruled over Israel for generations, beginning with Herod the Great in 37 BC. The Herodian dynasty followed that of the Hasmoneans, who were descended from the Maccabeans, about whom we read in the two books of the Maccabees. Not all the Herods used the name Herod. While Archelaus and Antipas did, Philip did not. He was commonly known as Philip the Tetrarch.

When King Herod the Great died in 4 BC, he had provided in his will for three of his sons to be put in charge of the different parts of his kingdom. Archelaus was to rule over Judea, Antipas over Galilee and Philip over the territory to the northeast of the Sea of Galilee, comprising Iturea, Trachonitis, Batanea and possibly Gaulanitis (the Golan Heights). Philip's territory fell within what is now northern Israel, Lebanon, and southern Syria.

Philip and Antipas had the title tetrarch, meaning ruler of a fourth of a larger territory. Since there seem to have been only three rulers of Israel at the time, the title tetrarch may have been given to Philip and Antipas because each ruled over a fourth of Herod the Great's kingdom. Judea, the territory of their brother Archelaus, was much larger, comprising about half the kingdom.

Philip the Tetrarch ruled from 4 BC until his death in 34 AD. He was the son of Herod the Great and his fifth wife Cleopatra of Jerusalem. Born around 26 BC, he was the half-brother of Antipas and Archelaus and, like them, was educated in Rome.

It is sometimes thought that it was this Philip who had married Herodias, who later divorced her husband to marry Herod Antipas, incurring the condemnation of John the Baptist. This appears not to have been the case. The Jewish historian Flavius Josephus says that the first husband of Herodias was rather Herod II, the son of Herod the Great by his first wife, and also called Philip by some historians. This is corroborated by the fact that Herod II lived in Rome, and it was on a visit to Rome to visit his brother that Herod Antipas fell in love with Herodias and later married her.

Philip's territory was the poorest of the three entrusted to the sons of

Herod the Great, but he ruled it well. It had few Jewish subjects, most of the people being of Syrian or Arab descent. This allowed Philip to pursue a policy of Hellenisation, of adopting Greek customs and ways of life. For example, his coins bore the face of the emperor and some had an image of a pagan temple, something contrary to Jewish law.

Philip rebuilt the town of Bethsaida on the northern shore of the Sea of Galilee and named it Julias, in honour of the emperor's daughter. He also rebuilt the town of Paneas, calling it by his own name Caesarea Philippi, to distinguish it from Caesarea Maritima on the sea coast, which was the seat of the Roman government. Near the source of the Jordan River he founded another town, to which he gave a great degree of self-government, following the Greek pattern.

Philip was not as extravagant as his brothers, avoiding prolonged trips to Rome and spending more time with his subjects in the various parts of his territory. He would travel with a small entourage and, when someone asked for help, he would order his throne to be put down, would hear their grievance and give his opinion. Naturally, his subjects considered this behaviour remarkable. Late in his reign he married a Salome, possibly Herodias' daughter.

Philip died at Julias in 34 AD, having ruled for thirty-seven years. Josephus considered him a person of moderation and quietness in the way he lived and governed. Since he left no sons, the emperor Tiberius ordered his realms to be added to the province of Syria. Then when Tiberius himself died in 37 AD, his successor Caligula almost immediately restored the principality and appointed Philip's nephew Herod Agrippa I as king.

781 Hellenists and Hebrews in the Bible

I recently came across the words "Hellenists" and "Hebrews" while reading the Acts of the Apostles. Can you please tell me who these groups were?

The words "Hellenists" and "Hebrews" occur together, for example, in chapter six of the Acts: "Now in these days when the disciples were increasing in number, the Hellenists murmured against the Hebrews because their widows were neglected in the daily distribution" (*Acts* 6:1). Who were these two groups and why the distinction between them?

First, it is clear that the people of both groups, whatever their background, were Christians. Hence the Hellenists bring their issue to the twelve apostles, who will resolve it by laying their hands on seven men, presumably to ordain them deacons, to dedicate themselves to looking after the welfare of those in need (cf. *Acts* 6:2-6). All of the seven had Greek names and hence were most likely from among the Hellenists. It would have been only natural for the deacons, who were chosen to look after the Hellenists, to have been Hellenists themselves.

The name Hellenist comes from the Greek name for Greece. The Hellenists were Jews who had been born and lived for a time outside Palestine, and who spoke Greek, used the Greek Septuagint version of the Bible and had a certain Greek culture. The Hebrews were Jews from Palestine who spoke Aramaic and used the Hebrew Bible. Afterwards, Jews from both groups would embrace the faith and became Christian, as we see in the passage from Acts 6.

The Hellenists had synagogues of their own, even in Jerusalem, as is clear in the Acts: "Then some of those who belonged to the synagogue of the Freedmen (as it was called), and of the Cyrenians, and of the Alexandrians, and of those from Cilicia and Asia, arose and disputed with Stephen" (*Acts* 6:9). Cyrene, in present-day Libya, was an important Greek city, as was Alexandria, in Egypt. Stephen himself was a Hellenist Syrian-Cilician, one of the seven newly ordained deacons. Since Stephen had left the Jewish synagogue to become Christian, the Jews disputed with him.

The origin of Hellenism goes back especially to the conquest of a great part of the Eastern Mediterranean, and as far as Persia, by Alexander the Great in the fourth century BC. Alexander, who is mentioned in the Bible (cf. *1 Mac* 1-7) and who had been taught by Aristotle, was convinced of the superiority of Greek culture and he introduced it, along with the common Greek language, Koine, in all the lands he conquered. The Hellenist Jews who later became Christians facilitated greatly the spread of the Church outside of Palestine, to the vast areas where Greek was the common language.

In Alexandria, named after Alexander the Great, the Greek culture was especially strong. It was there in the third century BC that Ptolemy II Philadelphus asked the Jews to translate the Hebrew Bible into Greek. Ptolemy II was the son of Ptolemy I Soter, the Macedonian Greek general of Alexander the Great who founded the Ptolemaic Kingdom after the death of Alexander. Ptolemy II ruled from 283 to 246 BC. In response to his request, seventy, or seventy-two, Hebrew scholars translated the Hebrew text of the Old Testament into Greek, giving rise to what is known as the Septuagint version of the Bible, from the Latin word for seventy.

The Hellenists appear again in chapter nine of the Acts, when the newly-converted St Paul goes to Jerusalem to preach the faith: "So he went in and out among them at Jerusalem, preaching boldly in the name of the Lord. And he spoke and disputed against the Hellenists; but they were seeking to kill him" (*Acts* 9:28-29).

The reason why these Hellenists were seeking to kill Paul is undoubtedly that they were still Jews, not Christians, and they wanted to kill him, just as Paul himself had previously tried to arrest Jews who had converted to Christianity.

In summary, the Christians of Our Lord's time came from two different groups: Hebrews, who were born in Palestine, spoke Aramaic and used the Hebrew Bible; and Hellenists, who were born outside Palestine, spoke Greek and used the Septuagint Bible.

782 Jews and Samaritans not on good terms. Why?

In a number of passages of the New Testament it is clear that Jews and Samaritans were not on good terms. Who were the Samaritans and why did they not get on with the Jews?

First of all, Samaria is the region in Israel between Galilee in the north, with towns like Nazareth, Cana and Bethsaida, and Judaea in the south, the location of Jerusalem and Bethlehem. Jesus often passed through Samaria on his way to Galilee or Judaea. In a number of passages, as you say, it is clear that Jews and Samaritans were not on good terms with each other. We see it, for example, when James and John wanted to call down fire to destroy a Samaritan town (cf. *Lk* 9:51-55), and in the encounter of Jesus with the Samaritan woman at the well (cf. *Jn* 4:1-42).

There are differing accounts of exactly when and how the hostility between the people of the two regions arose, but a number of facts are clear. The opposition can be traced back, first, to the division which arose after the death of King Solomon, around 930 BC. The kingdom, which had been united under Solomon, became divided between Solomon's two sons into the northern Kingdom of Israel, with its capital, Samaria, and the southern Kingdom of Judah, with its capital, Jerusalem. The northern kingdom was portrayed in the Old Testament as a sinful kingdom, for its practice of idolatry and various forms of iniquity, and for this it was punished by God.

Part of the punishment was the conquest of the northern kingdom by the Assyrian king Sargon II around the year 721 BC. The records of that king indicate that he deported more than 27,000 inhabitants of the kingdom of Israel to Assyria at that time. The deported people were replaced by the forced resettlement in Samaria of other peoples of different ethnic and religious backgrounds.

The Second Book of Kings, for example, speaks of the Assyrian king sending people from Babylon, Cuthah, Avva, Hamath and Sepharvaim to settle in Samaria. Because these peoples did not worship the true God, God sent lions which killed some of them. King Sargon then had one of the Jewish priests he had taken to Assyria sent back to teach the new settlers the law of God. The result was that the new settlers worshipped both the God of Israel and the various gods of the lands from which they came. The account concludes: "So these nations feared the Lord, and also served their graven images; their children likewise, and their children's children – as their fathers did, so they do to this day" (cf. *2 Kings* 17:24-41).

In the Second Book of Chronicles, following the destruction of

Samaria, King Hezekiah in Jerusalem is depicted as endeavouring to draw the Ephraimites, Zebulonites, Asherites and Manassites, all peoples from the region of Samaria, closer to Judah (cf. *2 Chron* 30:1). That at least some Samaritans still had reverence for the God of Israel is evidenced by the fact that temple repairs in Jerusalem at the time of King Josiah were financed by money from the Samaritan peoples of Ephraim and Manasseh as well from the peoples of Judah, Benjamin and Jerusalem (cf. *2 Chron* 34:9). The prophet Jeremiah also speaks of people from Shechem, Shiloh and Samaria bringing offerings of frankincense and grain to the house of Yahweh (cf. *Jer* 41:5).

The Samaritans worshipped God on Mount Gerizim, where they believed Abraham was asked to sacrifice his son Isaac, whereas the Judaeans worshipped God in the temple in Jerusalem. In Jesus' conversation with the Samaritan woman at the well, the woman said: "Our fathers worshipped on this mountain", referring to Mount Gerizim, "whereas you say that in Jerusalem is the place where men ought to worship." Jesus replied: "You worship what you do not know; we worship what we know, for salvation is from the Jews" (*Jn* 4:20-23).

In Jesus' time, both the Jewish and the Samaritan religious leaders taught that it was wrong to have any contact with the other people, and neither was even to speak to the other. We see an example of this when Jesus is passing through a Samaritan village with his disciples, on the way to Jerusalem, "but the people would not receive him, because his face was set toward Jerusalem" (*Lk* 9:52-53).

So, the hostility between Jews and Samaritans went back a long way, it was based on ethnic and religious differences and it was deep-seated.

783 The tomb of St Peter

Over the years several people have told me they visited St Peter's tomb beneath the Vatican Basilica. I have never been to Rome myself and admit to being somewhat sceptical about this. Is there really such a tomb and, if so, what evidence is there that it is St Peter's?

There is substantial and very trustworthy evidence of the tomb of the apostle Peter beneath St Peter's Basilica. We know that Emperor Nero ordered St Peter's crucifixion around the year 64 AD. After the massive fire which destroyed a great part of Rome that year, Nero blamed the Christians for the fire and he had St Peter, their presumed leader, along with many other Christians, put to death. St Peter was crucified, probably head downwards, in the Circus of Nero, a large area used for public executions and hearings on the Vatican Hill. Following the Christian custom, St Peter's body was buried near the site of his martyrdom.

Around 325 AD, Emperor Constantine I had a large basilica with five aisles built over St Peter's tomb to honour his memory. The altar of the basilica was directly over the tomb. When the basilica collapsed, Pope Julius II in 1503 initiated the construction of a new one on the site, the present St Peter's Basilica. When Michelangelo was designing it, he ensured that the dome was over St Peter's tomb. Beneath the dome, the main altar was directly over the tomb. When the foundation was being laid for Gian Lorenzo Bernini's four twisted bronze columns of the baldacchino over the altar, several tombs were discovered beneath the Basilica.

When Pope Pius XI, who died in 1939, indicated that he wished to be buried near St Peter's tomb, excavations of the site over the next ten years led to the discovery of a complex of mausoleums under the Basilica. They were part of the ancient Vatican necropolis, where both pagans and Christians were buried in the first centuries after Christ. A person visiting this necropolis today, commonly known as the scavi, or excavations, walks through an ancient Roman cemetery, with many mausoleums and tombs, some obviously pagan and others Christian.

The highlight of this visit is the tomb of St Peter, where there is a Red Wall, so-called because of the red plaster which covered it, with many Greek graffiti only partially intact. One of them has been interpreted to read "Peter is here". Built into this wall was a *Tropaion*, a shrine with a shelf of travertine extending out from the wall and supported by two marble columns. Above and below the shelf, niches were built into the wall. The Tropaion was made around the year 160, at the same time as the wall. In front of it was a large rectangular area paved with tiles, which were white with green borders. It was obviously a sacred space where people could gather to pray.

Around this area are the tombs of other Christians, many of them early Popes. Some of the tombs are arranged in a semicircle around the central tomb of St Peter, a sign of the importance of that tomb. It is estimated that there are as many as 91 Popes buried in the necropolis, along with other important people.

As regards the bones of St Peter, his skull is believed to be in the Basilica of St John Lateran in Rome, alongside the skull of St Paul, since at least the ninth century. In 1942, during the excavations which followed the burial of Pope Pius XI, the Administrator of St Peter's Basilica, Ludwig Kaas, discovered some bones in another tomb near the Tropaion. He ordered them to be stored elsewhere for safe keeping during the excavations.

After his death, archaeologist Margherita Guarducci discovered these remains by chance. An examination revealed that they were of a man in his sixties from the first century. With this and other evidence, Guarducci then informed Pope Paul VI of the findings, and on 26 June 1968 the Pope announced that they were the bones of St Peter. On 24 November 2013, the bones were displayed publicly for the first time after the closing Mass of the Year of Faith, celebrated by Pope Francis. On 2 July 2019 it was announced that Pope Francis had given nine fragments of the bones to the Orthodox Ecumenical Patriarch, Bartholomew of Constantinople, as a gesture of good will in view of the ongoing work towards communion between the Orthodox and Catholic Churches. The rest of the bones lie beneath the high altar of St Peter's Basilica.

So, as you can see, there is abundant evidence of the tomb of St Peter beneath the Basilica.

784 The Confession in St Peter's Basilica

Friends who recently returned from Rome told me they had seen the Confession in St Peter's Basilica. I have been to St Peter's several times but have never heard about the Confession or seen it. Where and what is it?

The Confession, or *Confessio* in Latin, is a chapel, or shrine, beneath the main altar of St Peter's Basilica, accessed via a double staircase surrounded by a semi-circular balustrade in front of the altar on the floor of the Basilica. It takes its name from the confession of faith of St Peter, for which he was martyred, and it is very close to the tomb of St Peter. If you have visited St Peter's, you have certainly seen the Confession, without knowing what it was.

There is evidence of a Confession close to the tomb of St Peter since the time of the fourth-century Basilica of Constantine I. When the new St Peter's was built in the sixteenth and seventeenth centuries, the Pope wanted to make this space visible to the faithful, and so an opening was made in the floor of the Basilica in front of the main altar with its iconic canopy with spiral bronze columns designed by the 26-year-old genius Gian Lorenzo Bernini.

The Confession, designed by Carlo Maderno, was built between 1615 and 1617. Maderno designed a balustrade around it, with steps leading down so that Mass could be celebrated close to the tomb of St Peter. Previously, the area was accessed only via a small passageway from the grottoes beneath the main floor of the Basilica. The new arrangement gave St Peter's tomb its former prominence.

The balustrade has 74 white marble balusters alternating with 24 small pillars of Eastern alabaster. The steps were made from parts of the architrave of the Constantinian Basilica, and undoubtedly still retain its moulding on the underside. The entrance gate to the stairs is decorated with heraldic lilies from the coat of arms of Pope Pius VI (1775-1799). The balustrade overlooking the Confession is a popular place of prayer to St Peter for the Church.

One of the principal features of the Confession, on its far wall and directly under the main altar of the Basilica, is a niche known as the Niche of the Pallium. In this niche a bronze coffer, or chest, is placed containing the "pallia", circular stoles woven from white wool with six black silk crosses on them, to be given to Metropolitan Archbishops and Patriarchs by the Holy Father, usually on the feast of Saints Peter and Paul, 29 June (cf. J. Flader, *Question Time 2*, q. 175).

The coffer, donated by Pope Benedict XIV (1740-1758), used to be on permanent display there, but this led to the confusion of people thinking it contained the bones of St Peter. At present the coffer is placed there on the night before the Holy Father confers the pallia.

The woollen pallium symbolises the two-fold responsibilities of shepherding the flock entrusted to the Archbishop or Patriarch and of fostering communion with the Vicar of Christ. The placing of the pallia in the coffer close to the tomb of St Peter provides a direct link to St Peter. It is a symbol of Apostolic Succession, and of continuity with the Apostles.

On the left of the gate to the Niche of the Pallium is a bronze statue of St Peter and on the right a bronze statue of St Paul. On the left and right walls of the Niche itself are mosaics of St Peter and St Paul.

On the ceiling of the Confession are three frescoes by Giovanni Battista Ricci. The fresco on the left depicts St Anacletus having a small chapel built over the tomb of St Peter. Pope St Anacletus was the second successor of St Peter and he reigned from 79 to 92 AD. In the centre St Sylvester consecrates the altar in the presence of Constantine, and on the right Pope Paul V (1605-1621) kneels in prayer with his cardinals before the recently decorated Confession.

There are numerous gilded oil lamps just inside the balustrade, along the stairs leading down and in front of the Niche of Pallium. They are burning day and night, representing the constant prayer to St Peter for the Church and the Holy Father.

In 1979, Pope St John Paul II inaugurated a new opening from the grottoes into the Confession. Above an arch over this opening is the inscription SEPULCRVM SANCTI PETRI – APOSTOLI: Tomb of St Peter the Apostle. Two high reliefs of angels, probably from the monument of Boniface VIII (1295-1303) in the old Basilica, are on the sides of the opening.

785 The Chair of St Peter

Some friends are going to Rome for Holy Week and they were talking about the Chair of St Peter in St Peter's Basilica. Is there such a chair, did St Peter ever sit on it, and what is known about its origin and significance?

First, as regards its significance, the chair (*cathedra* in Latin) or throne of a bishop represents his authority as the shepherd of his flock and, more particularly, his teaching authority, his "magisterium". It is from this word that we get the word "cathedral", which is the mother church of a diocese, where the diocesan bishop celebrates Mass and where there is a special chair for him.

It is also from this word that we have the expression *ex cathedra*, "from the chair", referring to a definitive, infallible teaching of the Pope in the exercise of his magisterium. The feast of the Chair of St Peter, which the Church celebrates on February 22 each year, thus honours the authority of the Pope as bishop of Rome and supreme pastor and teacher of the Church.

As regards whether there is a chair of St Peter in the Vatican Basilica, the answer is yes. In fact, there are two chairs. An ancient wooden one is now encased in an ornate gilded bronze chair designed by the architect Gian Lorenzo Bernini and constructed between 1647 and 1653. It is prominently displayed in the centre of the apse of the Basilica, behind the main altar and beneath the round illuminated window depicting the Holy Spirit in the form of a dove. The light streaming through the window illuminates the sunrays and sculpted clouds around it.

The ancient chair was a gift from the Emperor Charles the Bald to

Pope John VIII in 875. It is made of oak and is inlaid with eighteen ivory carvings on a panel below the seat. The back rest, also trimmed with ivory, has five columns supporting a triangular structure. There are metal rings on the sides, through which poles were placed when the chair was used to carry the Pope on men's shoulders for ceremonial occasions like the coronation of a Pope. When it is used in this way it is known in Latin as the *sedia gestatoria*, or "carrying chair".

During the Middle Ages the chair was exhibited each year for the veneration of the faithful, and the newly-elected Pope was solemnly carried into the Basilica and enthroned on it.

In order to preserve it for posterity, Pope Alexander VII (1655-67) had the chair enclosed within the bronze chair designed by Bernini and placed in the apse of the Basilica. The original chair was last removed and displayed for veneration in 1867.

Between 1968 and 1974 it was again removed, and a study concluded that it was made no earlier than the sixth century. Hence there is no suggestion that St Peter ever sat on it. The wood is damaged by cuts and worms, and parts have been removed, probably to be kept as relics. For example, one of the columns supporting the triangular top is missing.

The gilded bronze chair of Bernini is in the Baroque style, with elaborate scrolling members. Its upholstery pattern is rendered as a low relief of Christ instructing St Peter to tend his sheep. There are large angels on the sides, flanking a bronze seat, with its cushion strikingly empty. The chair is supported effortlessly by four large bronze figures of Doctors of the Church. The Western Doctors St Ambrose and St Augustine are on the outside wearing mitres, and the Eastern Doctors St John Chrysostom and St Athanasius are on the inside, closest to the chair. For some reason the latter two are not wearing mitres, even though they too were bishops.

Above the chair and the window, on the golden frieze just below the ceiling, are the Latin words *O Pastor Ecclesiae, tu omnes Christi pascis agnos et oves*: O Shepherd of the Church, you feed all Christ's lambs and sheep. They are followed by the same words in Greek.

Pope Benedict XVI, in his Angelus message on 19 February 2012, summed up the significance of the chair, describing it as "a symbol of the special mission of Peter and his successors to tend Christ's flock, keeping it united in faith and in charity".

The chair is a reminder to all of us to pray assiduously for the Holy Father in his difficult pastoral ministry at the service of the universal Church.

786 The ministry of catechist

I have been a catechist in state schools for 27 years and now someone has told me that Pope Francis has introduced the ministry of catechist. I thought I had this ministry already. What is new?

I think many catechists might be asking the same question. You have been exercising the role of catechist for all those years and, in a broad sense, you have been exercising an important ministry in the Church. What is new is that Pope Francis has introduced a new formal ministry of catechist, much like the formal ministry of acolyte and lector in the Mass. In order to exercise this new ministry, you must be instituted into the ministry, via a special ceremony. Just as there are many readers in Mass who are not formally instituted as lectors and others who are, so you too can continue to be a catechist without being instituted into the new ministry, or you can choose to be instituted into the ministry if you are accepted into it.

Pope Francis instituted the ministry on 10 May 2021 in the Motu Proprio *Antiquum ministerium*. In that document, whose title means "ancient ministry", he gives the background to his decision to institute a new ministry. He explains that the ministry of catechist in the Church is an ancient one and that theologians commonly hold that the first examples of these teachers of the faith are present in the New Testament. For example, St Paul writes: "Some people God has designated in the Church to be, first, apostles; second, prophets; third, teachers" (*1 Cor* 12:28).

Pope Francis, quoting St Paul, writes that "one who is being instructed in the word should share all good things with his instructor" (*Gal* 6:6). The Pope says that this text speaks of the communion of life as a sign of the fruitfulness of an authentic catechesis (cf. *Antiquum ministerium*, 1).

The Pope sees in these and other texts of the New Testament that "certain baptised persons exercised the ministry of transmitting in a more organic and stable form related to different situations in life the teaching of the apostles and evangelists. The Church wished to acknowledge this service as a concrete expression of a personal charism that contributed greatly to the exercise of her mission of evangelisation" (*AM*, 2). So now, in our own day, the Pope wishes to recognise and strengthen the important mission of catechists in the work of evangelisation, and give it a more organic and stable form, by instituting the ministry of catechist.

Pope Francis reminds us that the bishop is the primary catechist in his diocese, along with his priests, as are also parents in the formation of their children. But other catechists cooperate in this work, and they are more urgently needed today in the work of evangelisation. He writes: "Today, too, the Spirit is calling men and women to set out and encounter all those who are waiting to discover the beauty, goodness, and truth of the Christian faith. It is the task of pastors to support them in this process and to enrich the life of the Christian community through the recognition of lay ministries capable of contributing to the transformation of society through the 'penetration of Christian values into the social, political and economic sectors'" (*Evangelii gaudium*, 102; *AM*, 5).

It is interesting to note that Pope St Paul VI, on instituting the ministries of lector and acolyte in 1972, encouraged episcopal conferences to promote other ministries, including that of catechist. Pope Paul repeated this call in his Apostolic Exhortation *Evangelii nuntiandi* in 1975. Now Pope Francis has taken up the suggestion and instituted the new ministry.

He says that those called to the ministry should be "men and women of deep faith and human maturity, active participants in the life of the Christian community, capable of welcoming others, being generous and living a life of fraternal communion. They should also receive suitable biblical, theological, pastoral and pedagogical formation to be competent communicators of the truth of the faith and they should have some prior experience of catechesis" (*AM*, 8). It will be up to the bishops' conference to determine the process of formation and the criteria for admission to the ministry (cf. *AM*, 9).

As is obvious, this is a very welcome addition to the lay ministries in the Church.

787 Nazism and the Church

I know that Pope Benedict XVI, who died recently, was opposed to Nazism in his youth, as was his father, and that many Catholics were killed in concentration camps. Was there some reason why the Nazis were opposed to Catholics?

Nazism was, in a real sense, its own religion, and it was hostile to Christianity. Once again, I will draw here on Roy Schoeman's book *Salvation is from the Jews* (pp. 215-233).

Alfred Rosenberg (1893-1946) was the official ideologue of the Nazi party and the primary "theologian" of its new nationalist, pagan religion based on the superiority of the Aryan race. In his 1930 book *Myth of the Twentieth Century* he wrote: "We now realise that the central supreme values of the Roman and the Protestant Churches, being a negative Christianity, do not respond to our soul, that they hinder the organic powers of the peoples determined by their Nordic race, that they must give way to them, that they will have to be remodeled to conform to a Germanic Christendom."

His program for the "National Reich Church" included these statements: "The National Church will clear away from its altars all crucifixes, Bibles and pictures of saints. On the altars there must be nothing but *Mein Kampf* and to the left of the altar a sword. On the day of its foundation, the Christian Cross must be removed from all churches, cathedrals, and chapels ... and must be superseded by the only unconquerable symbol, the swastika."

Martin Bormann, Hitler's Deputy Führer, worked closely with Rosenberg in establishing the new religion. In letters to Rosenberg, he spoke of the need to abolish religious services in schools, confiscate religious property, circulate anti-religious material to the soldiers, and close down Christian periodicals and theological faculties. For Bormann, it was clear that Christianity stood in the way of Nazism and had to be "conquered". He wrote to Rosenberg: "The churches cannot be conquered by a compromise between National Socialism and Christian teachings, but only through a new ideology whose coming you yourself have announced in your writings."

In the Nazi religion, Hitler was the Messiah, replacing Christ, and the thousand-year reign of the Third Reich was the Messianic Era on earth. The Aryan race took the place of the Jews as the Chosen People, and purity of bloodline replaced holiness as the essence of salvation. Hitler himself said: "Those who see in National Socialism nothing more than a political movement know scarcely anything of it... It is more even than a religion. It is the will to create mankind anew... We will wash off the Christian veneer and bring out a religion peculiar to our race."

The 1935 German *Farmer's Almanac* made clear this replacement of Christianity by the new pagan religion, replacing every Christian feast day, including Christmas, Easter and Pentecost, with a pagan celebration. The Catholic bishop of Trier, Franz Rudolf, protested: "I am surprised and deeply shocked that the Reich Agricultural Organisation, to which every German farmer, man and woman, must belong, should have offered this Almanac... it is a deep insult to every Christian and Catholic feeling."

In his New Year's Eve sermon at the end of 1937 Bishop Bornewasser, also of Trier, complained that the celebration of Christmas was now to be replaced by a pagan celebration of the winter solstice: "This artificially stirred-up old Germanic pagan Consecration of Fire is meant as a direct challenge to the highest mystery of our religion, the Incarnation of Jesus Christ on the Holy Night of Bethlehem. I leave it to you to judge for yourselves." He went on to quote from the Nazi periodical *Führerdienst*, dated 12 December 1937: "At another meeting the Winter Solstice will be celebrated. We have to train our young members in order to enable them to celebrate this Christmas stripped of all the parasitical excrescences which were implanted in the hearts and minds of the German people by the Christian denominations."

In the Nazi religion Hitler was not only the Messiah, he was the new god. One of the members of the Agricultural Organisation stated succinctly: "Hitler is our Savior; it is to him that we must pray."

Given this openly hostile attitude of the Nazis toward Christianity, it is no wonder that people like Pope Benedict and so many other Catholics and Christians opposed Nazism.

788 Planned Parenthood, eugenics, Nazis

I always knew that Planned Parenthood promoted birth control and abortion, but I didn't know, as someone told me recently, that it also promoted eugenics. Is this true?

It is true. Planned Parenthood, founded by Margaret Sanger (1879-1966) in 1921 under the name American Birth Control League (ABCL), was a great contributor to the eugenics movement and its philosophy was taken up by Hitler's Third Reich in its effort to eliminate Jews. Sanger and her ABCL were also extremely hostile to the Catholic Church.

Incidentally, the Nazi plan to eliminate Jews was not based on their religion, but on what was considered to be their inferior race. It is for this reason that Jewish converts to the Catholic faith, like St Edith Stein (St Teresa Benedicta of the Cross), were also put to death. This was part of the Nazi plan to create a race of "supermen" of the Aryan race by selective breeding and the elimination of people of other, so-called "inferior", races.

Sanger was an avowed atheist and promoter of eugenics. At a March 1925 international birth control meeting, Dr Adolphus Knopf, a member of Sanger's ABCL, warned of the menace posed by the "black" and "yellow" peril, and another doctor lamented that preventive medicine was saving the lives of "worthless unfits". He suggested that euthanasia be used to dispose of some of these "hopeless dependants."

Elsewhere Sanger herself spoke of her plan for sterilising those she considered "unfit" as the way for the "salvation of American civilisation" and she also mentioned those who were "irresponsible and reckless", among whom were those "whose religious scruples prevent their exercising control over their numbers". She maintained that "there is no doubt in the minds of all thinking people that the procreation of this group should be stopped".

Among Sanger's associates was Lothrop Stoddard, author of *The Rising Tide of Color against White World Supremacy* (1920), which depicted a slowly increasing white race being overwhelmed by more rapidly increasing "colored" races. In a later book, *Into the Darkness: Nazi Germany Today* (1940), Stoddard wrote that the Nazis succeeded in increasing "both the size and the quality of the population", with a "drastic curb of the defective elements ... weeding out the worst strains in the Germanic stock in a scientific and truly humanitarian way".

Another associate was Dr Harry Laughlin, who described Slavic and Italian immigrants as "even inferior to our native Negro population". Laughlin was apparently the inspiration for the Nazi compulsory sterilisation law passed in 1933. Another contributor to Sanger's *Birth Control Review* was Ernst Rudin, the director of the foremost German eugenics research institute, the Kaiser Wilhelm Institute for Genealogy.

In June 1933 Hitler set up the Expert Committee on Questions of Population and Racial Policy, with Rudin as one of its members. On the committee's recommendation, a law was passed the following month requiring the compulsory sterilisation of those who carried hereditary conditions or diseases, including feeblemindedness, schizophrenia, alcoholism and epilepsy. It is estimated that under the law, nearly two million people were forcibly sterilised between 1933 and 1945. Moreover, in 1939 Hitler set up an advisory committee which promoted a program to "euthanise" retarded and deformed children up to the age of three. It was later amended to include those up to the age of twelve. The committee also initiated a program which "euthanised" between 70,000 and 100,000 inmates of German mental institutions. At the Nuremberg trial the total number of euthanasia victims was estimated at 275,000.

Sanger herself saw the "improvement" of the race through eugenics as the primary goal of birth control. In the 1920s she published several articles in her *Birth Control Review* on eugenics, including one titled "Birth Control: The True Eugenics". It is no wonder that she considered the Catholic Church as her worst enemy. She wrote in 1918, "The Catholic Church is the bigoted, relentless enemy of birth control", and in 1924, "Our only real enemy is the [Catholic] Church". As early as 1917 she wrote: "I look forward to seeing humanity free some day of the tyranny of priests no less than of capitalists". There can be no doubt about Sanger's eugenic, anti-Catholic intentions.

789 Freemasons and the Church

I know that Catholics are not supposed to belong to the Freemasons, but can you explain why this is so? Are the Masons really opposed to the Church?

As you say, Catholics are forbidden to belong to the Freemasons. This was stated most recently by the Congregation for the Doctrine of the Faith in the "Declaration on Masonic Associations", dated 26 November 1983. The Declaration stated that "the Church's negative judgment in regard to Masonic associations remains unchanged since their principles have always been considered irreconcilable with the doctrine of the Church and therefore membership in them remains forbidden."

Bishop Athanasius Schneider, in his book *Christus Vincit* (Angelico Press 2019), explains the background of the Church's position. Freemasonery had its origin officially with the establishment of the first Grand Lodge in London in 1717. Freemasonry is a secret society which sees itself as the universal religion, while Christianity is simply one of dozens of religious sects whose particular opinions have divided humanity down the ages. Freemasonry requires that its members accept a basic belief in a "supreme architect of the universe", some sort of divine figure who cannot be known, who rules over the temple of humanity. Ultimately, Freemasonry rejects the true God and worships humanity as god.

From the beginning, Freemasons have been anti-Catholic. They were instrumental in bringing about the French Revolution, which began in 1789 and suppressed the Church, nationalised Church property, exiled 30,000 priests, and killed hundreds more. Masons had a great role too in the Russian Revolution of 1917, where Vladimir Lenin was a Freemason of the 31st degree, and the Prime Minister of Russia, Alexander Kerensky, was also a Freemason.

The opposition of Freemasonry to the Church and to God is seen in an instruction given to candidates for the 33rd degree of "The Ancient and Accepted Scottish Rite" of Freemasonry, quoted by Bishop Schneider (p. 62): "Neither the law, nor property, nor religion may govern man; and since they destroy man by depriving him of his most precious rights, the law, property, and religion are murderers to whom we have sworn to take the most terrible revenge. … Of these three disreputable enemies, religion must be the constant object of our deadly attacks. If we have destroyed religion, we will have the law and property at our disposal, and we can regenerate society by building Masonic religion, law, and property."

To the extent that Freemasonry admits Catholics, it does so to influence them to infiltrate and transform the Church. The excommunicated Catholic priest Antonio Fogazzaro, a leading Italian Modernist, wrote in the book *Il Santo* in 1905: We want to organise our whole action purposefully. A Catholic Freemasonry? Yes, a Freemasonry of the catacombs... One must work towards reforming Roman Catholicism in a progressive, theosophical sense through a pope who is convinced by these ideas."

This same agenda was expressed in a document of the highest Italian masonic lodge, titled *The Permanent Instruction of the Alta Vendita*. It was obtained by the Catholic Church sometime before 1859 and was translated into English by Irish priest Monsignor George Dillon, who used it in a lecture in 1884. Among the statements in the document are these: "The Pope, whoever he may be, will never come to the secret societies. It is for the secret societies to come first to the Church, with the aim of winning them both... Now then, in order to secure to us a Pope according to our own heart, it is necessary to fashion for that Pope a generation worthy of the kingdom of which we dream. Leave on one side old age and middle life, go to the youth, and, if possible, even to children... The reputation of a good Catholic and good patriot will open the way for our doctrines to pass into the hearts of the young clergy and go even to the depths of convents. In a few years the young clergy will have, by the force of events, invaded all offices. They will govern, administer, and judge. They will form the Council of the Sovereign. They will be called upon to choose the Pontiff who will reign."

It is clear from all this that the agenda of Freemasonry is totally opposed to the Church.

790 Christadelphians

I have a work colleague who is a Christadelphian and, frankly, I had never heard of this religious group until now. What is their history and what do they believe?

The name Christadelphian comes from the Greek words for Christ (*Christos*) and brothers (*adelphoi*). The group is of relatively recent origin, tracing its origin to John Thomas (1805-1871), who emigrated from England to North America in 1832. Following a near shipwreck, he vowed to find out the truth about life and God through personal study of the Bible. In the U.S. Thomas found sympathy in the Restoration Movement, whose members sought religious reform based on the Bible alone, rejecting all creeds.

This soon led to dissent, since Thomas developed his own personal beliefs, which he considered essential for salvation, and he began to question mainstream Christian beliefs. He believed that Scripture, as the word of God, did not support a multiplicity of differing beliefs, and he challenged the leaders to continue the process of restoring first-century Christian beliefs and of interpreting them correctly through a process of debate.

During this period of formulating his ideas Thomas was baptised twice, the second time after renouncing the beliefs he had previously held, leading the Restorationists to reject him. He based his new position on an appreciation of the reign of Christ on the throne of King David. On a lecturing tour to the United Kingdom in 1848-1850, Thomas founded the Christadelphians. They were especially well received in Scotland.

One of Thomas' passionate followers was Robert Roberts, who in 1864 published a magazine for the community and carried on the work of developing the movement after the death of Thomas. After his death, the movement became divided over doctrinal issues and several groups broke away. At present there are some 50,000 Christadelphians in around 120 countries.

A principal tenet of Christadelphians is that all beliefs are based solely on the Bible, which is regarded as inspired by God and error-free. Christadelphians reject belief in the Trinity, believing that the Father is a separate being from the Son, Jesus Christ, and that the Holy Spirit is only the power of God in creation and salvation. Jesus is the promised Jewish Messiah, he is the Son of Man, and he is the Son of God by virtue of his miraculous conception by the power of God. But he is not God from all eternity. Although Christ was tempted, he committed no sin and he was therefore a perfect representative to bring salvation to mankind.

Christadelphians believe that God raised Jesus from the dead and gave him immortality, that he ascended into heaven and that he will return to set up the kingdom of God on earth, in fulfilment of the promises made to Abraham and David. They believe that this kingdom will be the restoration of God's first kingdom of Israel under Kings David and Solomon.

Christadelphians believe that the devil is not an independent spiritual being or fallen angel, but rather the general principle of evil and the inclination to sin found in all mankind. Hell is not a place of eternal suffering for sinners, but rather a state of eternal death, of non-existence due to the annihilation of the body and the soul.

As regards salvation, Christadelphians believe that people have been separated from God because of their sins but they can be reconciled with him by becoming disciples of Jesus Christ. This they do by belief in the gospel, repentance for their sins and baptism by total immersion in water. Christadelphians reject assurance of salvation, believing instead that salvation comes by remaining "in Christ". It is their belief that, after death, believers remain in a state of non-existence, knowing nothing until the resurrection at the return of Christ.

Following the judgment when Christ returns, those who are saved receive the gift of immortality and live with Christ on a restored earth, assisting him to establish the kingdom of God and to rule over the mortal population for a thousand years, the "Millennium". Some Christadelphians believe that while the kingdom will be centred on Israel, Christ will reign over all nations, while others believe the kingdom will be limited to the land of Israel.

791 Who are the Mormons?

Over the years I have seen Mormons knocking on doors and occasionally they have come to my house. They are exceptionally polite and very impressive. What is the background of the Mormons and what are their main beliefs?

The Mormons, properly known as The Church of Jesus Christ of the Latter-day Saints, were founded by Joseph Smith in upstate New York early in the nineteenth century. In March 1830, Smith published the *Book of Mormon*, which he claimed was a translation of some golden plates containing the religious history of an ancient American civilisation compiled by the prophet-historian Mormon. Smith claimed that an angel had directed him to the golden plates, which were buried in the Hill Cumorah. In 1832 he added an account of a vision he had had of the Father and the Son when he was about 14, sometime in the early 1820s. This vision came to be regarded by some Mormons as the most important event in human history after the life and death of Jesus Christ.

According to Smith, a departure from the original principles of Jesus Christ, known as the Great Apostasy, took place shortly after the ascension of Christ into heaven. It brought about the corruption of Christian doctrine by various philosophies, with followers dividing into different groups. Mormons claim that the martyrdom of the apostles led to a loss of the priesthood, but the early Church as Christ intended it, with a valid priesthood, was restored through Joseph Smith.

On 6 April 1830 Smith founded what he called the Church of Christ. The movement gradually spread West and communities were established in Ohio, Illinois and Missouri, with some of the people practising polygamy. There was often opposition from the local people and in 1844 Smith was arrested and he and his brother Hyrum were killed by a mob in Carthage, Illinois.

Brigham Young, a close associate of Smith's, then became the leader of most of the movement. To prevent conflict with the local people, Young led the members first to Nebraska and then to Utah, where they became firmly established. From there they sent missionaries to other countries, resulting in numerous converts, many of whom later migrated to the U.S. and settled in Utah.

Although polygamy continued to be practised by many Mormons, in 1904 the church president disavowed the practice before the U.S. Congress and issued a manifesto calling for all plural marriages to cease. The church excommunicated those practising polygamy, and today it distances itself actively from any "fundamentalists" who continue the practice.

Among the practices to be lived by Mormons are studying the scriptures, daily prayer, regular fasting, attendance at Sunday worship services, participation in church activities on weekdays, refraining from work on Sundays when possible, and high standards of honesty, integrity, obedience to the law, chastity outside marriage and fidelity within marriage. Mormons do not accept same-sex marriage. Observant Mormons contribute ten percent of their income to the church and many, especially the young, engage for a time in a proselytising mission, during which they dedicate all their time to the church, without pay.

Mormons follow the Word of Wisdom, a code of health that forbids the use of tobacco, alcohol, coffee and tea, the use of illegal drugs and the abuse of prescription drugs, gambling and the viewing of pornography. Family life is especially fostered by Mormons, who often have large families.

The Mormon scriptures are the Bible, the Book of Mormon and the revelations and writings of Joseph Smith. Jesus Christ is their central figure. Mormons believe in a "friendly universe" governed by a God whose aim it is to bring his children to immortality and eternal life. They believe in an eternal cycle where God's children become gods, create worlds, and have spirit children whom they will govern. Though Mormonism proclaims the existence of many gods, it does not advocate for their worship besides Earth's god.

Mormons believe that before humans began their life on earth they pre-existed as spirit children of God. They believe that Jesus, the eldest of God's children, came to earth as the literal Son of God to conquer sin and death so that God's other children could return to him.

According to Mormons, every person on earth will be resurrected, and nearly all of them will be received into various kingdoms of glory. In order to be accepted into the highest kingdom a person must fully accept Christ through faith, repentance, and ordinances such as baptism and the laying on of hands.

792 Reflections on Cardinal Pell

I was shocked and saddened to hear this week of the sudden death of Cardinal George Pell. I know you were close to him and I would be interested to hear your reflections on this great man.

I too was saddened by the death of this great warrior for the faith. Cardinal Pell did so much good for the Church, but we can only accept that God wanted to take him home to heaven, where he will undoubtedly continue to intercede for the Church here below, along with his beloved friend and ally Pope Benedict XVI, who died only ten days before. May they rest in peace!

I worked for Cardinal Pell for thirteen years, the first four as chaplain of RMIT University in Melbourne (1998-2001) and then, when he was transferred to Sydney, nine more as Director of the Catholic Adult Education Centre of that archdiocese (2002-2010).

During those years I came to know the Cardinal very well, as I met with him numerous times. He was always available to see me and interested in what I was doing. He would listen attentively, make a few suggestions, and encourage me in my job. "Keep up the good work", was a frequent final comment. He was not a micro-manager, who gave detailed instructions. He let me find my own way. And even when I came with bold initiatives of new programs, he let me do what I thought best and he always supported me.

When I say that he was always available, this applied not only to me but to anyone else who wanted to see him, especially priests. When he was Archbishop of Melbourne, he announced that every Thursday afternoon he would be available for any priest to see him without an appointment. This included, of course, priests who had problems, including those who had issues with him. This practice continued in Sydney.

What is more, he invited all the priests of the archdiocese, both religious and secular, to have dinner with him on Monday nights, calling them in alphabetical order. The number was limited only by the size of the table, usually at least a dozen. The dinner included drinks beforehand and then a fairly formal dinner, in a relaxed atmosphere where the priests felt at home and he could get to know them. He regarded his priests as co-workers in the vineyard of the Lord and he looked after them very well. In 2005 when I was in hospital following major surgery, he was kind enough to send me flowers and a message of prayerful support. He was truly a father.

He was a father to everyone, a shepherd who cared about his flock. An habitual practice of his was to stand outside the cathedral after Mass to greet and chat with anyone who wished to see him. He would remain there as long as there were people waiting to do so. He was truly a "people person". He loved to accept invitations to dinner with families, no matter who they were. He would show his warmth and good humour, and he loved to engage with the children.

At the same time, he made an enormous contribution to building up the Church. In his only five years as Archbishop of Melbourne, he brought about major changes, testified to by the many people who spoke at a farewell Mass for him in St Patrick's Cathedral. Among them were changes in the regime and personnel of the seminary, resulting in increased numbers of seminarians and the ordination of many fine, dedicated priests. He continued this in Sydney with the same results. Another great initiative in Melbourne was the drafting of new texts for religious education in the Catholic schools, titled *To Know, Worship and Love*. They were later used in dioceses all over Australia.

He loved young people and promoted parish youth groups and university chaplaincies, greatly increasing the number of young people involved in the Church. The appointment of Steve Lawrence, well-known Hawthorn AFL player who starred in the team's 1991 premiership win, as head of the youth ministry both in Melbourne and later in Sydney, did wonders for this work. Cardinal Pell's greatest initiative in the work with youth was the holding of World Youth Day in Sydney in 2008, greatly revitalising the faith of young people from Australia and all over the world.

His work for the universal Church was notable, including being a member of several bodies of the Vatican curia, his appointment by Pope Francis to his Council of Cardinal advisors, and especially his appointment as Prefect of the Secretariat for the Economy of the Church. And he spoke out strongly and frequently on matters of faith and morals. His voice is now silent. He will be sorely missed.

The angels

793 Hierarchy of the angels

In the Bible we see numerous names for the different types of angels, like seraphim and cherubim, archangels and angels. What do we know about these different types? Is there a hierarchy of the angels?

To answer your question, let us begin with Sacred Scripture. The prophet Isaiah writes that he saw the Lord sitting on a throne and "Above him stood the seraphim; each had six wings... And one called to another and said: 'Holy, holy, holy is the Lord of hosts; the whole earth is full of his glory" (*Is* 6:2-3). We recognise these last words as those used at the end of the Preface in every Mass. Christian tradition places the seraphim in the highest rank of angels.

Another rank of angels are the cherubim, who are mentioned in the book of Exodus with reference to the Ark of the Covenant: "And you shall make two cherubim of gold; of hammered work shall you make them, on the two ends of the mercy seat... The cherubim shall spread out their wings above, overshadowing the mercy seat with their wings, their faces one to another..." (*Ex* 25:18-20). Without being called cherubim, these angels with two pairs of wings also appear in the prophecy of Ezekiel (cf. *Ez* 1:23). Tradition places the cherubim in the second rank of angels.

We find more types of angels in the letters of St Paul. For example, he writes that in Christ "all things were created, in heaven and on earth, visible and invisible, whether thrones or dominions or principalities or authorities – all things were created through him and for him" (*Col* 1:16). These four types of angels are also considered to be part of the angelic hierarchy. The Catechism uses this text to say that "Christ is the center of the angelic world. They are his angels...They belong to him because they were created *through* and *for* him" (*CCC* 331).

St Peter too speaks of different types of angels. He writes that Christ has gone into heaven and is at the right hand of God, "with angels, authorities and powers subject to him" (1 Pet 3:22).

The classic treatise on the hierarchy of the angels comes from Pseudo-Dionysius the Areopagite, who wrote *On the Celestial Hierarchy* around the turn of the sixth century. Basing himself partly on the texts of Scripture we have just seen, Pseudo-Dionysius distinguished three spheres of angels, each with three categories. It must be said at the outset that this treatise is his own work, based on his own imagination, not a work accepted and used by the Magisterium of the Church. For example, the *Catechism of the Catholic Church* does not distinguish a hierarchy of the angels.

In the first sphere, according to Pseudo-Dionysius, are angels who see and worship God directly, and who communicate God's will to the angels who are closer to the life of man. The angels in the first sphere, in descending order, are the Seraphim, Cherubim and Thrones. St Thomas Aquinas imagined Satan as a fallen Cherub (cf. *STh* I, q. 63, a. 7).

In the second sphere are angels who act as heavenly governors of creation by subjecting matter and by guiding and ruling other spirits. In this sphere are the Dominations, sometimes called Lordships or Dominions, as well as the Virtues and Powers. The Dominations are considered to regulate the duties of lower angels and only rarely do they make themselves physically known to humans. The Virtues are the spirits of motion and they also assist in governing nature, in working miracles and in strengthening humans' faith in God. The Powers are able to restrain evil forces.

In the third and lowest sphere are the Principalities, Archangels and Angels. The Principalities, or rulers, preside over the bands of angels and charge them with carrying out their divine mission. St Paul refers to them, writing that Christ sits at the right hand of God in the heavenly places, "far above all rule and authority and power and dominion" (*Eph* 1:21). In that same letter he writes: "that through the Church the manifold wisdom of God might now be made known to the principalities and powers in the heavenly places" (*Eph* 3:10).

It is interesting that the name "Archangel" appears only twice in the New Testament (cf. *1 Thess* 4:16 and *Jude* 1:9). The only Archangel whose name is given is Michael (*Jude* 1:9), although Raphael (*Tobit* 12:15) and Gabriel (*Lk* 1:26) are also considered to be Archangels.

So yes, there are many types of angels but we cannot be certain about their hierarchy.

794 Knowledge of the angels

Something I have always wondered about is whether angels can know what will happen in the future and also what we are thinking. For example, do they know our inmost thoughts and future events that could harm us, and so can they protect us from them?

St Thomas Aquinas (1225-1274) answers your questions in his *Summa Theologiae*, in a section on angels (*STh*, I, q. 57, art. 3-4). His answer for the most part is in the negative in both cases.

As regards angels' knowledge of the future, he writes in Article 3: "Whatever is the exclusive sign of the Divinity, does not belong to the angels. But to know future events is the exclusive sign of the Divinity, according to Isaiah 41:23: 'Show the things that are to come hereafter, and we shall know that ye are gods.' Therefore, the angels do not know future events."

St Thomas goes on to explain that the future can be known in two ways. "First, it can be known in its cause. And thus, future events which proceed necessarily from their causes, are known with sure knowledge; as that the sun will rise tomorrow." With events that proceed necessarily from their cause, not only angels but also we humans can know them with certainty. For example, in the area of science, where there are fixed laws, we can know with certainty that there will be an eclipse on a certain day at a certain hour, or that if we mix two chemicals together there will be an explosion. Naturally, not all events proceed necessarily from their cause.

St Thomas comments: "But events which proceed from their causes in the majority of cases, are not known for certain, but conjecturally; thus the doctor knows beforehand the health of the patient. This manner of knowing future events exists in the angels, and by so much the more than it does in us, as they understand the causes of things both more universally and more perfectly; thus doctors who penetrate more deeply into the causes of an ailment can pronounce a surer verdict on the future issue thereof."

Other events follow from their cause only seldom. Here St Thomas says that "events which proceed from their causes in the minority of cases are quite unknown; such as casual and chance events." Of this sort, for example, are events such as an earthquake or lightning striking a particular object, where scientists cannot know for certain when and how the event will occur, and neither can angels.

The other way that future events can be known is in themselves. St Thomas comments that to know the future in this way belongs only to God. The reason is that "God sees all things in His eternity, which, being simple, is present to all time, and embraces all time. And therefore God's one glance is cast over all things which happen in all time as present before Him; and He beholds all things as they are in themselves… But the mind of an angel, and every created intellect, fall far short of God's eternity; hence the future as it is in itself cannot be known by any created intellect." That is, for God, all time is present at once, so there is nothing "future" for him.

Naturally, God can communicate to angels certain particulars about the future so that he can then commission them to pass on this information to a human person. Such was the case with the Archangel Gabriel and Our Lady at the Annunciation.

As regards whether angels can know what we are thinking, St Thomas says in Article 4 that they cannot. Again, he makes a distinction: "A secret thought can be known in two ways: first, in its effect. In this way it can be known not only by an angel, but also by man… For thought is sometimes discovered not merely by outward act, but also by change of countenance; and doctors can tell some passions of the soul by the mere pulse. Much more then can angels, or even demons, the more deeply they penetrate those occult bodily modifications."

The other way in which thoughts can be known is as they are in the mind itself, and affections as they are in the will. Here, says St Thomas, only God, and not angels, can know these thoughts and affections. "The reason of this is, because the rational creature is subject to God only, and He alone can work in it who is its principal object and last end... Consequently, all that is in the will, and all things that depend only on the will, are known to God alone. Now it is evident that it depends entirely on the will for anyone actually to consider anything; because a man who has a habit of knowledge, or any intelligible species, uses them at will."

St Thomas' arguments are his own, not those of the Magisterium of the Church, but they are most convincing and can be taken as truth. For this reason, the Church recommends them.

795 Questions on the guardian angels

My daughter recently asked whether her guardian angel will be with her in heaven, and whether God is constantly creating new angels. Can you help me?

There are lots of questions about angels which people have asked over the years. Here I will answer those of your daughter and others.

Before answering particular questions we should recall that the angels were created at the beginning of time, before human beings. They were created good and were endowed with sanctifying grace so that they could merit eternal life with God, but some of them rejected God and were condemned to eternal punishment. These we call devils. St Peter writes that "God did not spare the angels when they sinned, but cast them into hell and committed them to pits of deepest darkness" (*2 Pet* 2:4). It was one of these fallen angels that tempted Adam and Eve to commit the original sin.

All of the good angels are in heaven, where they give glory to God, but at the same time some of them have roles here on earth. For example, the Archangel Gabriel announced to both Zechariah and Our Lady the birth of a child, while other angels give glory to Our Lord in the Blessed Eucharist and still others serve as guardian angels of human beings.

At the beginning God created vast numbers of angels. Our Lord himself speaks of "legions of angels" (*Mt* 26:53) and the prophet Daniel, speaking of the angels serving God, writes: "a thousand thousands served him, and ten thousand times ten thousand stood before him" (*Dan* 7:10). The book of *Revelation* too speaks of "many angels, numbering myriads of myriads and thousands of thousands" (*Rev* 5:11).

From this we can understand that God created all the angels at the beginning, and that he is not constantly creating new ones. Therefore, the number of angels must be vast. The Catechism teaches: "From its beginning until death, human life is surrounded by their watchful care and intercession" (*CCC* 336), the understanding being that not only Christians, but every human being, has a guardian angel. There are billions of people alive today, and there are many billions more who have preceded us and will follow us until the end of time. All of their angels were created at the beginning.

Will our guardian angel be with us in heaven? As we said, all the angels are already in heaven, even though they may also have a role on earth. Our Lord referred to this when he said: "See that you do not despise one of these little ones; for I tell you that in heaven their angels always behold the face of my Father who is in heaven" (*Mt* 18:10-11). Our guardian angel has been assigned by God to look after only us, and when we die, he will be with us in heaven, giving glory to God. We can say that this angel is "our angel", assigned to us by God, and he will remain with us in heaven.

This answers another question which people sometimes ask: When someone dies, does his guardian angel get assigned to someone else on earth? To use modern terminology, somewhat facetiously, does God "recycle" the angels? The answer is clearly no. Our angel will remain with us forever. Obviously, if someone goes to hell, his angel will not be with him there. As regards purgatory, some theologians, including St Bonaventure, teach that the guardian angel will accompany the person's soul there, to strengthen it in its purification before going to heaven.

Another question people sometimes ask is whether it is permissible to give our guardian angel a name. The Vatican's *Directory on Popular Piety and the Liturgy* (2002) states: "The practice of assigning names to the Holy Angels should be discouraged, except in the cases of Gabriel, Raphael and Michael whose names are contained in Holy Scripture" (n. 217). One can assign a name to a being over which one has dominion, and so parents give names to their children, and children assign names to their pets or toys. But only God can assign a name to an angel. Nonetheless, some people, to have a more familiar relationship with their guardian angel, do give him a name, as if saying: "I don't know your name, but do you mind if I call you so and so"? Understood in this way, there can be no objection, and even saints have done this.

Our Lady and St Joseph

796 The betrothal of Mary and Joseph

The Bible speaks of Our Lady and St Joseph being "betrothed" when Jesus was conceived. How did people prepare for marriage at that time, and was betrothal the same as our engagement?

Marriage customs in the Jewish tradition at the time of Our Lady and St Joseph were very different from ours today. Henry Skrzyński, in his wonderful book *The Jewess Mary, Mother of Jesus* (Chevalier Press 1994) tells us much about these customs and I will take much of what follows from that book.

First, it was the custom that husband and wife should be of the same social class, and this was widely practised. For this reason, marriages between close relatives, such as first or second cousins, or between uncles and nieces, were not uncommon. Great difference in age was also to be avoided. It was customary for girls to marry around the age of fifteen and so St Joseph was probably around eighteen, for this was considered the right age for a man to marry. According to the sages, "God curses him who is not married by twenty".

Also, young men were advised to look not only for physical beauty in their prospective bride but especially for virtue. As the book of Proverbs says, "Charm is deceitful, and beauty is vain, but a woman who fears the Lord is to be praised" (*Prov* 31:30).

When young people reached the age for marriage, the parents of the two would get together and arrange for them to meet each other, usually in the company of one of their relatives. Family-arranged marriages were common in Palestine at the time, as they were and still are in many parts of the world. With this introduction to each other, there was no commitment to proceed with betrothal. If after spending some time getting to know each other, the two young people agreed to marry, it fell to a member of the man's family to approach the father of the woman to suggest the possibility of marriage.

If this was accepted, arrangements were made for the official betrothal, the *Erusim*. On the day itself, or the day before, the heads of both families signed a document known as the *Shitre Erusim*, binding both parties and stipulating the amount of the woman's dowry. On the day of the full moon, considered especially propitious for betrothals, the man would go to the woman's family home and hand her a small coin, as a token of her dowry, and the Shitre Erusim. He would put a gold ring on her finger, saying: "Be thou betrothed unto me with this ring in accordance with the laws of Moses and Israel". From then on, the couple were officially betrothed.

The man and his family would then give presents to the woman's father, a custom established by Abraham, when he betrothed his son Isaac to Rebekah (cf. *Gen* 24:53). The woman's father would in turn prepare a feast, attended by both families, and he would bless his daughter, that she be favoured with many sons, as Raguel did when he gave his daughter Sarah to Tobias to be his wife (cf. *Tob* 10:11-13).

At law, betrothed people were legally married and were already referred to as husband and wife. We see this in the gospel of St Matthew: "When his [Jesus'] mother Mary had been betrothed to Joseph, before they came together she was found to be with child of the Holy Spirit; and her husband Joseph, being a just man and unwilling to put her to shame, resolved to send her away quietly..." (*Mt* 1:18-19).

During the betrothal period, the wife could be set free from the commitment only on the death of her husband or by him divorcing her. Therefore, Joseph faced the dilemma of how to leave Mary without subjecting her to shame, and he resolved to "send her away quietly".

After the betrothal ceremony, the wife continued to live with her parents until the wedding, which was usually a year later in the case of a woman marrying for the first time. Widows and divorcees could wed again after three months. During these months, the husband was expected to prepare the new home with all its furnishings, and the wife to prepare her trousseau: the clothing and linen, etc., which she would bring into the marriage. During this time, conjugal relations and cohabitation were forbidden, and infidelity carried all the consequences of adultery.

As you can see, betrothal was very different from our present-day engagement.

797 The wedding of Mary and Joseph

I am getting married soon and my fiancé and I are entrusting ourselves to Our Lady and St Joseph. Can you tell me anything about their wedding if, indeed, anything is known?

We know something about the marriage customs of Jews at the time of Our Lady and St Joseph and I will draw on this information, gathered from various sources. Of particular help has been the book *The Jewess Mary, Mother of Jesus* by Henry Skrzyński.

The wedding ceremony took place about a year after the betrothal. During this time the couple lived separately even though they were legally considered to be husband and wife.

A wedding at that time was not, strictly speaking, a religious ceremony, although marriage had a deeply spiritual meaning, symbolising the union of God with Israel, as proclaimed by the prophets and psalms. For example, the prophet Hosea writes of how God says to his people: "And I will take you for my wife forever; I will take you for my wife in righteousness and in justice, in steadfast love, and in mercy. I will take you for my wife in faithfulness; and you shall know the LORD (*Hos* 2:19-20).

On the day of the wedding, often a Wednesday, the bride was anointed, dressed and adorned with ornaments, with a crown of flowers on her head. She awaited the arrival of her husband in the evening. The husband would arrive at the bride's family home in his best attire, accompanied by friends and by a scribe, who would write out the marriage contract, the ketuvah. This was a written document spelling out the terms on which the marriage was arranged, with the rights and duties that had been agreed upon. At the same time, it served as something like today's marriage certificate, proving that a marriage had in fact been contracted, thereby guaranteeing the legitimacy of any children born from the union.

A marriage not based on a *ketuvah* was considered null and void. It ensured that all the property the wife brought into the marriage as a dowry was safeguarded by an obligatory mortgage on all her husband's property. It also provided, among other things, for medical care in case of the wife's illness, for the costs of her funeral, and for her to stay in the husband's house in the event of his death. The obligation to repay the ketuvah, should the husband die or divorce his wife, acted as a deterrent to a hasty divorce.

After the *ketuvah* had been signed, when the bride was ready to leave, her father would bless her and express the wish that she not return home as a widow or divorced. He would also release her from any vows she had taken in his house. Then the husband would take his bride, held aloft on a litter, in a joyous procession to his own house with torches, lamps on long poles, drums, pipes, lutes and singing. Accompanying the couple were their relatives, friends and wedding guests. Those who happened to be on the streets when the procession passed, would accompany it for at least a short distance. Nuts and roasted ears of wheat were thrown to children and bystanders as a sign that a bride was passing by.

Our Lord refers to this procession in the parable of the wise and foolish virgins (cf. *Mt* 25:1-13). It was the virgins' role to accompany the procession with their lamps lit on the way to the husband's house. In the parable, the bridegroom was delayed and arrived at midnight.

When they arrived, the bride was given away in marriage to her husband with the words: "Take her according to the Law of Moses and of Israel", to which he replied: "Be thou my wife in marriage according to the Law of Moses and of Israel." The relatives and guests would then say, "May the Lord, by this young woman that is coming into your house, build it up with children, as Rachel and Leah have built up the house of Israel. May you prosper and be renowned."

Upon entering the house, the husband would kiss the prominent guests, who had their heads anointed with oil. Then from large stone jars, water was brought for the prescribed ritual washing of hands. The meal consisted of great quantities of bread, stews with vegetables and garlic, fish, olives, dates, figs, grapes, nuts and plenty of wine. The marriage feast lasted for seven days, explaining in part why the wine ran out at the wedding feast of Cana, where Our Lord changed water into wine (cf. *Jn* 2:1-11).

All in all, it was a joyous occasion as the couple began their life together. The wedding of Our Lady and St Joseph would undoubtedly have followed this pattern very closely.

798 The wedding ring of Our Lady

I remember reading some time ago that the wedding ring of Our Lady is still in existence somewhere. Is this credible?

First let us look at the facts. There is a ring in the Cappella di Santo Anello (Chapel of the Holy Ring) in the Cathedral of San Lorenzo in the Italian city of Perugia. It is kept in a reliquary made in the early sixteenth century, and is hanging from a gilded silver crown made in 1716. The ring itself is thick and smooth, and is made of a form of iridescent quartz known as chalcedony. It is dark amber or yellow in colour, and can appear milky white in the sunlight. An investigation carried out in 1949-50 suggested that the ring is a man's signet ring from the first century AD.

How did the ring come to be in Perugia? According to the story, a Jewish dealer in precious stones in Rome gave the ring to Ainerio, a goldsmith in Chiusi, Italy, around the year 1000. The ring had supposedly been passed down through the generations of a Jewish family, and the Virgin Mary had appeared to the Jewish merchant in a dream, moving him to give the ring to the goldsmith.

Ainerio, the goldsmith, placed the ring in the family crypt for safekeeping. He doubted its authenticity until his recently deceased young son appeared to him in a vision and rebuked him for abandoning the precious relic. Ainerio then gave the ring to the convent of St Mustiola in Chiusi so it could be honoured publicly.

In July, 1473, the ring was stolen but it was left in a church in Perugia that same year. It was transferred to the chapel in the Cathedral there in 1488. Over the years there have been numerous miracles associated with the ring, especially regarding the restoration of sight.

A fascinating aspect of the story comes in the visions of the German mystic Blessed Anne Catherine Emmerich (1774-1824). She had never heard of the ring, but on 29 July 1821 she saw it in a vision. In her book of revelations, *The Life of the Blessed Virgin Mary*, Chapter 7.VII, she wrote: "I saw the Blessed Virgin's wedding ring; it is neither of silver nor of gold, nor of any other metal; it is dark in color and iridescent; it is not a thin narrow ring, but rather thick and at least a finger broad. I saw it smooth and yet as if covered with little regular triangles in which were letters. On the inside was a flat surface. The ring is engraved with something. I saw it kept behind many locks in a beautiful church. Devout people about to be married take their wedding rings to touch it."

A few days later, on 3 August, she had another vision, this time of the wedding of Mary and Joseph, somehow overlaid with a vision of a contemporaneous church celebration, which she described like this: "Today I saw a festival in a church in Italy where the wedding-ring is to be found. It seemed to me to be hung up in a kind of monstrance which stood above the Tabernacle. There was a large altar there, magnificently decorated; one saw deep into it through much silverwork. I saw many rings being held against the monstrance. During the festival I saw Mary and Joseph appearing in their wedding garments on each side of the ring, as if Joseph were placing the ring on the Blessed Virgin's finger. At the same time I saw the ring shining and as if in movement."

Blessed Anne Catherine had no idea whether the ring was still in existence, but a few years after her death her revelations led to a search for the church and altar described in her visions. Soon it became obvious that her visions described the altar, with its reliquary and ring, in the Cathedral of San Lorenzo in Perugia. The ring was well known there and young couples did make pilgrimages to the Cathedral to receive a blessing for their marriage and to touch their wedding rings to the Santo Anello.

As regards the "many locks" in Blessed Anne Catherine's vision, the reliquary is kept in a safe with seven locks, inside a niche closed by a gilded grate with another four locks. The ring is brought out to be viewed on July 29-30 and the penultimate Sunday of January each year.

We cannot be absolutely sure that this is the wedding ring of Our Lady, but the visions of Blessed Anne Catherine lend credibility to it.

799 The Assumption of Our Lady into heaven

I have a Protestant friend who thinks we Catholics are foolish for believing in the bodily Assumption of Our Lady into heaven when there is no reference to it in the Scriptures. How can I answer her?

As we have said in this column a number of times over the years, there are many truths we believe as Catholics that are not explicit in the Scriptures, but are part of the tradition of the Church going back to the earliest centuries. Among them are the belief in Purgatory and in the Immaculate Conception of Our Lady. The very canon, or list, of the books in the Bible is another fact not found in the Scriptures, but comes rather from the tradition of the Church. What is the evidence from tradition for the Assumption, which was defined by Pope Pius XII as late as 1950?

To begin with, we can say that when a truth has been defined as a dogma of faith, as is the case here, it is because the Church is absolutely certain that it is true. Popes do not "invent" dogmas. They find them in the constant and firm belief of the Church.

Although, as you say, there is no mention of Our Lady's Assumption in the Scriptures, Pope Pius XII, in his Bull *Munificentissimus*

Deus (1950) proclaiming the dogma of the Assumption, gave many biblical references, including some from the Old Testament, which Fathers of the Church and theologians have interpreted as referring symbolically to Our Lady's Assumption.

The tradition of Our Lady's Assumption goes back to the earliest centuries. The earliest known account is the *Liber Requiei Mariae* (*Book of the Repose of Mary*), which was probably composed in the fourth century, but possibly as early as the third. It is regarded as an apocryphal work, meaning not officially approved by the Church, but the very fact that it speaks of Our Lady's Assumption is evidence of the belief of many people at that time. Another work which attests to the Assumption is the *Six Books Dormition Narratives*, of the fifth and sixth centuries, and the *De Obitu S. Dominae* (*On the Death of the Holy Lady*), which is a summary of the Six Books.

The first Father of the Church in the West to witness to the tradition of the Assumption of Mary was St Gregory of Tours, who died in 594 AD. He writes: "Finally, when blessed Mary, having completed the course of her earthly life, was about to be called from this world, all the apostles, coming from their different regions, gathered together in her house. When they heard that she was about to be taken up out of the world, they kept watch together with her. And behold, the Lord Jesus came with his angels and, taking her soul, handed it over to the archangel Michael and withdrew. At dawn, the apostles lifted up her body on a pallet, laid it in a tomb, and again the Lord presented himself to them and ordered that her holy body be taken and carried up to heaven. There she is now, joined once more to her soul; she exults with the elect, rejoicing in the eternal blessings that will have no end" (L. Gambero, *Mary and the Fathers of the Church*, Ignatius 1999, p. 353).

An Eastern Father of the Church who testifies to this tradition is St John Damascene, who died in 749. He writes in a prayer to Mary: "The assembly of apostles carried you, the Lord God's true Ark, as once the priests carried the symbolic ark, on their shoulders. They laid you in the tomb, through which, as if through the Jordan, they will conduct you to the promised land, that is to say, the Jerusalem above, mother of all the faithful, whose architect and builder is God. Your soul did not descend to Hades, neither did your flesh see corruption. Your virginal and uncontaminated body was not abandoned in the earth, but you are transferred into the royal dwelling of heaven, you, the Queen, the sovereign, the Lady, God's Mother, the true God-bearer..." (*Homily 1 on the Dormition* 12-13).

Of importance in this regard is the fact that, even though the Church has always safeguarded and venerated the relics of the martyrs and other saints, there is no tradition of the relics of Our Lady being kept anywhere.

As early as the sixth century a feast of the Dormition, or death, of Our Lady began to be celebrated on August 15 in both Jerusalem and Rome.

By the sixteenth century the tradition of Mary's Assumption was firmly implanted in the Church's prayers. The Rosary, which was standardised by the Dominican Pope St Pius V in 1569, had the Assumption of Our Lady as the fourth Glorious Mystery, as it has been ever since. And a *Manual of Devout Prayers and Devotions*, printed in England in 1688, of which I have a copy, has the feast of the "Assumption of the Blessed Virgin" celebrated on August 15.

So, with this constant tradition going back to the early Church, there can be no question about the bodily Assumption of Our Lady, even though it is not explicit in the Scriptures.

800 The place of Mary's Assumption

Do we know from where Our Lady was assumed into heaven? I know that she lived for some time with St John in Ephesus but I have also heard that there is a church in Jerusalem commemorating her assumption there.

There are two traditions in this regard. An ancient one says Mary was assumed into heaven in Jerusalem and a more recent one in Ephesus. Let us consider the earlier tradition, which has more credibility.

Among the Jerusalem traditions are some apocryphal writings generically known as *Transitus Virginis*, "the passing of the Virgin", or *Dormitio Mariae*, "the falling asleep of Mary. It should be remembered that the expression "falling asleep" in the Scriptures and other writings usually means "dying". According to these writings, when Our Lady was nearing the end of her life, the apostles gathered around her bed, and Our Lord himself came down and took her soul to heaven. Then the apostles placed her body in a tomb and three days later Our Lord returned and took her body to reunite it with her soul in heaven.

We find echoes of these traditions in several Fathers of the Church. St Gregory of Tours, who died in 594, is the first Western Father to write about the assumption. He hands down information he received from an apocryphal Greek text, which he knew in a fifth-century Latin translation. He describes how the apostles were with Our Lady when Our Lord came with his angels and took her soul, handing it over to the Archangel Michael. At dawn, the apostles lifted her body onto a pallet, laid it in a tomb, and kept watch over it until Our Lord came and ordered it to be carried up to heaven.

St John Damascene, who died in Jerusalem in the middle of the eighth century, writes in a similar vein. He says Mary died in the Upper Room, after which the apostles prepared her body for burial and carried it on their shoulders in procession from Mount Zion to the Garden of Gethsemane, accompanied by the angels and the whole Church.

Today there are two churches in Jerusalem which commemorate these events. The Basilica of the Dormition of Mary, where Our Lady is believed to have died, is located next to the Cenacle on Mount Zion, a hill on the southwest edge of Jerusalem, just outside the walls of the Old City. In the second half of the fourth century, a basilica was built there called Holy Zion, and it was considered to be the mother of all churches. It included the Cenacle, or Upper Room, and also the place of the "transit of Our Lady". The basilica was destroyed and rebuilt several times in the following centuries, until only the Cenacle itself remained standing, where it is today. The present Basilica of the Dormition was built next to the Cenacle, starting in 1910, by the German Emperor Wilhelm II, who also built a Benedictine abbey alongside it.

The Basilica is round in shape and has on its upper floor the main church, crowned by a great dome adorned with beautiful mosaics. The sanctuary is in an apse with a half dome above it, and has a mosaic of the Virgin holding the Child Jesus. On the lower floor is a crypt with a statue of the Blessed Virgin, lying as though asleep, beneath a cupola supported by pillars.

The other church, where Our Lady's body was believed to have been laid before it was assumed into heaven, is the Basilica of the Tomb of Mary, just to the north of the Garden of Gethsemane, across the Kidron Valley from Jerusalem. It is about a 25-minute walk from the Cenacle. It is called the Church of the Assumption by the Greek Orthodox and other Orthodox Churches who have certain rights over it.

The tomb in the Basilica is two long flights of stairs down from the present street, owing to the fact that the Kidron riverbed has risen substantially over the centuries and also to the fact that the building today was probably the crypt of the earlier basilica, built in the fourth or fifth century. Archaeological excavations in the 1970s revealed that the tomb where Our Lady's body was laid was part of a first-century burial site. The central focus of the Basilica is a small chapel over the place where, according to the tradition, Our Lady's tomb was carved out of the rock.

801 Was St Joseph assumed into heaven?

Since St Joseph was so close to Our Lady and so holy, is it possible that he too was assumed body and soul into heaven when he died?

Although we cannot be absolutely sure, there is a strong possibility that St Joseph too was assumed into heaven. As you say, he was very close to Our Lady, as her husband, and he was extremely holy, to a point where he may have been without sin, so God may have rewarded him in this way. What is more, the Holy Family was always very united on earth, and so it is likely that Jesus and Mary, who are in heaven in their bodies, would have wanted St Joseph to be there too in that way.

That St Joseph may have been assumed body and soul into heaven was certainly the view of a number of saints.

Among them was St Bernardine of Siena OFM (1380-1444), an Italian saint who did much to spread devotion to St Joseph. He said in one of his sermons: "We may piously believe, but not assert, that the Most Holy Son of God Jesus crowned his foster-father with the same privilege which he gave his Mother: that as he assumed her into heaven, bodily and glorious in soul, so also on the day when he arose he took Joseph up with him in the glory of the Resurrection. So that, as this glorious family, Christ, the Virgin and Joseph, had dwelt together on earth in the labours of life and in loving grace, so now they reign in heaven in loving glory of both body and soul."

It is recorded that when St Bernardine preached in Padua that St Joseph was in heaven body and soul, a bright heavenly gold cross appeared above his head. This was taken as a sign that what he was saying was true. Blessed Bernardine de Bustis OFM (1450-1513) witnessed the event, and he also believed in the bodily assumption of St Joseph.

Another great saint who believed in St Joseph's bodily assumption was the Doctor of the Church, St Francis de Sales (1567-1622). In the nineteenth of a series of spiritual conferences, he said that "we must nowise doubt that this glorious saint has great credit in heaven with him who has so favoured him as to raise him to it both body and soul; which is the more probable as we have no relic of him here below on earth; and it seems to me that no one can doubt this truth. For how could he who had been obedient to him all the time of his life, have refused this grace to St Joseph?"

In that conference St Francis de Sales described what might have been said during the meeting of Jesus and St Joseph in the Limbo of the Fathers, where the holy souls of the Old Testament were waiting for Jesus' death and resurrection, when Jesus descended there after his death on the Cross. St Francis added: "And if it is true, as we must believe, that by virtue of the most Holy Sacrament which we receive, our bodies will rise again at the day of judgment, how can we doubt that our Lord caused to rise with him to heaven in body and soul the glorious St Joseph who had had the honour and the grace of carrying him so often in his blessed arms, in which our Lord took such pleasure? Oh, how many kisses he tenderly gave him with his blessed lips, to reward, in some measure, his labour!" So as to make his view abundantly clear, this great Doctor of the Church added: "St Joseph, then, is in heaven in body and soul; there is no doubt of it."

St Leonard of Port Maurice OFM (1676-1751), an Italian preacher and writer who did much to promote the proclamation of the dogma of the Immaculate Conception, was another who believed in St Joseph's bodily assumption.

Closer to our own time, Pope St John XXIII, in a homily on 26 May 1960, the feast of the Ascension, said that the bodily Ascension of Jesus into heaven "corresponds, also, to those deceased from the Old Testament who were closer to Jesus. We name two who were the most intimate in his life: John the Baptist, the forerunner, and Joseph of Nazareth, his putative father and custodian. It corresponds to them, as well, and can be piously believed. It is an honour and a privilege for them to experience this admirable path to heaven."

The Last Things

802 The dead were raised

When Christ died on the cross, St Matthew says that tombs were opened and people who had died were raised and went into the city and appeared to many. How are we meant to understand this? Did they really rise in their bodies and walk around again?

The passage to which you refer says that when Christ breathed his last, "behold, the curtain of the temple was torn in two, from top to bottom; and the earth shook, and the rocks were split; the tombs also were opened, and many bodies of the saints who had fallen asleep were raised, and coming out of the tombs after his resurrection they went into the holy city and appeared to many" (*Mt* 27:51-53).

The Navarre Bible commentary says that this passage is not clarified by any other passages in Scripture, nor has there been any statement from the Magisterium, but that the great Church writers have proposed three possible explanations.

The first is that, rather than resurrections in the strict sense, they would have been apparitions of these deceased people. This explanation, however, seems less faithful to the text, which uses the word "raised", surrexerunt, or "resurrected" in Latin. This implies a true resurrection of the whole person, body and soul, not just an apparition.

The second is that these people would have risen from the dead in the strict sense, in their body and soul, as did Lazarus, and would have gone on to continue living until they died again.

The third is that their resurrection would have been definitive, or glorious, in the sense that they would not need to die again, in this way anticipating the final resurrection of the body. This explanation, however, is difficult to reconcile with the clear affirmation of Scripture that Christ was the first-born from the dead (cf. *1 Cor* 15:20; *Col* 1:18).

For these reasons writers like St Augustine, St Jerome and St

Thomas Aquinas prefer the second explanation, because they consider that it fits best with the sacred text and it does not present the theological difficulties of the third explanation. It is also the solution proposed by the *Catechism of the Council of Trent*.

St Thomas deals with the question in his *Summa Theologiae*, III, q. 53, art. 3, making reference to both St Augustine and St Jerome. He begins by quoting St Paul: "But in fact Christ has been raised from the dead, the first fruits of those who have fallen asleep" (*1 Cor* 15:20).

He goes on to distinguish two kinds of resurrection. The first is what he calls imperfect resurrection, where a person is raised from the dead only to die again, like Lazarus. The second is perfect resurrection, where the person is raised immortal and remains forever in life, like Christ himself, as in Romans 6:9: "Christ rising from the dead dies now no more."

St Thomas concludes that if Christ was the first-born from the dead in a perfect resurrection, all those who were raised before him, including those who came out of the tombs after his death, had an imperfect resurrection. They rose in their bodies and lived on earth until they died again. St Thomas says of these that "by an imperfect resurrection, some others have risen before Christ, so as to be a kind of figure of his resurrection".

The *Catechism of the Council of Trent*, or *Roman Catechism*, echoes this teaching: "These words of the Apostle are to be understood of a perfect resurrection, by which we are raised to an immortal life and are no longer subject to the necessity of dying. In this resurrection Christ the Lord holds the first place. For if we speak of resurrection, that is, of a return to life subject to the necessity of again dying, many were thus raised from the dead before Christ, all of whom, however, were restored to life to die again. But Christ the Lord, having subdued and conquered death, so arose that he could die no more, according to this most clear testimony: 'Christ rising again from the dead, dies now no more; death shall no more have dominion over him'" (*Rom* 6:9; *Roman Catechism* I, 5).

803 Christ's Ascension and souls going to heaven

I remember someone saying that the souls of the good people who died before Christ, like Moses and St Joseph, only went to heaven when Christ ascended there. Is this true?

While not a dogma of faith, the proposition you mention is a common teaching of the Church, which has taught and believed it for many centuries.

As background, we should remember that when Adam and Eve committed the original sin of disobedience to God's command not to eat of the fruit of a certain tree, heaven was closed and no one was able to go there. It is a common teaching of the Church that the good people who died before Christ, like the ones you mention, were in a state of natural happiness called the "Limbo of the Fathers" awaiting their Redemption, which took place when Christ died on the Cross and rose from the dead (cf. J. Flader, *Question Time 2*, q. 184). When we say that Christ "descended into hell", or "he descended to the dead", we are referring to that state or place, where he went to announce the good news of Redemption.

The reason why we say that these souls only went to heaven when Christ himself did, is that he is the head of the Mystical Body and it is only right that the head should precede the body in entering heaven. In this regard the *Catechism of the Catholic Church* teaches: "Left to its own natural powers humanity does not have access to the 'Father's house,' to God's life and happiness. Only Christ can open to man such access that we, his members, might have confidence that we too shall go where he, our Head and our Source, has preceded us" (*CCC* 661).

Ludwig Ott, in his *Fundamentals of Catholic Dogma* writes: "From the soteriological angle it [the Ascension] is the crowning conclusion of the work of the Redemption. According to the general teaching of the Church, the souls of the just of the pre-Christian era also moved with the Saviour into the glory of Heaven." Ott cites as a reference St Paul's letter to the Ephesians, which in turn quotes Psalm 68: "When he ascended on high he led a host of captives, and he gave gifts to men" (*Eph* 4:8; cf. *Ps* 68:18; *Ott*, p. 194).

St Thomas Aquinas, in answer to the question: "Whether Christ's Ascension is the cause of our salvation" answers in the same vein: "In regard to those things which, in ascending, he did for our salvation. First, he prepared the way for our ascent into heaven, according to his own saying (*Jn* 14:2): 'I go to prepare a place for you' and the words of Micah (2:13), 'He shall go up that shall open the way before them.' For since he is our head, the members must follow where the head has gone; hence he said (*Jn* 14:3): 'That where I am, you also may be'. In the saints delivered from hell, according to Ps 68:18 (cf. *Eph* 4:8): 'Ascending on high he led captivity captive', because he took with him to heaven those who had been held captives by the devil, to heaven, as to a place strange to human nature; captives indeed of a happy taking, since they were acquired by his victory" (*STh* III, q. 57, art. 6).

Catholic doctrine on this subject was stated authoritatively by Pope Benedict XII in his Apostolic Constitution *Benedictus Deus* (1336), in which he defined the Church's belief that the souls of the departed go to their eternal reward immediately after death, as opposed to remaining in a state of unconscious existence until the Last Judgment. He wrote: "By this Constitution, which is to remain in force for ever, we, with apostolic authority, define the following: According to the general disposition of God, the souls of all the saints who departed from this world before the passion of our Lord Jesus Christ [...] since the ascension of our Lord and Saviour Jesus Christ into heaven, already before they take up their bodies again and before the general judgment, have been, are and will be with Christ in heaven, in the heavenly kingdom and paradise, joined to the company of the holy angels."

How then can we explain Our Lord's words from the Cross to the good thief: "Today you will be with me in paradise" (*Lk* 23:43)? Since "with the Lord one day is as a thousand years (*2 Pet* 3:8),

Christ was not referring to that particular day, Good Friday, but rather to God's time. The good thief no doubt went to heaven, along with all the other good people of the Old Testament, on the day of Christ's Ascension.

II. THE SACRAMENTS

Baptism

804 Changing the formula for Baptism

I read recently that the Vatican has declared that Baptisms celebrated with the formula "We baptise you..." are invalid. I can understand that the minister should not change the words of a sacrament, but in this case why would such a small change render Baptism invalid?

By way of background, there was a recent news item about an American priest who resigned from his parish after it was disclosed that he had been performing baptisms for many years with the formula, "We baptise you..." instead of "I baptise you..." In June 2020 the Congregation for the Doctrine of the Faith (CDF), with the approval of Pope Francis, declared that Baptisms conferred with the formula "We baptise you..." were invalid and that all persons baptised with that formula were to be baptised again unconditionally; that is, not with some condition like "if you are not already baptised".

Why is this formula invalid? In its accompanying doctrinal note, the CDF explains: "Recently there have been celebrations of the Sacrament of Baptism administered with the words: 'In the name of the father and of the mother, of the godfather and of the godmother, of the grandparents, of the family members, of the friends, in the name of the community we baptise you in the name of the Father and of the Son and of the Holy Spirit'".

The Note goes on to say that "apparently, the deliberate modification of the sacramental formula was introduced to emphasise the communitarian significance of Baptism, in order to express the participation of the family and of those present, and to avoid the idea of the concentration of a sacred power in the priest to the detriment of the parents and the community that the formula in the *Rituale Romanum* might seem to imply. With debatable pastoral motives, here resurfaces the ancient temptation to substitute for the formula handed down by Tradition other texts judged more suitable."

The Note mentions that St Thomas Aquinas, who lived in the thirteenth century, had already posed the question of whether several persons can simultaneously baptise one and the same person, and he answered in the negative, because this practice is contrary to the nature of the minister. He wrote: "The point to be observed, however, is this, that by this form, 'We baptise you,' the intention expressed is that several concur in conferring one Baptism: and this seems contrary to the notion of a minister; for a man does not baptise save as a minister of Christ, and as standing in his place; wherefore just as there is one Christ, so should there be one minister to represent Christ. Hence the Apostle says pointedly 'one Lord, one Faith, one Baptism' (*Eph* 4:5). Consequently, an intention which is in opposition to this seems to annul the sacrament of Baptism" (cf. *STh*, III, q. 67, a. 6 c).

The Second Vatican Council's Constitution on the Liturgy *Sacrosanctum Concilium*, also taught this, saying that "when a man baptises it is really Christ himself who baptises" (*SC*, 7). The Note explains that this text, inspired by a writing of Saint Augustine, wants to return the sacramental celebration to the presence of Christ, not only in the sense that he grants his power to give it efficacy, but above all to indicate that the Lord has the principal role in the event being celebrated. The text of St Augustine is very clear: "Peter may baptise, but this is He [Christ] that baptises; Paul may baptise, yet this is He that baptises; Judas may baptise, still this is He that baptises" (*In Evangelium Ioannis tractatus*, VI, 7).

Since it is Christ, acting through the minister, not the community, who baptises, the formula must be expressed in the singular: "I baptise you…" The Doctrinal Note explains that when the priest or deacon pronounces the formula of Baptism, he "does not speak as a functionary who carries out a role entrusted to him, but he enacts ministerially the sign-presence of Christ, who acts in His Body to give His grace".

That is, the minister of the sacrament does not act on behalf of the community, but in the very person of Christ, and it is Christ who gives the grace.

In conclusion, no minister should alter the formula of any sacrament, let alone a traditional one like that of Baptism, which was given by Christ himself to the apostles (cf. *Mt* 28:19).

805 Consequences of invalid Baptism

If someone has not been validly baptised, does that render all the other sacraments they have received invalid and ineffective?

Your question refers to the unfortunate situation that in recent times ministers of baptism have used formulas which the Holy See has later declared to be invalid. Among these are the formula "We baptise you...", which I dealt with in the previous question, and "I baptise you in the name of the Creator and of the Redeemer and of the Sanctifier" or "I baptise you in the name of the Creator and of the Liberator and of the Sustainer" (cf. J. Flader *Question Time 2*, q. 193).

When this has happened, you ask whether the invalid Baptism renders invalid or ineffective all the other sacraments the person has received, and therefore whether they should be repeated. Obviously, if the Baptism was invalid, the person should be baptised validly as soon as possible. When that has been done, whether the other sacraments should be repeated varies with each one. We can consider them in the order in which the Catechism treats them.

Following Baptism, the second Sacrament of Christian Initiation is Confirmation. Since the Baptism was invalid and it is a prerequisite for Confirmation, a subsequent Confirmation will also be invalid and it should be repeated.

As regards the Eucharist, the person may have subsequently received Communion very often and, even though the person was not validly baptised, the Communions will still have been of great benefit due to the person's subjective dispositions. In any case, it is obvious that a person cannot repeat all the previous Communions they may have received.

Of the two Sacraments of Healing, the first is the sacrament of Penance and Reconciliation, or confession. As with the Eucharist, the person may have gone to confession numerous times before the invalidity of the Baptism was discovered. These confessions will, nonetheless, have been fruitful through the sorrow expressed in the sacrament. God will have forgiven the person, as he would any person on earth who is sincerely sorry and seeks forgiveness from him.

As regards the second Sacrament of Healing, the Anointing of the Sick, again we can say that the personal dispositions of sorrow for sin and love for God will have moved God to grant the person many graces.

Turning to the Sacraments at the Service of Communion, the first is Holy Orders. Here, as with Confirmation, the invalidity of the Baptism means that the bishop, priest or deacon was not validly ordained and he should be baptised and ordained as soon as possible. Also, any sacraments he conferred prior to his valid Baptism were invalid. The exception is that of Baptism, since even a lay person can baptise validly. As regards the other sacraments, this obviously presents enormous problems in rectifying the damage done in conferring the sacraments invalidly.

For example, an invalidly ordained bishop who later ordained priests and deacons would have to ordain these men again, and all the sacraments those priests conferred, except Baptism, would have been invalid.

The second Sacrament at the Service of Communion, Matrimony, can also present problems. Even though the ministers of the sacrament are the spouses themselves, with the priest or deacon acting only as a witness to their exchange of consent on behalf of the Church and the state, the Church requires a dispensation from the impediment of Disparity of Cult for the validity of a marriage when one of the spouses has not been baptised (cf. *Code of Canon Law*, Can. 1086). If the invalidly baptised person has married a baptised person, this dispensation will not have been sought or granted, and so the marriage will be invalid. When the invalidly baptised person has been validly baptised, the couple should obtain the dispensation of the impediment as soon as possible and then have the marriage validated, following Canons 1156-1165.

In all of this, the Catechism gives us much consolation: "God has bound salvation to the sacrament of Baptism, but he himself is not bound by his sacraments" (*CCC* 1257). God can always give grace independently of the sacraments, as we have seen. But because of the enormous confusion and problems that can follow invalid Baptism, it is of primordial importance to ensure that all Baptisms are conferred with a valid formula.

The Eucharist

806 The Mass as sacrifice

We sometimes hear the expression "the sacrifice of the Mass". Why do we call the Mass a sacrifice and has it always been considered to be such?

If you asked your Catholic friends what the Mass is, you would probably hear answers like "a gathering of the parish community to pray to God", a "fraternal meal", a "reminder of the Last Supper", etc. All of these answers contain some kernel of truth, but the essence of the Mass is that it is a sacrifice, the sacrifice of Christ on Calvary made present on the altar.

Why does the Church call the Mass a sacrifice? Simply because from the time Moses received the Ten Commandments on Mount Sinai, God asked the Israelites, our forebears in the faith, to offer sacrifice throughout the ages as a way of worshipping him. They were to offer two sacrifices a day, one in the morning and one in the afternoon, except on the Sabbath, when it was to be two in the morning and two in the afternoon (cf. *Ex* 29:38-42).

These sacrifices were a figure, a symbol, of the definitive sacrifice Christ was to offer for our redemption on Mt Calvary. His sacrifice was to be perpetuated in the sacrifice of the Mass, as the sacrifice of the New Testament.

Christ himself instituted the Eucharist in the Last Supper to make present his sacrifice. St Paul relates "that the Lord Jesus on the night when he was betrayed took bread, and when he had given thanks, he broke it, and said, 'This is my body which is for you. Do this in remembrance of me.' In the same way also the chalice, after supper, saying, 'This chalice is the new covenant in my blood. Do this, as often as you drink it, in remembrance of me'" (*1 Cor* 11:23-25).

The *Catechism of the Catholic Church* comments: "The sacrificial character of the Eucharist is manifested in the very words of institution: 'This is my body which is given for you' and 'This cup which is poured out for you is the New Covenant in my blood'" (*Lk* 22:19-20; *CCC* 1365).

In telling the apostles to "do this in remembrance of me", Our Lord was asking them to continue to celebrate his sacrifice down the ages. St Paul, in the passage we have just read, goes on to comment that in the Eucharist we are proclaiming Our Lord's sacrifice until the end of time: "For as often as you eat this bread and drink the chalice, you proclaim the Lord's death until he comes" (*1 Cor* 11:26).

Thus, the daily sacrifices of animals in the Old Testament were to be replaced by the one and only sacrifice of Christ, the Lamb of God, on Calvary, made present in the Mass. The Council of Trent expressed it like this: "Sacrifice and priesthood are, by the ordinance of God, joined together in such a way that both have existed in every law. Whereas, therefore, in the New Testament, the Catholic Church has received, from the institution of Christ, the holy visible Sacrifice of the Eucharist, it must also be confessed that there is, in that Church, a new, visible and external priesthood, into which the old has been translated" (Sess. 23, Chap. 1).

The reality of the Mass as a sacrifice was understood from the beginning of the Church. The *Didache*, an early Christian document dating probably to the end of the first century, says: "On the Lord's day, assemble together and break bread and give thanks, first confessing your sins, that your sacrifice may be pure."

We express the idea of sacrifice in the Eucharistic Prayers of the Mass. In Eucharistic Prayer 1 we read: "we offer you this sacrifice of praise", and in Eucharistic Prayer 3: "we offer you in thanksgiving this holy and living sacrifice". We express it too in the acclamations after the Consecration, saying, for example, "We proclaim your Death, O Lord."

The sacrificial nature of the Mass is seen too in the separate consecrations of the Body and the Blood of Christ. When the body and blood of a person are separate, the person is dead.

The Catechism sums it up, quoting the Council of Trent: "The sacrifice of Christ and the sacrifice of the Eucharist are *one single sacrifice*: 'The victim is one and the same: the same now offers through the ministry of priests, who then offered himself on the cross; only the manner of offering is different'" (Council of Trent, *DS* 1740; CCC 1367).

807 Offering the Mass

Our priest has suggested that we should offer the Mass for our personal intentions. I had never heard of this before and thought only the priest could determine the intentions of the Mass. Can you explain this please?

We should remember that all the baptised are members of the Mystical Body of Christ. Christ is the head of the Body, which is the Church, and all the baptised are members of his Body. The Mass makes present the one and only sacrifice of Christ on the cross of Calvary, and so it is Christ who offers the Mass through the ministry of the priest. But since the lay faithful are members of Christ's Body, they are united with him and the priest in offering the Mass. Thus they have an active role in offering the Mass together with the priest.

The Catechism teaches: "The Eucharist is also the sacrifice of the Church. The Church which is the Body of Christ participates in the offering of her Head. With him, she herself is offered whole and entire. She unites herself to his intercession with the Father for all men. In the Eucharist the sacrifice of Christ becomes also the sacrifice of the members of his Body" (*CCC* 1368).

The priest usually offers the Mass for a particular intention, such as the good of the faithful of his parish, the repose of the soul of a deceased person, the end of a natural disaster, peace in the world, etc. This is the principal intention for which the Mass is offered. But he may also pray for other personal intentions like the success of a parish function, the healing of a sick person, the health of his parents, etc.

The lay faithful, as members of Christ's Body, can join their own personal intentions to those of the priest, so that these intentions too will benefit from the powerful prayer which is the Mass.

The Mass is the most powerful prayer of the Church, since it is the action of Christ offering himself to the Father on the cross. As the action of God the Son, it can be said that the Mass is of infinite value and is always most pleasing to the Father. Our own prayers, like the rosary, the Divine Mercy chaplet, the Angelus, etc., are pleasing too, but in the end they are the actions of God's creatures and so are of more limited value. If we offer our intentions in union with the Mass they acquire the value of Christ's sacrifice on the cross.

As the Catechism puts it: "The lives of the faithful, their praise, sufferings, prayer, and work, are united with those of Christ and with his total offering, and so acquire a new value. Christ's sacrifice present on the altar makes it possible for all generations of Christians to be united with his offering" (*CCC* 1368). This invites us to offer not only our prayers but all our activities – our work, rest, family life, joys and sufferings – in union with the Mass, whether we attend the Mass that day or not. In some sense, all our activity then becomes a Mass offered to God in union with Christ's sacrifice. Cardinal Joseph Cardijn, who founded the Young Christian Workers, expressed it succinctly: "Your workbench is your altar".

And St Josemaría Escrivá, founder of Opus Dei, said in a meditation: "We serve [God] not only at the altar, but throughout the world – which for us is an altar. All the works of men are done as if on an altar, and each one of you, in that union of contemplative souls that is your day, in some way says 'his Mass', which lasts twenty-four hours, in expectation of the Mass to follow, which will last another twenty-four hours, and so on until the end of our lives" (Meditation "St Joseph, our Father and Lord", in *In Dialogue with the Lord*, Scepter 2018, p. 98).

When we attend Mass it is good to arrive early so that we can compose ourselves and consider the intentions we would like to unite with those of the priest in the Mass. They can be in the area of any of the four principal ends for which the Mass is offered: petition, thanksgiving, adoration and atonement. Then we spiritually place them on the altar along with the host, and they are raised to God in the Mass.

A good moment to pray for these intentions is in the brief silence before the Opening Prayer, or Collect, of the Mass, when the priest says: "Let us pray". These intentions help us value the Mass more and attend it more often, since we are now attending it to pray for specific intentions.

808 Mass intentions

In your article about offering the Mass for particular intentions, you didn't mention asking the priest to offer a Mass for our own intentions. Is this still being done? And is there something wrong with giving the priest money to celebrate a Mass for our intention?

It should be understood that the general intention of any Mass is the worship of God and the salvation of souls. However, each Mass can also be offered for a particular intention which the priest determines. Very often this intention is one that has been requested by a member of the faithful, who usually gives the priest a small stipend as an offering.

The custom of offering the Mass for a particular intention is very ancient, going back to the early centuries. Around the year 216 Tertullian described how the Church prayed for the dead and offered Mass for them on the anniversary of their death: "A woman, after the death of her husband ... prays for his soul and asks that he may, while waiting, find rest; and that he may share in the first resurrection. And each year, on the anniversary of his death, she offers the sacrifice" (*Monogamy* 10:1–2).

The sacrifice is, of course, the Mass. We may be familiar too with St Monica's request to her son Augustine when she was nearing the end of her life: "This only I ask of you, that you remember me at the altar of the Lord, wherever you may be" (St Augustine, *Confessions* 9, 10-11).

Since the Mass is the most powerful prayer of the Church, making present the sacrifice of Christ on Calvary, it is a very effective way of praying to God for our intentions. The faithful can ask the priest to celebrate a Mass, or Masses, for their own intentions and the priest then carries out their request, so that the intention of that person becomes the intention of the priest offering the Mass. Many priests receive a steady flow of such requests so that they are celebrating practically all their Masses for these intentions.

I say "practically all" their Masses because parish priests are required by law to offer the Mass on all Sundays and holydays of obligation for the people entrusted to them. So strong is this obligation that if the priest is lawfully impeded from this celebration, (for example, if he is sick) he is to have someone else apply the Mass on these days, or he is to apply it himself on other days (cf. *Code of Canon Law*, Can. 534, §1). By "parish priest" in this context is meant the priest in charge of the parish, not the assistant priests who help him in his ministry.

As I have said, it is customary for the person requesting the Mass to offer the priest a small amount of money, known as a stipend. There can be misunderstanding of the nature of this offering, including the idea that there is something wrong with it; that is, that it would constitute simony, defined in the Catechism as "the buying or selling of spiritual things" (*CCC* 2121).

If the priest charged a fee for celebrating the Mass and he refused to celebrate without receiving it, it might be construed as simony. But the money is not a fee. It is rather a voluntary offering for the upkeep of the priest. The *Code of Canon Law* clarifies: "In accordance with the approved custom of the Church, any priest who celebrates or concelebrates a Mass may accept an offering to apply the Mass for a specific intention. It is earnestly recommended to priests that, even if they do not receive an offering, they celebrate the Mass for the intentions of Christ's faithful, especially of those in need" (Can. 945).

The purpose of the offering is indicated in the following canon: "The faithful who make an offering so that Mass can be celebrated for their intention, contribute to the good of the Church, and by that offering they share in the Church's concern for the support of its ministers and its activities" (Can. 946). What is more, "even the semblance of trafficking or trading is to be entirely excluded from Mass offerings" (Can. 947).

Lest a priest be tempted to be greedy and celebrate multiple Masses each day in order to enrich himself with the stipends, the Code stipulates that he may keep for himself the stipend for only one Mass a day. The stipends for any other Masses he celebrates are to be given over for purposes prescribed by the bishop (cf. Can. 951, §1).

So yes, you can still ask your priest to offer the Mass for your intentions.

809 The Mass as centre of all activity

Some people say that the main thing we need to do in the Church is not so much get people back to Sunday Mass but rather foster care for the poor and for those of other ethnic backgrounds, be more compassionate, etc. How should we view this?

In simple terms, these other aims are very important, but they will be fostered more effectively if people first put God, and the Mass, at the centre of their lives. The Mass is fundamental. The third commandment tells us to remember to keep holy the Lord's Day, and the principal way we do this is by attending Mass. If someone is not attending Mass, they are leaving God very much out of their life. And if God is not the centre of their life, they will not be inclined to do his will in everything, including being generous and compassionate to others.

Here the first commandment also comes to mind: "You shall not have strange gods before me". Whatever other activities are keeping someone away from the worship of God on Sunday are, in some way, assuming the role of a strange god. This might be sport, earning more money, working outside the home, or simply relaxation. Our Lord said in the Sermon on the Mount, "For where your treasure is, there will your heart be also" (*Mt* 6:21). We do well from time to time to ask ourselves where our heart is. Is it in God, so that God is the centre of our life, and we find time each day for prayer and, at least each week, to worship him by attending Mass? Or is it rather in ourselves, in our plans, in making more money, in sport, etc.?

If the Mass is the centre of people's lives, both they and the life of their parish take on a new vitality. Pope Francis writes in his Apostolic Letter *Desiderio desideravi* that "a comprehensive, organic, and integrated pastoral practice is the consequence of placing the Sunday Eucharist, the foundation of communion, at the centre of the life of the community. The theological understanding of the Liturgy does not in any way permit that these words be understood to mean to reduce everything to the aspect of worship. A celebration that does not evangelise is not authentic, just as a proclamation that does not lead to an encounter with the risen Lord in the celebration is not authentic. And then both of these, without the testimony of charity, are like sounding a noisy gong or a clanging cymbal (*1 Cor* 13:1)".

As the Pope says, when the Sunday Eucharist is at the centre of the life of the community, the Mass is not just an act of worship. An authentic celebration of the Mass leads to evangelisation. That is, when people put Christ at the centre of their lives, they are eager to share his love and truth with others in the work of evangelisation. This in turn can lead to bringing more people back to or into the Church, thus helping them and building up the parish community.

Likewise, the Mass leads to "an encounter with the risen Lord" through the readings, the prayers and especially Holy Communion. This personal encounter cannot but lead to greater love for Christ and for others, and this in turn will be lived out in the family, in the workplace, in care for the poor and the marginalised, etc.

Furthermore, when the Mass becomes, in the words of St Josemaría Escrivá, the "centre and root" of the interior life, all other activities become an extension of the Mass and they are done with greater love and generosity. As the Catechism puts it, "The Church which is the body of Christ participates in the offering of her Head. With him, she herself is offered whole and entire… The lives of the faithful, their praise, sufferings, prayer, and work are united with those of Christ and with his total offering, and so acquire a new value" (*CCC* 1368).

So, when the Mass is the centre of people's lives, all their activity, including their love for others, is an extension of the Mass and it improves greatly. Yes, the Mass is fundamental.

810 The priest in the Mass

I have sometimes seen the priest act something like a "showman" in the Mass, using gestures and words in such a way as to seem to be drawing attention to himself. This just doesn't seem right to me. Is it acceptable?

I have often heard comments like yours over the years. And no, it isn't acceptable. One could begin by going back to the way Mass was celebrated, and still is in the traditional Latin rite, when the priest celebrated Mass *ad orientem*, "facing East", facing God with his back to the people. In that Mass there was no place for the priest as showman, nor was there any temptation on his part to act as one. The priest was facing God and offering the Mass on behalf of the people to lead them to God. He was talking to God, not to the people, and he used a soft voice, since the people didn't need to hear him. In a sense the priest "disappeared" in a liturgy directed to God.

The temptation to be a showman only came about when the Mass began to be celebrated facing the people. Here, even though the prayers are still addressed to God, the priest sees the people and he can be tempted to use gestures and explanations that draw attention to himself, rather than to God. He can see himself as the "president of the assembly". Mind you, he does not have to do this, and most priests do not. He can still celebrate Mass with great reverence, absorbed in God, and lead the people effectively to God.

Years ago I came across an article by Fr Donald MacDonald, SMM, reprinted from the Irish magazine *The Furrow*, which addressed this issue. The writer used an analogy which I thought was very appropriate. He quoted the famous violinist Yehudi Menuhin saying: "An artist's presence is more strongly felt the more he is concentrated, centred and disregarding the audience... The more absorbed you are in the music and thus the more you withdraw your presence from the audience, the more strongly they will feel your presence."

The centre of attention in the concert, what the audience came to hear, is the music of Bach, Brahms or Beethoven. The violinist is there to help the audience appreciate the music. Similarly, in the Mass the centre of attention is Christ, truly present in his word and on the altar after the consecration. It is not the priest. The priest's role is to bring the people into the presence of Christ and help them worship him. As one simple way of doing this, after the consecration the priest should preferably look down at the host on the paten when he is not looking at the missal to read the prayers.

In his Apostolic Letter *Desiderio desideravi* on liturgical formation, Pope Francis mentions, among some of the characteristics of a priest-centred celebration of the Mass, an "exasperating creativity", "sloppy carelessness" and "superabundant friendliness" (cf. *DD* n. 54). He comments: "I think that the inadequacy of these models of presiding have a common root: a heightened personalism of the celebrating style which at times expresses a poorly concealed mania to be the centre of attention. Often this becomes more evident when our celebrations are transmitted over the air or online, something not always opportune and that needs further reflection. Be sure you understand me: these are not the most widespread behaviours, but still, not infrequently assemblies suffer from being thus abused" (*ibid*).

Pope Francis goes on to say: "For this service to be well done – indeed, with art! – it is of fundamental importance that the priest have a keen awareness of being, through God's mercy, a particular presence of the risen Lord... This fact gives 'sacramental' weight (in the broad sense) to all the gestures and words of the one presiding. The assembly has the right to be able to feel in those gestures and words the desire that the Lord has, today as at the Last Supper, to eat the Passover with us. So, the risen Lord is in the leading role, and not our own immaturities, assuming roles and behaviours which are simply not appropriate. The priest himself should be overpowered by this desire for communion that the Lord has toward each person. It is as if he were placed in the middle between Jesus' burning heart of love and the heart of each of the faithful, which is the object of the Lord's love. To preside at Eucharist is to be plunged into the furnace of God's love" (*DD* n. 57).

811 Care in the Mass

In my travels I have attended Mass in many parishes and have seen it celebrated in very different ways, in some places with great care and reverence, but in others with little care for the rubrics, even leaving out some prayers and introducing others. Is this allowed?

I have been asked this question many times over the years, and I now use Pope Francis' recent Apostolic Letter *Desiderio desideravi* to answer it. The Pope wrote that letter, dated 29 June 2022, the feast of Saints Peter and Paul, to stress the importance of formation in the liturgy for everyone, both priests and lay faithful.

He mentions in the letter that on various occasions he has warned against the dangerous temptation of "spiritual worldliness", about which he had written at length in his Apostolic Exhortation *Evangelii Gaudium* (nn. 93-97). One form of it, Gnosticism, "shrinks Christian faith into a subjectivism that ultimately keeps one imprisoned in his or her own thoughts and feelings" (*DD* 17). Here the priest celebrating Mass can be tempted to ignore the prayers and gestures in the Missal and adapt them to his own subjective way of thinking.

Pope Francis goes on to say that the liturgy, by its very nature, is the most effective antidote against this: "If Gnosticism intoxicates us with the poison of subjectivism, the liturgical celebration frees us from the prison of a self-referencing nourished by one's own reasoning and one's own feeling. The action of the celebration does not belong to the individual but to the Christ-Church, to the totality of the faithful united in Christ. The liturgy does not say 'I' but 'we,' and any limitation on the breadth of this 'we' is always demonic. The Liturgy does not leave us alone to search out an individual supposed knowledge of the mystery of God. Rather, it takes us by the hand, together, as an assembly, to lead us deep within the mystery that the Word and the sacramental signs reveal to us" (*DD* 19).

That is, the liturgy, and in this case especially the Mass, is not an action of the individual priest, but an action of Christ together with his Mystical Body, the Church. The prayers and gestures have been determined by the Church and are spelled out in the Missal. It is not up to the individual priest to leave out or add anything, according to his own tastes.

The Pope goes on to say: "Let us be clear here: every aspect of the celebration must be carefully tended to (space, time, gestures, words, objects, vestments, song, music…) and every rubric must be observed. Such attention would be enough to prevent robbing from the assembly what is owed to it; namely, the paschal mystery celebrated according to the ritual that the Church sets down" (*DD* 23).

The faithful have a right to the Mass celebrated according to the indications of the universal Church, a right to the Catholic Mass. They should not be subjected to a Mass celebrated according to the personal whims of the priest. The Mass belongs to the Church, not to the individual priest to do with as he sees fit. "Let us always remember that it is the Church, the Body of Christ, that is the celebrating subject, not just the priest" (*DD* 36).

One of the ideas that the Pope treats at some length is the *ars celebrandi*, the art of celebrating. Here he says there are two dangers to be avoided: on one hand a rigid adherence to the rubrics without piety, and on the other a wild creativity without rules: "The *ars celebrandi* cannot be reduced to only a rubrical mechanism, much less should it be thought of as imaginative – sometimes wild – creativity without rules. The rite is in itself a norm, and the norm is never an end in itself, but it is always at the service of a higher reality that it means to protect."

He also says that the art of celebrating must be in harmony with the action of the Holy Spirit, who obviously only inspires us according to the mind of the Church: "Only in this way will it be free from the subjectivisms that are the fruit of individual tastes dominating" (*DD* 49).

It is clear from all this that the priest can celebrate Mass making use of his own personality and personal piety, but always in fidelity to the norms of the Church, so that the Mass is not his own but that of the Church.

812 Fragments of the host in Mass

After Mass in our parish the acolytes used to run their hand over the altar to make sure there were no fragments of the Eucharist that had accidentally fallen. They no longer do so. I am wondering down to what size a fragment would still be the Blessed Sacrament.

The reply to your question comes in the *Catechism of the Catholic Church*: "The Eucharistic presence of Christ begins at the moment of the consecration and endures as long as the Eucharistic species subsist. Christ is present whole and entire in each of the species and whole and entire in each of their parts, in such a way that the breaking of the bread does not divide Christ" (*CCC* 1377).

In saying "in each of their parts", no mention is made of the size of the part. Every particle of the host and every drop of the Precious Blood, no matter how small, is equally Jesus Christ. We see this lived out in practice when the priest is distributing Communion and he sees that there are more people coming up than the number of hosts remaining in the ciborium. He can then divide the hosts as needed, giving each person a part of a host. Those who receive a part are receiving Jesus Christ whole and entire just as much as those who receive a whole host.

Your question, however, refers rather to the tiny fragments that may fall from the host at various moments. Concern not to lose any of these fragments goes back to the early centuries of the Church.

St Cyril of Jerusalem, in his catechesis to new converts around the year 352, says: "With care, then, having sanctified your eyes through contact, receive the holy body, taking care that nothing be lost of it. For if you should lose something, you should consider it as if you had lost a part of your own body. Because tell me: if someone gave you some gold filings, wouldn't you safeguard them with every care, taking care not to lose any particle of them, nor to suffer any loss? Won't you make an effort, then, with much more diligence, that not even one crumb fall of what is more precious than gold or precious stones?" (*Cat. Myst.* 5, 21)

For this reason, in the distribution of Communion it used to be common practice for the server to hold a Communion plate under the communicant's chin or hand to catch any fragments that may fall. My own experience in this regard is that there are often tiny crumbs that fall onto the Communion plate, making its use both justified and recommended.

The *General Instruction of the Roman Missal (GIRM)* instructs the priest: "Whenever a fragment of the host adheres to his fingers, especially after the fraction or the Communion of the faithful, the priest is to wipe his fingers over the paten or, if necessary, wash them. Likewise, he should also gather any fragments that may have fallen outside the paten" (n. 278). The paten, by the way, is the round, usually gilded, metal plate on which the large host is placed during Mass.

As a safeguard, a corporal, or square linen cloth, is placed on the altar and the sacred species are consecrated over this cloth to catch any crumbs of the host or drops of the Precious Blood that may fall on it outside the paten.

After Communion the GIRM also prescribes: "Upon returning to the altar, the priest collects any fragments that may remain. Then, standing at the altar or at the credence table, he purifies the paten or ciborium over the chalice, then purifies the chalice" (n. 162). The ciborium is the chalice-like vessel in which the small hosts are placed for Communion. Often there are numerous particles of the hosts remaining in it, and these are swept with a finger into the chalice.

Also, after Communion the priest may scrape the corporal with the paten to collect any fragments of the host that may have fallen on it. He then wipes the fragments off the paten into the chalice. He also washes his fingers with water over the chalice to remove any particles adhering to them, and he then drinks the water, so that all the fragments are consumed.

As an added precaution, the corporal itself is usually washed separately from the other linens. It is customarily first rinsed in a bowl of water and then this water, which may contain particles of the host, is poured either into the sacrarium in the sacristy, which drains directly into the ground, or it is poured onto the ground under a tree or bush where no one will step on it.

As you can see, great care is to be taken not to lose any of these tiny fragments.

813 Changing the words of the Consecration

In more than one parish I have attended recently, the priest in the Consecration of the Precious Blood says "for all" instead of "for many". Does this make the Consecration invalid? And, in any case, is the priest being disobedient if he does this?

First, we should remind ourselves of the background to your question. Both of the Gospels which relate Our Lord's words in the institution of the Eucharist speak of Christ's blood being shed "for many" (cf. *Mt* 26:28, *Mk* 14:24). Following this, the first Eucharistic Prayer, which dates back to the sixth century, and all the others of more recent origin say in the Latin "pro multis", for many.

When the Mass was translated into English after the Second Vatican Council, this phrase was rendered as "for all". Christ did of course, die for all in the sense that his death was sufficient to redeem all mankind. When he said "for many" on instituting the Eucharist, he obviously meant "for the multitude", as distinct from "for the few", so the translation of his words as "for all" was theologically correct, if not the best literal translation of "pro multis".

In 2006, at the request of Pope Benedict XVI, the Congregation for Divine Worship sent a letter to the presidents of all bishops' conferences asking that in those countries where the vernacular translation was "for all", this should be changed to "for many".

In this way, following the directives of the Instruction *Liturgiam authenticam*, which sets out the criteria for translations of liturgical texts into the various languages, the translation would conform to the Latin original, which is "pro multis", "for many". The new edition of the Roman Missal in English, published in 2011, has the words "for many" in all the Eucharistic Prayers. Since then, we have become accustomed to hearing "for many" in all Masses.

If a priest continued to say "for all" the Consecration would obviously be valid, since this formula was considered valid for many years. But it is not lawful for priests to change the words of the official texts of the liturgy, and in particular the words of the Eucharistic Prayer, especially those of the Consecration. The criterion is given in the Vatican's Instruction *Redemptionis sacramentum*, issued by the Congregation for Divine Worship on 25 March 2004 with the approval of St John Paul II.

In its Preamble, the Instruction states why it is important to observe the norms and texts of the liturgy faithfully: "The liturgical words and rites, moreover, are a faithful expression, matured over the centuries, of the understanding of Christ, and they teach us to think as he himself does; by conforming our minds to these words, we raise our hearts to the Lord" (n. 5).

The general criterion regarding fidelity to the prayers of the liturgy is given in the Second Vatican Council's *Constitution on the Sacred Liturgy*: "Regulation of the sacred liturgy depends solely on the authority of the Church, that is, on the Apostolic See, and, as laws may determine, on the bishop... Therefore, no other person, not even a priest, may add, remove or change anything in the liturgy on his own authority" (*SC* n. 22).

The reason is clear: "The Mystery of the Eucharist is too great for anyone to permit himself to treat it according to his own whim, so that its sacredness and its universal ordering would be obscured... For arbitrary actions are not conducive to true renewal, but are detrimental to the right of Christ's faithful to a liturgical celebration that is an expression of the Church's life in accordance with her tradition and discipline... The result is uncertainty in matters of doctrine, perplexity and scandal on the part of the People of God..." (*Redemptionis sacramentum* n. 11).

As regards the Eucharistic Prayer in particular, the Instruction states: "It is not to be tolerated that some priests take upon themselves the right to compose their own Eucharistic Prayers or to change the texts approved by the Church, or to introduce others composed by private individuals" (n. 51).

If priests take it upon themselves to introduce even minor changes in the official texts of the liturgy, they would expose the faithful to different versions of the Mass in every parish. They would deny the faithful their right to the official liturgy of the Church and possibly expose them to theological errors. Individual changes, even minor ones, are not to be introduced.

814 The Supper of the Lamb

When the priest holds up the host before Communion and says, "Blessed are those called to the supper of the Lamb", is he referring to the supper of Communion in the Mass or to the wedding feast of the Lamb in heaven? Or possibly both?

While, as far as I am aware, there is no official Church teaching on this point, it has always seemed clear to me that those words refer both to the Communion of the Mass and to the wedding banquet of the Lamb in heaven.

The most obvious and immediate reference is to Communion in the Mass, which the faithful in the Mass will receive a few minutes later. But why the reference to the Lamb, when what is received in

Communion is the Body of Christ in the host and the Precious Blood in the chalice?

The answer takes us back to what the priest has just said when holding up the host: "Behold the Lamb of God, who takes away the sins of the world. Blessed are those called to the Supper of the Lamb." The Lamb of God who takes away the sins of the world is Christ himself, present in the host. Those are the words St John the Baptist used when he pointed Jesus out to his disciples: "Behold, the Lamb of God, who takes away the sin of the world" (*Jn* 1:29). It is Christ himself, the Lamb, whom the people will receive in Holy Communion.

The reference to the Lamb also takes us back to the Passover, which was a figure of the Eucharist. As we may recall, on the night before Moses led the Israelites out of Egypt, he told them to slaughter a lamb and eat it roasted over a fire. They were to sprinkle the blood of the lamb on the door posts and lintel of the house so that when the angel of death came that night and killed the first-born of the Egyptians, he would pass over the first-born of the Israelites (cf. *Ex* 12:1-13).

This is an obvious symbol of the blood which Christ, the Lamb of God, would shed on the Cross of Calvary on Good Friday to redeem us and save us from eternal death. Christ referred to this in the Last Supper when he blessed the chalice and gave it to the apostles, saying, "This is my blood of the covenant, which is poured out for many for the forgiveness of sins" (*Mt* 26:28).

And just as the Israelites ate a lamb they had previously sacrificed, so in the Mass we receive in Communion the Body and Blood of Christ, which have previously been offered in the sacrifice of the Mass. Thus, the Mass is not just a fraternal meal, a banquet, but a communion sacrifice, in which the victim is first sacrificed and then received in Holy Communion. This is mentioned in the Prayer after Communion in the Mass for the thirteenth Sunday in Ordinary Time: "May this divine sacrifice we have offered and received fill us with life."

As regards whether the "Supper of the Lamb" refers also to the wedding banquet of heaven, we find practically the same words we use in the Mass in the Book of Revelation: "Blessed are those who are invited to the marriage supper of the Lamb" (*Rev* 19:9). Throughout the Book of Revelation we see the heavenly worship offered to the Lamb, who is Jesus Christ.

The two meanings are related in that our Communions on earth prepare us for entry into heaven, where we too will share in the heavenly banquet. Just as the Israelites ate the manna which fell from heaven for forty years before they entered the Promised Land, so Eucharistic Communion is our "daily bread" which nourishes us on our journey through life to the Promised Land of heaven.

At the same time, the reception of Holy Communion is accompanied by a promise of heaven. In the synagogue of Capernaum Our Lord said: He who eats my flesh and drinks my blood has eternal life, and I will raise him up at the last day" (*Jn* 6:54).

And the Eucharist is also an anticipation of heaven: "He who eats my flesh and drinks my blood abides in me, and I in him" (Jn 6:56). To abide in Jesus is what we will experience in heaven. We will be in communion with the Son, the Father and the Holy Spirit, when we see God face to face. In fact, the Catechism describes heaven in those very terms: "This communion of life and love with the Trinity, with the Virgin Mary, the angels and all the blessed is called 'heaven'" (*CCC* 1024).

815 Masses on-line

Now, with the Covid-19 restrictions that have closed churches, I have a few questions. If we cannot attend Mass, are we obliged to watch a Mass on-line or is this something optional? Also, if we watch an on-line Mass, what can we do to get more out of it and not just be passive spectators?

In answer to your first question, when there is no Mass available in the place where we are or within a reasonable distance, the Sunday Mass obligation ceases. No one is obliged to do something impossible. Most of the ten commandments are phrased in negative terms – You shall not... – and these always oblige, since it is always possible *not* to do something. But a positive commandment like the third, to keep holy the Sabbath by attending Mass, only obliges when it is possible to fulfil it.

That said, are we then obliged to watch an on-line Mass? No, we are not. But even to speak in terms of the obligation to attend Sunday Mass or to do so on-line is to lose sight of what the Mass really is. It is not an onerous duty imposed on us by the Church but rather an opportunity to worship God, and to do so in the most powerful possible way through the sacrifice of Christ on Calvary, which the Mass makes present on the altar.

When we consider how much God has loved us in creating the world with all its beauty, in giving us life, in redeeming us through the death of Christ on the Cross, in giving us the Church and the sacraments to help us along the way to eternal life, we should be eager to express our gratitude by worshipping him through the sacrifice of the Eucharist. What is more, when we think of the many blessings God gives us throughout the week, how he looks after us in his loving providence all day and every day, surely we can spend one hour a week with him in praise and thanksgiving, remembering Jesus' words to the apostles in the garden of Gethsemane: "Could you not watch with me one hour?" (*Mt* 26:40)

Moreover, while we attend Mass primarily to worship God and thank him for all he is and has done for us, we also ask him for so many favours through the powerful prayer that the Mass is. We pray for the Pope and the Church, for an end to pandemics and wars, for those who are sick and have died, for the unemployed to be able to work again, for all our personal and family intentions ... And, of course, we also receive so many blessings when we attend. We spend time in prayer along with the parish community, we hear the word of God in the readings, we are helped to apply the readings to our daily life through the homily, and above all we receive Jesus himself in Holy Communion. In short, the Mass is a marvellous opportunity to be with our loving God.

I have been edified in recent weeks by the effort so many people are making to attend an on-line Mass not only on Sundays, but every day of the week. And we have all been edified and grateful to God for the more than a million people, undoubtedly including many non-practising Catholics and non-Catholics, who watched the television coverage of the Good Friday service and Easter Sunday Mass in St Mary's Cathedral in Sydney during the pandemic.

In times of crisis like this, people seem to turn more than ever to God, entrusting themselves and their loved ones to him and praying for an end to the pandemic, with all its unfortunate consequences.

To attend these on-line Masses better many families are doing some of the following things. Rather than be dressed sloppily or in their pyjamas, many are dressing better to honour God even by their external appearance. Some families have lit candles and set up what amounts to a little shrine near the television set or computer screen to have a visual reminder that the Mass is a sacred act of worship to God.

Many people do not simply remain seated throughout the Mass but rather stand, sit and kneel as they would if they were in a church. And, of course, they recite out loud the prayers and responses that correspond to them. At the time of Communion they say a spiritual Communion, expressing their desire to receive Our Lord with love and devotion whenever this may be possible again. In this way, they truly live the Mass and God showers them with graces.

So no, it is not compulsory to attend on-line Masses, but it is certainly recommended and very beneficial.

816 Women Acolytes and Lectors

I understand the Pope has recently allowed women to be acolytes and lectors in church. I have seen women carrying out these roles for many years. What is new?

On 10 January 2021 Pope Francis issued an Apostolic Letter titled *Spiritus Domini*, which modified the *Code of Canon Law* to allow women, as well as men, to be installed in the ministry of acolyte and lector, or reader, at Mass.

As you say, in many countries women, as well as men, have been assisting the priest as altar servers and doing the readings for many years. But they fulfilled these roles on a casual basis, invited by the priest. They were not installed formally in the ministry of acolyte or lector, roles reserved until now only to men. What is new is that women may now have the formal ministry of acolyte and lector.

A little history will help to clarify the significance of this development. For many centuries before the Second Vatican Council (1962-65), the roles of acolyte and lector were two of what were called minor orders, exercised by clerics on their way to priestly ordination. The other minor orders were those of porter, or doorkeeper, and exorcist. They were called minor orders to distinguish them from the major orders of subdiaconate, diaconate and priesthood.

In 1972 Pope St Paul VI, in the Motu proprio *Ministeria quaedam*, abolished the minor orders and the subdiaconate altogether. He retained, however, the roles of acolyte and lector, which were to be called ministries, and which, "in keeping with the venerable tradition of the Church" (n. 7), could be conferred on lay men. A man entered these ministries, after a suitable period of formation, in a ceremony known as installation, which was conducted by the bishop.

In that same document Pope Paul said that the duty of the acolyte was to assist the deacon and the priest in liturgical celebrations, especially the Mass. The acolyte could distribute holy communion as an extraordinary minister if required. Among the acolyte's functions, as specified in the *General Instruction of the Roman Missal*, are to prepare the altar and the sacred vessels, carry the cross in the entrance procession, present or hold the missal for the priest, place the corporal, purificator, chalice, pall and missal on the altar for the presentation of the gifts, assist the priest or deacon in purifying the sacred vessels after communion, etc. (cf. *GIRM* nos. 98, 187-193).

The role of the lector is to carry the book of the Gospels in the entrance procession and to read the readings that precede the Gospel. The lector, in the absence of a deacon, may also read the intentions of the Prayer of the Faithful (cf. *GIRM* nos. 194-198).

Until now, where a duly installed lector or acolyte was not available, their roles were often taken on an ad hoc basis by another suitably prepared person. Originally this was to be only a man, but over time women were allowed to perform these functions.

In 1994 a letter from the Congregation for Divine Worship clarified that girls could serve at the altar, but individual bishops were not bound to permit them to do so. The letter added that it would always be appropriate to follow the noble tradition of having boys serve at the altar, since it contributed to the fostering of priestly vocations. A further letter in 2001 said that individual priests were not bound to have girls serve at the altar even when their bishops granted permission for them to do so.

As regards the ministries, the 1983 *Code of Canon Law* stipulated: "Lay men whose age and talents meet the requirements prescribed by decree of the Bishops' Conference, can be given the stable ministry of lector and of acolyte, through the prescribed liturgical rite" (Can. 230, §1).

The new Apostolic Letter of Pope Francis changes this paragraph to read: "Lay persons who possess the age and qualifications established by decree of the conference of bishops can be admitted on a stable basis through the prescribed liturgical rite to the ministries of lector and acolyte."

In saying "lay persons" instead of "lay men", the document was implicitly including women. Thus both women and men may now be formally installed in the ministries of acolyte and lector. It is up to the Bishops' Conference to determine the age and qualifications required for these ministries.

817 New Latin Mass restrictions

I often attend a Latin Mass in the traditional rite with my family, and we find it very spiritual and helpful. I understand the Pope has now put severe restrictions on the use of this Mass. Does this mean that we may not be able to attend it in the future?

The restrictions to which you refer came in Pope Francis' Motu Proprio *Traditionis custodes*, issued on 16 July 2021. The restrictions are, as you say, quite severe and they have caused considerable concern and disappointment among those who celebrate or attend the Mass regularly. In this column I will explain the background to the latest development and, in the next, the substance and reasons for the new directives.

For almost five hundred years, ever since Pope Pius V issued a new missal in 1570 following the Council of Trent, the Church of the Latin Rite all over the world celebrated the Latin Mass you have been attending.

Then in the Second Vatican Council (1962-1965), the bishops asked for changes to be made in the Mass, so that "the faithful should be led to that full, conscious, and active participation in the liturgical celebrations which is demanded by the very nature of the liturgy" (*SC* 14).

Pope St Paul VI, who was Pope at the time, entrusted a group of liturgical experts with the task of reforming the Mass to achieve the aim proposed by the Council. The result was the so-called Novus Ordo, or new rite, of the Mass, which was introduced in 1970 and is now commonly used all over the world. Nonetheless, as considerable changes had been made to the Mass, some priests, especially older ones, preferred to continue using the older missal.

As the numbers grew, in 1984 Pope St John Paul II saw fit to regulate the use of the 1570 missal, in the version authorised by Pope St John XXIII in 1962, by granting official permission for its use. Pope John Paul further regulated it by his Motu Proprio *Ecclesia Dei* in 1988.

As Pope Francis explains in his letter to bishops accompanying *Traditionis custodes*, Pope John Paul was motivated above all "by the desire to foster the healing of the schism with the movement of Mons. Lefebvre". French Archbishop Marcel Lefebvre in 1970 had established the Society of St Pius X, whose members celebrated only the traditional Mass. In 1988, when the Archbishop ordained bishops without permission from the Holy See, the Society ended up in schism. Pope Francis continues: "With the ecclesial intention of restoring the unity of the Church, the Bishops were thus asked to accept with generosity the 'just aspirations' of the faithful who requested the use of that [1962] Missal."

To accommodate these "just aspirations", the Holy See in 1988 established the Priestly Fraternity of St Peter, whose priests celebrate Mass with the 1962 missal. This was done also with a view to drawing Catholics away from the Society of St Pius X into union with the Church.

The permission granted by John Paul II was further broadened by Pope Benedict XVI in 2007 with his Motu Proprio *Summorum Pontificum*. Pope Benedict called the missal of Pope Paul VI the "ordinary form" of the Roman Rite, and the missal of John XXIII the "extraordinary form". Thus, there were to be two forms of the one Roman Rite.

As Pope Francis says in his letter, quoting Pope Benedict, the latter Pope intended to afford greater access to the traditional Mass to those, "including young people, who when 'they discover this liturgical form, feel attracted to it and find in it a form, particularly suited to them, to encounter the mystery of the most holy Eucharist'".

Over the years, there has been a growing number of priests, in addition to the over 300 in the Priestly Fraternity of St Peter, who celebrate Mass, regularly or occasionally, with the 1962 missal. They find that a large number of those attending these Masses are young people, who were born long after the Second Vatican Council and who never knew the former Mass. At a time when most young people are estranged from the Church and do not attend Mass at all, a growing number feel drawn to the traditional Mass and they attend it eagerly.

818 Regulations on the traditional Latin Mass

Can you tell me what the new regulations issued by Pope Francis for the celebration of the traditional Latin Mass will mean for those of us who attend it regularly, or at least from time to time?

With his document *Traditionis custodes*, issued on 16 July 2021, Pope Francis sought to heal divisions in the Church which certain bishops had reported arising in some communities using the traditional Latin rite. In 2020 the Pope asked the Congregation for the Doctrine of the Faith to circulate a questionnaire to the bishops regarding the implementation of Pope Benedict's 2007 document *Summorum Pontificum*. That document granted ample faculties to celebrate the traditional Latin rite of the Mass, using the 1962 missal issued by Pope John XXIII.

In his letter to the bishops accompanying *Traditionis custodes*, Pope Francis described his reaction to the findings of the survey: "The responses reveal a situation that preoccupies and saddens me, and persuades me of the need to intervene. Regrettably, the pastoral objective of my Predecessors, who had intended 'to do everything possible to ensure that all those who truly possessed the desire for unity would find it possible to remain in this unity or to rediscover it anew', has often been seriously disregarded. An opportunity offered by St John Paul II and, with even greater magnanimity, by Benedict XVI, intended to recover the unity of an ecclesial body with diverse liturgical sensibilities, was exploited to widen the gaps, reinforce the divergences, and encourage disagreements that injure the Church, block her path, and expose her to the peril of division."

In particular, he says he is "saddened that the instrumental use of *Missale Romanum* of 1962 is often characterised by a rejection not only of the liturgical reform, but of the Vatican Council II itself, claiming, with unfounded and unsustainable assertions, that it betrayed the Tradition and the 'true Church'... To doubt the Council is to doubt the intentions of those very Fathers who exercised their collegial power in a solemn manner *cum Petro et sub Petro* in an ecumenical council, and, in the final analysis, to doubt the Holy Spirit himself who guides the Church."

As Pope Francis says, to doubt the teachings of the Second Vatican Council and to say that the Council betrayed the Tradition and the true Church. is to doubt the Holy Spirit himself. It is not clear how many people in fact have this attitude, but the attitude is certainly very misguided and lacking in faith. In view of those findings the Pope introduced the new norms, which restrict the use of the Missal of 1962. Among the norms are those which follow.

Whereas before, every priest in the world was authorised to use the 1962 missal freely at his own discretion, now priests must seek permission from their bishop to use it.

Masses celebrated with the 1962 missal are never to be celebrated in a parish church, something which has been done commonly until now, even in cathedrals, for the benefit of parishioners. It should be borne in mind that there are very few churches which are not parish churches.

The bishop can now decide whether or not to allow an existing group using the 1962 missal to continue doing so, and he is not to authorise the establishment of any new groups.

Priests ordained from now on who wish to celebrate Mass with the 1962 missal must seek permission from the diocesan bishop, who is to consult the Holy See before granting the permission. And priests who already use this missal must request permission from their bishop to continue doing so.

In summary, it will be up to each bishop to decide how he wants to implement these norms and, depending on what he decides, the traditional rite will be more or less available. It is possible that in many places the faithful will have to travel further to attend a traditional Mass.

As many commentators have said, these norms are a matter of Church discipline, not of doctrine, and they may be changed by a future Pope.

819 Martin Luther on the Mass

I know that Martin Luther did not regard the Mass as a sacrifice. Why did he say that and how do we defend the Catholic belief that the Mass is truly a sacrifice?

Luther admitted that the language and notion of sacrifice had been applied to the Mass from the very beginning, a belief that was practically unquestioned until his own writings on the matter.

For example, Christ had said on instituting the Eucharist, "This chalice is the new covenant in my blood. Do this, as often as you drink it, in remembrance of me" (*1 Cor* 11:23-25). He was instituting the sacrifice of the New Covenant, where the blood would be not that of animals, as in the daily sacrifices of the Old Covenant, but now his own blood, to be shed on the cross the following day. And he asked the apostles to continue celebrating it.

Also, the belief of the early Church that the Mass was a sacrifice is clear in the *Didache*, a Christian document dating probably to the end of the first century: "On the Lord's day, assemble together and break bread and give thanks, first confessing your sins, that your sacrifice may be pure."

Martin Luther's rejection of the sacrificial nature of the Mass was based especially on his belief that we are justified by faith, not by good works. According to him, nothing we do, including offering the Mass, is capable of "exacting" anything from God. He considered the Church to be teaching that the Mass as a sacrifice was a "good work", offered to God to propitiate him and win favours from him. According to Luther, the Mass could not be Christ's sacrifice, since that had been offered once and for all on Calvary. It was only an action of the Church or the priest, who offered Christ to the Father. It was a human action, a good work, on the part of the Church or the priest, something Luther considered unnecessary and even, in his words, an "abomination".

In his work *The Misuse of the Mass*, Luther wrote: "This has been the fate of the mass; it has been converted by the teaching of godless men into a good work. They themselves call it an *opus operatum* [a work done or performed] and by it they presume themselves to be all-powerful with God. Next, they proceed to the very height of madness, and after inventing the lie that the mass is effective simply by virtue of the act having been performed, they add another one to the effect that the mass is nonetheless profitable to others…"

Luther continues: "If, however, you recognise that this Sacrament is a promise and not a sacrifice, you are not uncertain and are aware of no anger [on the part of God] … And as he promises and shows himself to be gracious and merciful, so you will find him to be, if you hold and believe him to be thus. And if you notice that he promises you nothing but grace, then you will understand with a light and joyous conscience that he demands nothing from you in the way of gift or sacrifice but that he lovingly entreats and encourages you to accept his gift."

In another work, "The Abomination of the Secret Mass", Luther wrote: "The priest offers up once again the Lord Christ, who offered himself only once (cf. *Heb* 9:25-26), just as he died only once and cannot die again or be offered up again (cf. *Rom* 6:9-10). For through his one death and sacrifice he has taken away and swallowed up all sins. Yet they [Catholic priests] go ahead and every day offer him up more than a hundred thousand times throughout the world. They thereby deny, both with their deeds and in their hearts, that Christ has washed sin away and has died and risen again. This is such an abomination that I don't believe it could be sufficiently punished on earth if it rained pure fire from heaven. This blasphemy is so great that it must simply wait for eternal hell fire."

The *Augsburg Confession* summarised Lutheran belief: "The Scriptures also teach that we are justified before God through faith in Christ. Now, if [as Catholics believe] the Mass takes away the sins of the living and the dead by a performance of the outward act, justification comes from the work of the Mass and not from faith. But the Scriptures do not allow this."

The Council of Trent (1545-1563), in answer to Luther, stated the traditional Catholic teaching: "And since in this divine sacrifice which is celebrated in the Mass, the same Christ who offered himself once in a bloody manner on the altar of the cross is contained and offered in an unbloody manner ... this sacrifice is truly propitiatory" (in *CCC* 1367).

820 Luther on the Real Presence

I have some Lutheran friends who tell me they believe in the Real Presence of Christ in the Eucharist. Is this what Martin Luther taught?

Martin Luther's understanding of the Eucharist is surprisingly close to the Catholic understanding, although with a very important difference. Luther (1483-1546) had been an Augustinian priest, so it is only natural that many of his beliefs were, at least initially, those of a Catholic.

His major work on the Eucharist was *On the Babylonian Captivity of the Church*, published in 1520. In that book Luther listed three "captivities" of the Eucharist by the Church: the denial of Communion under both species to all the faithful, the doctrine of transubstantiation and the notion that the Mass is a sacrifice.

As regards transubstantiation and the Real Presence, Luther mentions how he was quite taken by the ideas of Cardinal Pierre d'Ailly of Cambrai, who argued that to believe that real bread and real wine, and not merely their accidents or appearances, are present on the altar would be much more probable and require fewer superfluous miracles, if only the Church had not decreed otherwise. That is, it would be easier to believe that after the consecration it is the bread and wine themselves, not only their accidents or appearances, that remain, along with the Body and Blood of Christ, but the Church has decreed otherwise. Luther accepted that this was the case, when Cardinal d'Ailly and the Church did not.

Luther goes on to explain that "after floating in a sea of doubt, I at last found rest for my conscience in the above view, namely, that it is real bread and real wine, in which Christ's real Flesh and real Blood are present in no other way and to no less a degree than the others assert them to be under their accidents."

He also writes: "For my part, if I cannot fathom how the bread is the Body of Christ, yet I will take my reason captive to the obedience of Christ [cf. *1 Cor* 10:5], and clinging simply to his words, firmly believe not only that the Body of Christ is in the bread but that the bread is the Body of Christ ... What does it matter if philosophy cannot fathom this? The Holy Spirit is greater than Aristotle."

Luther never departed from this position, holding that Christ's Body and Blood are truly present in the bread and wine. He frequently calls this presence a "substantial" one, even though he still believed that the full reality of the bread and wine also remained. This doctrine has come to be called "consubstantiation." It holds that the substance of the Body and Blood of Christ are present alongside the substance of the bread and wine, which remain truly present.

The traditional Catholic theology is that the substances of bread and wine have been transformed into the substances of the Body and Blood of Christ, with only their accidents, not the substances, remaining. This change is called "transubstantiation" or "change of substance".

In his 1528 *Confession Concerning Christ's Supper*, in which he espoused this doctrine of consubstantiation, Luther faced the opposition not only of Catholics, but also of the followers of Ulrich Zwingli and Johannes Oecolampadius, who taught that the bread and wine were only a symbol of the Body and Blood of Christ.

In that work Luther stated: "It is not necessary … that one of the two disappear or be annihilated, but both the bread and the Body remain, and by virtue of the sacramental unity it is correct to say, 'This is my Body', designating the bread with the word 'this'. For now it is no longer ordinary bread in the oven but a 'Flesh-bread' or 'Body-bread', i.e., a bread that has become one sacramental substance, one with the Body of Christ."

The 1530 *Ausburg Confession*, which remains the common profession of faith among Lutherans, declared: "Our churches teach that the Body and Blood of Christ are truly present and are distributed to those who eat in the Supper of the Lord."

In summary, Luther believed in the Real Presence, but he denied transubstantiation, holding rather to consubstantiation. Naturally, Lutheran ministers then and now, not having received Holy Orders, cannot bring about any form of Eucharistic presence.

821 The age for First Communion

My daughter is six and very much wants to make her First Communion, but in our parish First Communion is given when the children are in year four, when they are nine or ten. Is there anything we can do?

Before I answer your question, let us take a brief look at the history of this matter, as related in the decree *Quam Singulari*, issued by the Congregation for the Discipline of the Sacraments in 1910 by the authority of Pope St Pius X. From the very beginning of the Church, Communion was given to infants at the time of their Baptism, along with the Sacrament of Confirmation. This custom prevailed until the thirteenth century, and in some places even later. It is still the custom in the Orthodox and some other Eastern Churches.

Communion was given by placing a few drops of the Precious Blood on the infant's tongue, which is safer than giving them a small piece of the Host, which they might expel. Afterwards, when the parents went up to receive Communion, they would take their infant with them and the child would again receive Communion in this way.

Later this practice died out in the Latin Church and children were not permitted to receive Communion until they had reached the age of reason and had some understanding of the Sacrament. This practice was solemnly confirmed by the Fourth Lateran Council in 1215 and again, in the sixteenth century, by the Council of Trent.

The decree issued at the time of St Pius X in 1910 took up this criterion, establishing the age of reason for the reception of both Penance and the Eucharist. It mentioned that over time "deplorable abuses" had been introduced, with a later age and greater knowledge being required for Communion. In some places this age was ten or twelve, and even fourteen or older. This custom, it stated, "has kept the faithful from the Eucharist and been the cause of many evils."

According to the decree, "The age of discretion, both for Confession and for Holy Communion, is that at which a child begins to reason, that is, about the seventh year, perhaps a little above or even a little below ... For first Confession and first Communion there is not necessary a full and perfect knowledge of Christine doctrine... The knowledge that is required in a child in order to be properly prepared for first Communion is that by which the child will understand according to his capacity those Mysteries of Faith that are necessary as a means of salvation and can distinguish between Eucharistic bread and ordinary, bodily bread."

It should be noted that the "seventh year", when children have reached the age of reason and can receive these sacraments, begins when the child turns six. Indeed, the *Code of Canon Law* states that a person is presumed to have the use of reason at the age of seven (cf. *Can.* 97 §2). Thus, there will be many six-year-olds who are very capable of making their first Confession and receiving Communion.

Here one must take into account the obvious differences among families and their children. There are families who attend Mass every Sunday and whose children are well instructed in the faith and can very well make their first Confession and Communion when they are only six. When the families are not attending Mass regularly and the children are not well instructed, a later age is more opportune.

While there is much to be said for children receiving these Sacraments along with the others of their age group in the parish, it is not strictly necessary. The parents, perhaps assisted by catechists, can prepare their children on their own, and, when they think they are ready, ask a priest to examine them and give his opinion. According to the *Code of Canon Law*, "It is primarily the duty of parents and of those who take their place, as it is the duty of the parish priest, to ensure that children who have reached the use of reason are properly prepared and, having made their sacramental confession, are nourished by this divine food as soon as possible" (Can. 914).

When the children are prepared, they can simply make their first Confession on their own, and later receive Communion in any Mass, with the customary celebrations in the family afterwards.

822 Communion under both species

I am now in my 80s and was a little surprised when many years ago the practice of the laity receiving Communion from the chalice was introduced, since for most of my life it was not allowed. Can you tell me the history of the practice and the reasons for it?

I will begin my review of the history in this article and will continue it in the next, using especially Mario Righetti's history of the liturgy, *Storia Liturgica*. It is clear that the practice of giving Communion to the lay faithful under the species of both bread and wine goes back to the early centuries of the Church and it continued until the twelfth century.

In the early centuries it was considered wrong not to receive Communion under both species. Thus, in the fifth century, Pope St Leo the Great denounced the "sacrilegious simulation" of the Manicheans of his time, who received Communion only under the species of bread. He ordered them to be expelled from the assembly of the faithful. At the end of that century, Pope Gelasius I (492-496 AD) denounced the "grave sacrilege" of the Church in Calabria, Italy, where Communion was given only under the species of bread.

Interestingly, in 726 AD, St Boniface in Germany asked Pope Gregory II whether, in view of the large number of communicants, it was permissible to use more than one chalice for the consecration of the Precious Blood, and the answer was negative, since Our Lord only consecrated one chalice.

To make the reception of the Precious Blood more hygienic it was proposed at one stage that the faithful should receive it through a metallic straw made of silver or gold. It seemed preferable to many, however, rather to adopt the custom of the Greeks in the East who, from the end of the eighth century, gave Communion with pieces of the host dipped in the Precious Blood. That custom, also known as intinction, found its way to the West in the middle of the eleventh century, where it was accepted by some but rejected by others.

In England intinction was strenuously defended by Ernulphus,

Bishop of Rochester. It was also adopted in the monastery of Cluny in France, but the Council of Clermont in 1095 allowed it only in cases of necessity. Pope Paschal II (1099-1118), who had been a Cluny monk, in a letter to Pontius, the Abbot of Cluny, stipulated that the custom of offering the host and the Precious Blood separately was to be maintained always in the Church, except for children and the sick. The best theologians of the time disapproved of the practice of intinction, among them Gratian, Hugo of St Victor, Pope Innocent III and St Thomas Aquinas. The latter expressly forbade intinction, which soon fell into disuse in ordinary practice, except for the sick.

The difficulties that led to the practice of intinction gradually brought about the elimination altogether of giving Communion under the species of wine. This was attested to first by Rodolphus, Abbot of St Troud, near Liege, around 1110. He argued that the whole Christ was already present under the species of bread alone and so, with this reasoning, the custom of Communion only under the species of bread gradually spread everywhere. St Thomas Aquinas, who died in 1274, spoke of it as a practice already prevalent in his time, and he recommended it as a way of avoiding irreverence and spilling (cf. *STh* III, q. 80, art. 12).

At the University of Paris, Alexander of Hales, who died in 1245, said that it was only permissible for lay people to receive the Eucharist under the species of bread, as was done almost everywhere in his day. Nonetheless, the custom of receiving under both species continued here and there at least until the beginning of the fifteenth century, when the Council of Constance in 1415 forbade it altogether.

Various reasons were proposed at the time of the Council for not giving Communion from the chalice: the possibility of spilling when the chalice was carried from one place to another, the natural repugnance of receiving under the form of wine, especially by women, the fact that the chalice would become unclean after many had drunk from it, the difficulty in preserving the wine lest it turn to vinegar, the excessive cost, the possibility that the wine would freeze in the cold months of the winter, etc.

823 More about Communion under both species

In your last article you wrote that you would continue your coverage of the history of Communion under both species. I am interested in this topic and keen to read more about it.

As I mentioned in the previous article, Communion was received under both species, that is from the chalice as well as the host, until the twelfth century, when the practice died out except for a few exceptions here and there. I concluded with the Council of Constance (1414-18), which banned the practice altogether.

The Council was addressing the teaching of John Hus and his followers, who were known as Utraquists, from the Latin word for "both" species. They maintained that, in order to receive the full Christ, the faithful needed to receive both the Blood of Christ from the chalice and his Body in the host. In answer to them, the Council declared that "it must be firmly believed and in no way doubted that the whole Body and Blood of Christ are truly contained both under the species of bread and under the species of wine. Therefore, since this custom [of receiving only under the species of bread] has been reasonably introduced by the Church and the holy Fathers and has been observed for a very long time, it must be held to be a law that it is not permitted to reject or to change at will without the authority of the Church" (DS 1199).

The issue refused to go away, however, and there were repeated requests in different parts of the Church for the faithful to receive from the chalice. The Protestants at the time of the Reformation were particularly insistent on it. This moved the Council of Trent (1545-63) to declare in its twenty-first session, in 1562, that it was not necessary for the faithful to receive Communion under both species, that the Church was led by just and reasonable motives to legislate that the laity and even priests who were not celebrating should receive only under the species of bread, and that the whole and entire Christ was received under the one species of bread (Canons I-III, DS 1731-73).

Since there was considerable disagreement among the bishops as to whether the Church should permit, at least in some circumstances, the reception of Communion under both species, the Council decreed in its twenty-second session, also in 1562, that it should be left to the Pope to decide when and under what circumstances Communion might be given from the chalice to those requesting it (DS 1760). In fact, the practice of giving Communion only with the host prevailed for the next four centuries.

In the Second Vatican Council (1962-65), when the doctrinal errors of the Protestants, with their insistence on Communion under both species in order to receive the full Christ, were no longer an issue, the bishops decided that, in specific cases to be determined by the Apostolic See, Communion under both species was to be restored.

In the Constitution on the Sacred Liturgy *Sacrosanctum Concilium* (1963), the Council declared: "The dogmatic principles which were laid down by the Council of Trent remaining intact, Communion under both kinds may be granted when the bishops think fit, not only to clerics and religious but also to the laity, in cases to be determined by the Apostolic See. For example, to the newly ordained in the Mass of their ordination; to the newly professed in the Mass of their religious profession; to the newly baptised in the Mass which follows their baptism" (n. 55).

Following the Council, various post-conciliar documents proceeded to list the cases in which Communion could be given under both species. These were always for small groups of the faithful on special occasions. By way of example, the Congregation for Divine Worship's Instruction *Sacramentali Communione*, approved by Pope Paul VI on 26 June 1970, listed the following occasions: newly baptised adults in the Mass following their baptism, the bride and bridegroom in their wedding Mass, those being instituted into a ministry in the Mass of their institution, the deacon and ministers who exercise their office at Mass, and those participating in a retreat in a special Mass for retreatants.

At the local level, in 1986 the Australian bishops received special permission from the Holy See to give Communion to the faithful under both species at Masses on Sundays and feast days.

824 Communion for Protestants

I recently saw an article in The Catholic Weekly *saying that a German bishop is giving Holy Communion to Protestants who ask for it. I thought this was not allowed. My husband is Lutheran and he would like to receive Communion too. Can this be done?*

An article in *The Catholic Weekly* on 7 March 2021 reported that the President of the German Catholic Bishops Conference, Archbishop Georg Bätzing of Limburg, has said that he would continue to give Holy Communion to Protestants who ask for it, and that it was necessary to respect the "personal decision of conscience" of those seeking to receive it. He said this was already a practice in Germany every Sunday, and that it was in line with papal documents.

We should understand that while it may be a practice in the diocese of Limburg, and perhaps in some other dioceses, it is most certainly not a practice throughout the country. There are many bishops in that country who are faithful to the Church and opposed to the practice.

That the practice is not in line with papal documents is clear in a four-page critique by the Congregation for the Doctrine of the Faith sent to Archbishop Bätzing in September 2020. It emphasised that significant differences in understanding of the Eucharist and ministry remained between Protestants and Catholics: "The doctrinal differences are still so important that they currently rule out reciprocal participation in the Lord's Supper and the Eucharist."

We should remember that the word "Communion" means "union with", and that in the Catholic Church only those who are in full union with the Church on doctrinal matters and in their personal lives – with their soul in the state of grace – may receive Holy Communion.

What then is the teaching of the Church on who may be admitted to Communion? As a general rule, the *Code of Canon Law* states that "Catholic ministers may lawfully administer the sacraments only to Catholic members of Christ's faithful, who equally may lawfully receive them only from Catholic ministers" (Can. 844 §1).

There are a few exceptions to this rule. A distinction is made between the Eastern Churches not in full communion with the Catholic Church, i.e., the Orthodox, and the communities derived from the Reformation, usually known as Protestants. The reason for the distinction is that the Orthodox Churches, by virtue of their apostolic succession, have a valid priesthood and therefore valid sacraments. Moreover, they have the same faith as regards the sacraments; e.g., that the Eucharist is the Real Presence of Christ, and not just a symbol. The Protestants, on the other hand, do not have apostolic succession or a valid priesthood, and their theology of the sacraments is very different from ours.

With respect to the Orthodox, the Code says: "Catholic ministers may lawfully administer the sacraments of penance, the Eucharist and anointing of the sick to members of the eastern Churches not in full communion with the Catholic Church, if they spontaneously ask for them and are properly disposed. The same applies to members of other Churches which the Apostolic See judges to be in the same position as the aforesaid eastern Churches so far as the sacraments are concerned" (Can. 844 §3).

As regards Protestants, the criterion is more strict: "If there is a danger of death or if, in the judgment of the diocesan Bishop or of the Episcopal Conference, there is some other grave and pressing need, Catholic ministers may lawfully administer these same sacraments to other Christians not in full communion with the Catholic Church, who cannot approach a minister of their own community and who spontaneously ask for them, provided that they demonstrate the Catholic faith in respect of these sacraments and are properly disposed" (Can. 844 §4).

Since Protestants do not share our faith in the Real Presence in the Eucharist, they cannot be admitted to Holy Communion, even if they ask for it.

The Church in Germany is going through a very trying time, as many are aware. We should pray for the German bishops, that they may be in full communion with the Church as regards her teachings and discipline, and for Pope Francis, who has the difficult task of restoring and preserving this unity.

825 Communion for the divorced

I am unfortunately divorced due to violence in the home, which caused me to leave with my young son. I now find myself unable to go to Communion and I feel very deprived of the spiritual nourishment I need. Is there anything I can do?

Who told you that you cannot receive Communion? You can. The *Code of Canon Law* teaches: "Any baptised person who is not forbidden by law may and must be admitted to holy communion" (Can. 912). And who is forbidden by law? "Those upon whom the penalty of excommunication or interdict has been imposed or declared, and others who obstinately persist in manifest grave sin, are not to be admitted to Holy Communion" (Can. 915).

Is a divorced person, for the fact of being divorced, committing manifest grave sin? No, they are not, at least not for the mere fact of being divorced. Only if they are actually living with a new partner and having sexual relations with that person, whether married civilly or not, or they are not living together but are having such relations, would they be committing grave sin.

But isn't it a sin to be divorced? No, not in itself. We can distinguish two cases. Where a spouse has been the cause of the breakup of the marriage through domestic violence, adultery, sexual abuse, alcoholism, compulsive gambling, etc., they have committed grave sin. In order to be admitted to Holy Communion they must be sorry for what they have done and seek absolution in the sacrament of penance, as well as do all they can to repair the damage and, if possible, resume marital relations with their spouse. And, of course, they cannot enter into a new relationship that involves the acts reserved for marriage.

In the case of the spouse who is the victim of the violence or other form of abuse, they have not committed grave sin and so they can most certainly be admitted to Communion, again provided they are not living in sin with another person.

Naturally, it is not always easy, or even possible, to put all the blame for the breakup of a marriage at the feet of one spouse. Therefore, each one must be sorry for whatever contribution they may have made to the breakup of the marriage.

And if, as we have said, one of the spouses is now living in an immoral relationship with another person, they will have to end the relationship before they can receive Communion. Only if they have received an annulment of the marriage from a Church tribunal are they able to marry a new partner in the Church and be able to receive Communion. Alternatively, if they have children needing their common care, and the years have passed and they feel they can abstain from marital intimacy and live "as brother and sister" in the new relationship, they too can be admitted to Communion.

This should not be considered harsh. It was Jesus himself who said: "Whoever divorces his wife and marries another, commits adultery against her; and if she divorces her husband and marries another, she commits adultery." (*Mk* 10:11-12) From the beginning, the Church, in obedience to her divine founder, has not allowed divorce and remarriage in the Church. As a consequence, those who "remarry" outside the Church are considered to be living in a state of sin and cannot be admitted to Holy Communion.

In this matter the Church is only being faithful to Christ's teaching, which concerns the indissolubility and sanctity of marriage, so important for the life of the Church and of society. Moreover, the Church is not imposing anything on the couple in this irregular marriage situation. It was they, after all, who freely chose to enter into a relationship in which they knew they would not be able to receive Communion.

While they cannot receive Communion, the Church, as the good mother she is, opens her arms wide to welcome people in irregular marriage situations into other aspects of Church life, including attendance at Mass, prayer, reading of Scripture, and participation in the charitable and other works of the Church. Both the couple and the Church community wait in hope for a time when the couple will once again be able to receive the sacraments, through a declaration of nullity of the previous marriage by a Church tribunal, the decision to live together as brother and sister, or the death of the previous spouse.

826 Communion for the mentally impaired

My mother is in a nursing home and is suffering from dementia. She was a regular Mass goer and has been receiving Communion in the nursing home. At present, however, she can no longer understand what Communion is. Can she continue to receive the sacrament?

St Thomas Aquinas (1225-1274) deals with this question in Part III of his *Summa Theologiae* and I will base my answer on his reasoning there. In Question 80, Article 9, he answers the question of whether those who do not have the full use of reason ought to receive the Eucharist.

St Thomas distinguishes three different conditions of people as regards their use of reason: those who never had the use of reason, those who have a diminished use of reason, whom he calls "feeble-minded", and those who once had the use of reason but have now lost it.

As regards those who have never had the use of reason, he writes: "In another way men are said not to possess fully the use of reason. Either, then, they never had the use of reason, and have remained so from birth; and in that case this sacrament is not to be given to them, because in no way has there been any preceding devotion towards the sacrament."

In a similar state to them are infants who have not yet acquired the use of reason. St Thomas equates them to older people who are severely lacking in mental capacity, whom he calls insane: "The same reason holds good of newly born children as of the insane who never have had the use of reason: consequently, the sacred mysteries are not to be given to them ... Nor do they suffer any loss of life from the fact of Our Lord saying (*Jn* 6:54), 'Except you eat the flesh of the Son of Man, and drink his blood, you shall not have life in you'; because, as Augustine writes to Boniface (*Pseudo-Beda, Comment. in 1 Cor. 10:17*), 'then every one of the faithful becomes a partaker,' i.e. spiritually, 'of the Body and Blood of the Lord, when he is made a member of Christ's body in Baptism.' But when children begin to have the use of reason so as to be able to conceive some devotion for the sacrament, then it can be given to them."

As regards those who have a diminished use of reason, St Thomas writes: "Men are said to be devoid of reason in two ways. First, when they are feeble-minded, as a man who sees dimly is said not to see: and since such persons can conceive some devotion towards this sacrament, it is not to be denied them." With these people, obviously, there are degrees of the use of reason, and pastors should ensure that they have sufficient understanding of what Holy Communion is before giving it to them. The *General Catechetical Directory* of 1972 said that those who are to receive Communion should have an idea "about God as our Lord and Father, about his love towards us, about Jesus, the Son of God, who became man for us, died and rose again" (*Addendum* 2, n. 836). And, of course, they should be able to distinguish the Eucharist from ordinary bread.

Finally, there are those whom you mention in your question, who once had the use of reason but have now lost it. St Thomas says of them: "Those lacking the use of reason can have devotion towards the sacrament; actual devotion in some cases, and past in others." He says that "if when they formerly had their wits they showed devotion towards this sacrament, it ought to be given to them in the hour of death; unless danger be feared of vomiting or spitting it out. Hence we read in the acts of the Fourth Council of Carthage (Canon 76); and the same is to be found in the Decretals (xxvi, 6): 'If a sick man ask to receive the sacrament of Penance; and if, when the priest who has been sent for comes to him, he be so weak as to be unable to speak, or becomes delirious, let them, who heard him ask, bear witness, and let him receive the sacrament of Penance. Then if it be thought that he is going to die shortly, let him be reconciled by imposition of hands, and let the Eucharist be placed in his mouth."

Although St Thomas speaks only of giving Communion to those about to die, it is clear that people suffering from dementia may receive the Sacrament earlier. This is certainly the case when their dementia is just beginning, and it continues so long as they do not react against it, spit it out, etc. There can come a time when they no longer know how to receive the Sacrament, in the hand or on the tongue, and then it should be discontinued.

827 President Biden and Holy Communion

President Joe Biden of the U.S., who is a Catholic, has expressed publicly his support for abortion, yet he continues to go to Mass and receive Communion. I was surprised to hear this. Should he be allowed to receive Communion?

President Biden, as you say, is a Mass-going Catholic. He carries rosary beads, he made the sign of the cross after a public ceremony at the White House honouring the 500,000 Americans who had died from Covid-19, and he has a photo of Pope Francis behind his desk in the Oval Office. Yet, by executive order, he has already reinstated funding for international abortion providers and he has expressed his commitment to codify into law the *Roe versus Wade* Supreme Court decision declaring a right to abortion. Should he be allowed to receive Holy Communion?

The fact is he has been receiving Communion – at Holy Trinity Catholic Church, a few kilometres from the White House, with the support of the parish priest, Fr Kevin Gillespie, S.J. Fr Gillespie had checked this with the Archbishop of Washington, Cardinal Wilton Gregory, who agreed that the President was welcome to receive Communion. Nonetheless, the parish has received more than a hundred angry phone calls, letters and emails protesting the decision to allow it.

What is the official teaching of the Church on the matter? Canon 915 of the *Code of Canon Law* states: "Those … who obstinately persist in manifest grave sin, are not to be admitted to Holy Communion."

Can it be said that a person who expresses public support for abortion obstinately persists in manifest grave sin? Yes, provided the person is aware of the Church's teaching on the matter, as most Catholics are. The *Catechism of the Catholic Church* teaches: "Since the first century the Church has affirmed the moral evil of every procured abortion... Direct abortion ... is gravely contrary to the moral law" (*CCC* 2271).

Therefore, to contradict publicly a teaching as fundamental as this is clearly a grave sin. If the person is aware that they are contradicting Church teaching on so grave a matter, they cannot be admitted to Holy Communion. After all, reception of Communion implies that the person is fully in communion with the Church on all matters, including Church teaching.

What is more, to deny a fundamental teaching like that on abortion is really to fall into the sin of heresy, defined in the Catechism as "the obstinate post-baptismal denial of some truth which must be believed with divine and catholic faith" (*CCC* 2089; Can. 751). If someone has been warned that what they are advocating is contrary to Church teaching and they obstinately persist in their belief, they are guilty of heresy. The penalty is severe – automatic excommunication by the law itself (cf. Can. 1364). Since it is often not clear exactly who is guilty of heresy and who is not, the local bishop, after a proper investigation, may choose to declare publicly that the person is excommunicated. Whether the bishop considers this to be the most prudent way to proceed, however, is another matter.

One approach the priest or bishop may take, after speaking personally with the person and warning him of the scandal he is causing, is to ask him not to present himself for Communion in Masses in the parish or diocese. This is not the same as excommunication, which prevents the person from receiving any sacrament in the Church until such time as the person repents and has been absolved of the excommunication.

This approach was taken, for example, in 2008 by Archbishop Joseph Naumann of Kansas City against Kathleen Sebelius, Governor of Kansas, who had vetoed a bill passed by both houses of the state legislature greatly restricting access to abortion. After speaking personally several times with Governor Sebelius about her action, the Archbishop asked Sebelius not to present herself for Holy Communion until such time as she amended her life and publicly repudiated her previous actions.

What action the authorities in Washington will take remains to be seen. They may choose to do nothing. But meanwhile many Catholics will remain confused when a President who has expressed views and acted contrary to Church teaching on such an important issue continues to be admitted to Communion.

828 Spiritual Communion

Without being able to attend Mass during the pandemic I really miss Mass and Communion. They tell us to make a Spiritual Communion. What exactly is this?

As its name suggests, Spiritual Communion is a prayer expressing the desire to receive Our Lord in the Blessed Sacrament. A Spiritual Communion can be said not only when one is unable to receive sacramental Communion but also in preparation for sacramental Communion. Thus, one might say the prayer at night in preparation for Communion the following day, or on waking, or in the church itself before receiving Communion.

Pope St John Paul II recommended this practice in his encyclical *Ecclesia de Eucharistia*: "Precisely for this reason it is good to cultivate in our hearts a constant desire for the sacrament of the Eucharist. This was the origin of the practice of 'Spiritual Communion', which has happily been established in the Church for centuries and recommended by saints who were masters of the spiritual life. Saint Teresa of Jesus wrote: 'When you do not receive Communion and you do not attend Mass, you can make a Spiritual Communion, which is a most beneficial practice; by it the love of God will be greatly impressed on you" (*The Way of Perfection*, Ch. 35; *EE*, n. 34).

Interestingly, Pope John Paul in that same encyclical spoke of Our

Lady herself doing this in preparation for Our Lord's death on the cross and for her reception of Communion from the apostles: "In her daily preparation for Calvary, Mary experienced a kind of 'anticipated Eucharist' – one might say a 'Spiritual Communion' – of desire and of oblation, which would culminate in her union with her Son in his passion, and then find expression after Easter by her partaking in the Eucharist which the Apostles celebrated as the memorial of that passion" (*EE*, n. 56).

St John Vianney compared Spiritual Communion with blowing on embers to rekindle the fire: "If we are deprived of sacramental Communion, let us replace it, as far as we can, by Spiritual Communion, which we can make every moment; for we ought to have always a burning desire to receive the good God. Communion is to the soul like blowing a fire that is beginning to go out, but that has still plenty of hot embers; we blow, and the fire burns again. After the reception of the sacraments, when we feel ourselves slacken in the love of God, let us have recourse at once to Spiritual Communion. When we cannot go to the church, let us turn towards the tabernacle; no wall can shut us out from the good God" (*The Spirit of the Curé of Ars*).

More recently St Josemaría Escrivá wrote: "What a source of grace there is in Spiritual Communion! Practise it frequently and you'll have more presence of God and closer union with him in your life" (*The Way*, 540). And also: "Do not neglect to say, 'Jesus, I love you', and make one Spiritual Communion, at least, each day, in atonement for all the profanations and sacrileges he suffers because he wants to be with us" (*Furrow*, 689).

St Josemaría gave us the wording for a Spiritual Communion which he had learned from the Piarist Fathers when he made his first Communion and which is now used by people all over the world: "I wish, my Lord, to receive you with the purity, humility and devotion with which your most holy Mother received you, with the spirit and fervour of the saints."

Another popular Spiritual Communion is that of St Alphonsus Liguori: "My Jesus, I believe that you are present in the Most Holy

Sacrament. I love you above all things, and I desire to receive you into my soul. Since I cannot at this moment receive you sacramentally, come at least spiritually into my heart. I embrace you as if you were already there and unite myself wholly to you. Never permit me to be separated from you. Amen."

As regards the benefits of Spiritual Communion, Fr Stefano Manelli, OFM Conv., STD, in his book *Jesus our Eucharistic Love*, writes: "Spiritual Communion, as St Thomas Aquinas and St Alphonsus Liguori teach, produces effects similar to Sacramental Communion, according to the dispositions with which it is made, the greater or less earnestness with which Jesus is desired, and the greater or less love with which Jesus is welcomed and given due attention." What is more, the Vatican's *Enchiridion of Indulgences* (1968) indicates that "an act of Spiritual Communion, according to any pious formula, is enriched with a partial indulgence" (n. 15).

829 The Eucharistic miracle of Legnica

I understand there has been another Eucharistic miracle in Poland, apart from the one in Sokołka, about which you wrote. Is this true and has the Vatican given any judgment on it?

On Christmas Day, 2013, in St Hyacinth's church in Legnica, a city of 100,000 in southwest Poland, a priest accidentally dropped a consecrated Communion host on the floor. Following the normal procedure, he picked up the host and placed it in a bowl of water until it would dissolve. After two weeks, the host had dissolved only partially, and a red substance had appeared on it.

The bishop of Legnica at the time, Stefan Cichy, then formed a commission to study the matter. In February of the following year a tiny fragment of the host was removed and placed on a corporal to be studied by the Department of Forensic Medicine of the Universities of Szczecin and Wrocław. The researchers found human DNA as well as tissue from the heart, which had alterations that often appear when a person is in a state of agony before dying.

When a Polish daily newspaper challenged the findings on the grounds that a certain bacteria thrives on bread and can create large amounts of a red substance similar to blood, the diocese responded that the bishop had specifically asked the researchers in Wrocław and Szczecin to check whether the red substance was of bacterial or fungal origin, and they had found no such evidence.

In January 2016, Bishop Cichy's successor Zbigniew Kiernikowski referred the matter to the Vatican's Congregation for the Doctrine of the Faith. On April 10 of that year, following the Holy See's recommendations, he asked the parish priest, Fr Andrzej Ziombrze, to prepare a suitable place for the relic so that the faithful could give it due adoration. He also asked for instruction to be given to the faithful so that they would have the proper attitude to devotion to the Eucharist, and for a book to be prepared where favours and other supernatural events could be recorded.

Bishop Kiernikowski said that he hoped this would serve to deepen devotion to the Eucharist and have a deep impact on the lives of people viewing the relic. "We interpret this amazing sign as an expression of the generosity and love of God, who stoops so low to be with man", he said.

On July 2, the host was placed in a reliquary for public view in St Hyacinth's. More than 3,000 faithful attended a liturgy of expiation in the Legnica cathedral and the subsequent procession to St Hyacinth's Shrine, where the reliquary was placed on the church's main altar during a Mass celebrated by Bishop Kiernikowski.

Legnica is one of Poland's least-religious dioceses, where weekly Mass attendance stands at just 29.9%, compared to the national average of 39.1%.

Fr Ziombra said there have already been miraculous conversions and healings, and there is a large number of pilgrims from all over the world travelling to Legnica to pray before the miraculous host. All of this documentation will be presented to the Holy See to assist in its evaluation of the extraordinary event.

Among the conversions was that of a man from Legnica who had been hostile to the Church all his life and even fought against it. In an extraordinary way he was converted in a way not even he could understand. He made his first confession and received Holy Communion for the first time in fifty years. There have been other conversions as well.

Interestingly, St Hyacinth, the first Polish Dominican and a companion of St Dominic, had his own involvement with the Eucharist. In 1240, during the siege of Kiev by the Mongols, as the friars were fleeing, Hyacinth went to rescue the ciborium with the Blessed Eucharist from the tabernacle in the monastery chapel. He heard the voice of Mary, asking him to take her with him. Hyacinth lifted the large stone statue of Mary and saved both the Blessed Sacrament and the image of Our Lady.

Penance and Holy Orders

830 Repentance and absolution

I read recently that Pope Francis told some seminarians that priests should always forgive sins, even when the person is not sorry for them. This doesn't sound right to me. Is it?

It was reported that Pope Francis told seminarians from Barcelona, Spain that they must not be clericalist and should always forgive; even "if we see that there is no intention to repent, we must forgive all." He said that if we deny absolution to someone who is unrepentant, "we become a vehicle for an evil, unjust, and moralistic judgment." Since this is not the traditional teaching of the Church, and the Pope was speaking without a prepared text, it would be safer to assume that he was misquoted.

What is the traditional teaching? We should begin by saying that when someone goes to Confession, by that very fact they are showing they are sorry and want to be forgiven. It is exceedingly rare that anyone going to Confession would not be truly repentant and determined to try to avoid falling into the sin again. A priest friend recently told me that in his more than fifty-five years of priesthood he had had only one such case. The person admitted openly that he was not sorry, that he was planning to commit the sin again a few days later, and he understood that he could not be granted absolution.

In instituting the sacrament of penance on the evening of his Resurrection, Christ himself referred to the possibility that the apostles would not always be able to forgive the sins confessed: "Receive the Holy Spirit. If you forgive the sins of any, they are forgiven; if you retain the sins of any, they are retained" (*Jn* 20:22-23). Retaining sins, in this context, means not forgiving them. So Christ already allowed for this possibility.

The *Catechism of the Catholic Church*, quoting the Council of

Trent, teaches that true sorrow, contrition, is necessary for one's sins to be forgiven. It is one of the acts of the penitent: "Among the penitent's acts contrition occupies first place. Contrition is 'sorrow of the soul and detestation for the sin committed, together with the resolution not to sin again'" (*CCC* 1451).

What is more, *The Code of Canon Law* states that for penitents to receive "the saving remedy of the sacrament of penance, they must be so disposed that, repudiating the sins they have committed and having the purpose of amending their lives, they turn back to God" (Can. 987).

We see the importance of repentance and God's readiness to forgive in Christ's parable of the prodigal son. The younger son, having received his share of the inheritance, went off and squandered the money, living loosely with women. Finding himself penniless and reduced to feeding swine, an unclean animal for the Jews, he repented sincerely, saying: "I will arise and go to my father and I will say to him, 'Father, I have sinned against heaven and before you; I am no longer worthy to be called your son; treat me as one of your hired servants" (*Lk* 15:18-19). The father, an image of God the merciful Father, moved with compassion, embraced him and kissed him, put a ring on his finger, clothed him in the best robe, put shoes on his feet and called for the fatted calf to be killed and eaten to celebrate his return (cf. *Lk* 15:20-24). God will always forgive us, no matter how many or how grave the sins we have committed, provided we are truly sorry.

The Catechism, quoting the Council of Trent, distinguishes between perfect contrition and imperfect contrition: "When it arises from a love by which God is loved above all else, contrition is called 'perfect' (contrition of charity). Such contrition remits venial sins; it also obtains forgiveness of mortal sins if it includes the firm resolution to have recourse to sacramental confession as soon as possible" (*CCC* 1452). "The contrition called 'imperfect' (or attrition) ... is born of the consideration of sin's ugliness or the fear of eternal damnation and the other penalties threatening the sinner (contrition of fear). Such a stirring of conscience ... disposes one to obtain forgiveness in the sacrament of Penance" (*CCC* 1453).

One could also speak of sorrow for a merely human motive; for example, sorrow moved by pride when the person has not been able to overcome a particular sin. This sorrow is not sufficient for absolution, since it is not directed to God but rather to oneself.

So true contrition with a resolution to try to avoid the sin in the future is necessary to receive absolution. And God will always forgive a contrite person: "A broken and contrite heart, O God, you will not despise" (*Ps* 50: 17).

831 The Third Rite of Reconciliation for Australia

I understand the recent Plenary Council of Australia has asked Pope Francis to approve a wider use of the Third Rite of Reconciliation for Australia. I thought this had been ruled out years ago. Might it be approved now?

My own answer is that it is most unlikely to be approved now, but that depends on Pope Francis, not on me. Why do I say this?

The third rite, which involves general absolution of a group of people without prior individual confession, was approved only for cases of "grave necessity". The sequence of events that led up to its approval is the following. In 1972 the Congregation for the Doctrine of the Faith, with the special approval of Pope Paul VI, issued some *Pastoral Norms* on general absolution which were substantially those now in force. They were incorporated into the *Rite of Penance*, approved by Pope Paul VI in 1974, as the third rite of the sacrament. They were later approved by Pope John Paul II when he promulgated the Code of Canon Law in 1983 (Canons 961-963) and the *Catechism of the Catholic Church* in 1992 (*CCC* 1483-1484).

Taking the text from the Catechism, which is the most recent document, there are two circumstances in which general absolution may be given. The first can arise "when there is imminent danger of death without sufficient time for the priest or priests to hear each penitent's confession" (*CCC* 1483). This could happen, for example, in the case of an earthquake, a tsunami, a terrorist attack, a sinking ship, an airplane about to crash, etc.

The second arises "when, given the number of penitents, there are not enough confessors to hear individual confessions properly in a reasonable time, so that the penitents through no fault of their own would be deprived of sacramental grace or Holy Communion for a long time" (*CCC* 1483). The *Pastoral Norms* explain that this can happen in certain mission territories, where a priest goes seldom and only for a short period of time, such that he cannot hear all the individual confessions in the time available.

Personally, I cannot see how either of these circumstances exists in Australia at the present time. Undoubtedly for this reason, the Vatican explicitly told the Australian bishops during their *ad limina* visit to Rome in 1998 that they were not to allow the use of the third rite.

The *Pastoral Norms* of 1972 explain that the principal reason for limiting the use of general absolution to these exceptional circumstances is Christ's words to the apostles: "Whose sins you shall forgive, they are forgiven; whose sins you shall retain, they are retained" (*Jn* 20:22-23). This implies that the priest must hear the individual confession in order to be able to judge whether to forgive or not. The document also mentions "the very great good of souls deriving, according to centuries-long experience, from individual confession and absolution rightly administered" (n. 1).

As a priest who hears hundreds of confessions every month, I see constantly the "very great good" that penitents derive from this sacrament of mercy, of joy. They confess their sins personally, exercising the virtues of humility and sincerity in so doing. They receive personal counsel and direction, with the opportunity to ask questions and engage the priest in a conversation about their concerns, which helps them in their spiritual struggle. They hear the words of forgiveness of their sins, coming from God through the priest. They are given some penance to do, which helps to make up for their sins. They leave the sacrament full of joy and hope for a new beginning in their spiritual life. What is more, as St John Paul II told priests in Lent, 1981, "Confession periodically renewed, the so-called confession 'of devotion', has always accompanied the ascent to holiness in the Church."

I cannot, for the life of me, imagine any of the penitents I see having any desire whatsoever to make use of the third rite. Nor can I imagine any priest who hears many confessions have this desire. What the Church needs is more holiness, more preaching on the value of individual confession, more availability of priests to hear confessions, not an easy way out for both priest and penitents.

832 Women Deacons?

I sometimes hear talk of the Church possibly approving the ordination of women as deacons. Is this something that might happen or is it out of the question?

Any talk of the ordination of women as deacons is based on the presumption that there were women deacons in the early Church. But were there?

Yes, there were women deacons, or more properly deaconesses, in the early Church but they were not deacons in the modern sense of having the power of Holy Orders. They remained lay people. We should remember that the Greek word *diakonos* was a generic term meaning helper or servant, and it did not necessarily imply the reception of Holy Orders.

St Paul mentions a deaconess in his letter to the Romans: "I commend to you our sister Phoebe, a deaconess of the church at Cenchreae ... for she has been a helper of many and of myself as well" (*Rom* 16:1-2). The word "deaconess" at that time meant simply a woman helper in the broad sense.

From the third century on, in various parts of the East, deaconesses were officially instituted or commissioned to assist in such roles as instructing and baptising women, visiting sick women who needed bathing and taking Holy Communion to them. Thus they came to form a structured group in the Church much like the order of widows. In some places at least they entered that order by a ceremony involving the laying on of hands.

That deaconesses did not receive Holy Orders and were clearly differentiated from priests and deacons in the strict sense was made clear in the *Apostolic Constitutions*, written around 400 AD: "A deaconess does not bless, nor perform anything belonging to the office of presbyters or deacons, but is only to keep the doors, and to minister to the presbyters in the baptising of women, for the sake of decency" (*Apost. Const.* VIII, 28). In the baptism of women, the priest anointed the head or forehead of a woman while, for the sake of modesty, the deaconess performed the additional anointings that followed.

The office, roles and meaning of deaconess varied greatly from one region to another, and deaconesses were unknown to the Church in Egypt, as well as to the Maronites and Slavs. There were no deaconesses in the Latin Church for the first five centuries. These differences in the very existence of deaconesses in different parts of the Church and in their meaning and roles show clearly that there was no sacrament involved, since the theology and essential discipline of the sacraments have always been universal throughout the Church.

This is seen too in Canon 15 of the Council of Chalcedon, celebrated in the year 451: "No woman under forty years of age is to be ordained a deaconess, and then only after close scrutiny. If after receiving ordination and spending some time in the ministry she despises God's grace and gets married, such a person is to be anathematised along with her spouse." It is clear from the minimum age of forty, which was different from that for male deacons, and the requirement of celibacy, that deaconesses were not in Holy Orders but rather in an order of mature women who assisted the Church in various ways.

Deaconesses gradually declined in numbers in both East and West until they finally disappeared altogether, probably in the eleventh century. Because of present-day confusion on the matter, the Holy See issued a Notification on 17 September 2001 which stated in part: "Our Dicasteries have heard reports from some countries of programs and developments under way, aimed directly or indirectly at the diaconal ordination of women. Thus, certain expectations are being established, which are lacking in solid doctrinal foundation and which, consequently, can generate pastoral confusion. Since ecclesial authority does not foresee the possibility of such an ordination, it is not licit to implement initiatives that, in some way, look to preparing female candidates for the diaconal Order."

III MORAL LIFE IN CHRIST

General moral issues

833 The call to holiness

In the Gospel there are radical counsels, like take up your cross, blessed are the poor in spirit, sell what you have, etc. In view of this, is it okay just to be a sacramental Catholic, attending Mass on Sundays and saying some prayers, or should we do more than that?

I think many people are content to be "sacramental Catholics", as you call them. They consider it enough to attend Mass on Sundays, go to confession from time to time and say a few prayers. To be honest, those who do that are already in the top echelon of Catholics in this country, where only some eleven per cent attend Mass regularly on Sundays.

But even they should not rest easy. After all, we are called to holiness, and this means getting out of our comfort zone. The call to holiness is clear in the Second Vatican Council's document *Lumen gentium*: "It is therefore quite clear that all Christians in any state or walk of life are called to the fullness of Christian life and to the perfection of love, and by this holiness a more human manner of life is fostered also in earthly society" (n. 39).

Before the Council, someone might have been forgiven for thinking that holiness was only for those extraordinary people, the canonised saints, whose feasts we celebrate in the Mass. I am not called to be like them, we are inclined to think. No, we are probably not called to be like them, but we can still be saints whoever, wherever, we are.

St John Paul II wrote in his Apostolic Letter *Novo millennio ineunte* in 2001: "As the Council itself explained, this ideal of perfection must not be misunderstood as if it involved some kind of extraordinary existence, possible only for a few 'uncommon heroes' of holiness. The ways of holiness are many, according to the vocation of each individual. I thank the Lord that in these years he has enabled me to beatify and canonise a large number of Christians, and among them many lay people who attained holiness in the most ordinary circumstances of life" (n. 31).

Among the lay people beatified or canonised in recent times have been Pier Giorgio Frassatti, Louis and Zelie Martin, Francisco and Jacinta Marto, Guadalupe Ortiz de Landázurri and Juan Diego Cuauhtlatoatzin.

Indeed, Pope Francis, in his Apostolic Exhortation *Gaudete et exsultate*, wrote: "To be holy does not require being a bishop, a priest or a religious. We are frequently tempted to think that holiness is only for those who can withdraw from ordinary affairs to spend much time in prayer. That is not the case. We are all called to be holy by living our lives with love and by bearing witness in everything we do, wherever we find ourselves" (n. 14).

What does it mean then to strive for holiness? First, it does not mean that we commit no sins. We all sin. A saint is someone who struggles to avoid sinning and who gets up and begins again after each fall, going frequently to the sacrament of penance. Confession itself is a great means of growing in holiness, as St John Paul II said in an address to priests at the beginning of Lent, 1981: "We recall that confession periodically renewed, the so-called confession 'of devotion', has always accompanied the ascent to holiness in the Church."

On the positive side, seeking holiness certainly means that we strive to attend Mass as often as we can, not limiting ourselves to going only on Sundays. The Eucharist is an especially powerful means of growing in holiness, through the readings and homily, the prayers, and especially the reception of Our Lord himself in Holy Communion. Naturally, a saint is someone who spends more time in prayer each day. This may include mental prayer, the rosary, reading of scripture, spiritual reading, etc. And a saint will be generous in serving those in the family, those in need, etc.

And while we should always take up the little crosses that come our way in the form of tiredness, sickness, difficulties in life, etc., and we should always be poor in spirit in the sense of being humble and detached from material goods, we obviously do not need to sell all our goods in order to follow Jesus and be holy.

In summary, holiness consists essentially in love for God, and love for God consists in doing his will. We can all strive to respond promptly to whatever God is asking of us in each moment, in the ordinary circumstances of our life.

The more we strive for holiness, the more our light will shine out in this world of so much moral and spiritual darkness. We will make the world a better place and more people will be helped to come closer to God by our example and word.

834 Discerning a vocation

I am 22 and trying to discern whether God is calling me to marriage or perhaps to a religious vocation. I really don't know how to go about this. Can you help me?

You mention that God may be calling you to marriage. That is a good way to look at it. God has a mission, a vocation, a calling, for each person. Pope Francis, in his Apostolic Exhortation to young people *Christus vivit* (2019), explains: "The word 'vocation' can be understood in a broad sense as a calling from God, including the call to life, the call to friendship with him, the call to holiness, and so forth. This is helpful, since it situates our whole life in relation to the God who loves us. It makes us realise that nothing is the result of pure chance but that everything in our lives can become a way of responding to the Lord, who has a wonderful plan for us" (*CV*, n. 248).

For most people, this calling is to marriage. For some it is a calling to apostolic celibacy: in the priesthood, the religious life or in the lay state. In every case, it is a calling to holiness.

Discerning this calling is the question each of us must face. The choice is vital, since we will only be truly happy and useful in God's service if we choose what he is asking of us. The first question we must ask then is not, "What would I like to do?", but rather, "What is God calling me to do?"

Pope Francis, in *Christus vivit*, says that this discernment, "even though it includes reason and prudence, goes beyond them, for it seeks a glimpse of that unique and mysterious plan that God has for each of us... It has to do with the meaning of my life before the Father who knows and loves me, with the real purpose of my life, which nobody knows better than he" (*CV*, n. 280).

Since this is a very personal and vitally important matter, the first step is to pray about it, to ask God what he desires for us. Pope Francis writes: "Since this is a very personal decision that others cannot make for us, it requires a certain degree of solitude and silence... which enables us better to perceive God's language, to interpret the real meaning of the inspirations we believe we have received, to calm our anxieties and to see the whole of our existence afresh in his own light" (*CV*, n. 283). In order to find this solitude and silence, it may be helpful to go away from our usual surroundings to a church or chapel, or to a monastery, where we can find the peace and quiet we need.

Pope Francis continues: "We must remember that prayerful discernment has to be born of an openness to listening – to the Lord and to others, and to reality itself, which always challenges us in new ways. Only if we are prepared to listen, do we have the freedom to set aside our own partial or insufficient ideas..." (*CV*, n. 284). In prayer we must be truly open to God, not allowing our own preferences to drown out God's gentle voice.

"In this way, we become truly open to accepting a call that can shatter our security, but lead us to a better life. It is not enough that everything be calm and peaceful. God may be offering us something more, but in our comfortable inadvertence, we do not recognise it" (*CV* n. 284). As the Pope says, we must be open to a call that can "shatter our security", setting us off on a challenging and joy-filled path. We should not simply seek the most comfortable way.

In addition to prayer, we should ask the advice of people who know us and who know the circumstances of the vocation to which we feel called. These can include our parents, our spiritual director if we have one, and especially persons already in that vocation.

We must remember that, so to speak, three persons are involved in a vocation: God, who does the calling; the person who is called; and persons in the institute or way of life to which we are called. It can be that a person feels strongly drawn to a particular vocation, but is told by those in the vocation that they are not suited to it. In that case we must accept that God is not calling us to that way of life. He speaks through those people.

And always, to be prepared for any vocation, we should endeavour to grow assiduously in holiness through such means as mental prayer, recitation of the rosary, spiritual reading, frequent attendance at Holy Mass, and regular use of the sacrament of penance. Then God's seed will fall on fertile ground where it can more readily take root and bear much fruit.

835 Learning to forgive

I recently saw the beautiful television program about the families whose four young children had been killed by a driver who was speeding and under the influence of alcohol, and yet were able to forgive him. How can we learn to forgive like that?

The program you mention was for all who watched it a great lesson in love and joy in a family, in the importance of faith in God and, as a result, in the ability to forgive someone who caused great harm. It was truly inspirational. How can we learn to forgive like that? It is not easy in those circumstances, yet profoundly necessary. Let us consider what Christ taught us about forgiveness.

In the Sermon on the Mount Jesus gave us the Our Father, in which we say: "Forgive us our trespasses as we forgive those who trespass against us." Immediately afterwards he added: "For if you forgive men their trespasses, your heavenly Father also will forgive you; but if you do not forgive men their trespasses, neither will your Father forgive your trespasses" (*Mt* 6:14-15).

These are strong words and a reminder that forgiveness of others is essential if we expect God to forgive us. We desperately want God to forgive us our sins, and we know he will if we are truly sorry, because he is ever rich in mercy. But then we must be ready to forgive our neighbour for his offences against us.

To exemplify this teaching, Jesus gave us the parable of the servant who owed his master ten thousand talents, an enormous sum of money, and when he pleaded to be given time to pay, the master forgave him the whole debt. But even after that the servant was unwilling to show mercy to a fellow servant who owed him only one hundred denarii, a much smaller amount. In anger, the master ordered that servant to be put in jail until he paid the whole amount. Jesus concluded: "So also my heavenly Father will do to every one of you, if you do not forgive your brother from your heart" (*Mt* 18:23-35).

What Our Lord is telling us in this parable is that no matter how much someone may have offended us, it is nothing compared to how much we have offended God. This is understandable. Our neighbour is a fellow human being like us and so his offence is done against someone who is his equal, even though the offence may be very great. Our sins, on the contrary, are not an offence against our equal but against almighty God himself, our Creator, our Lord, our Saviour. We could never make up in justice to God, yet in his mercy he forgives us if we tell him we are truly sorry. If God has forgiven us our offences against him, we should be ready to forgive our neighbour his much smaller offences against us, great though they may be.

And we must be ready to forgive our neighbour not once or twice, but as often as he offends us. We recall how Peter asked Jesus how often he should forgive his brother, if as many as seven times, and Jesus answered: "I do not say to you seven times, but seventy times seven" (*Mt* 18:22). In other words, we must be ready to forgive our neighbour always, no matter how many times he offends us.

We should remember too, as I wrote in an earlier article, that to forgive does not mean to feel kindly towards the person who has hurt us. We may feel angry every time we think of what he has done. It means to tell God that we don't hold anything against him, that we wish him well, not harm, that we love him, that we pray for him. Forgiveness is an act of the will, relieving the other person of any debt against us. It is not a feeling of kindness in the heart (cf. *Question Time 2*, q. 242).

And forgiveness of course means that we do not seek revenge. It was admirable to see the father who had lost three children in that accident not want anyone to take revenge. Our Lord was clear on this too: "You have heard that it was said, 'An eye for an eye and a tooth for a tooth'. But I say to you, Do not resist one who is evil. But if any one strikes you on the right cheek, turn to him the other also..." (*Mt* 5:38-39).

In order to live out in practice this demanding spirit, we need to grow greatly in love for God through prayer and reception of the sacraments. The more we love God, the easier it will be to love our neighbour and to forgive him. And we should ask God too to give us this grace of forgiveness.

836 How to grow in patience

I am a teacher, and also a mother, and I really struggle sometimes to live patience with the children. Do you have any suggestions for me?

When it comes to frequently-asked questions, this one is right at the top of the list. We all struggle to live patience.

Each person has to take into account their own flashpoint, their habitual level of patience. Some people are temperamentally very prone to losing their temper and exploding, and others are habitually more placid, more patient. No one can be expected to change radically overnight, so the first ones must be patient with themselves in their struggle to improve. What no one should do, however, is resign themselves to accepting that they will never be able to change. St Josemaría Escrivá puts it bluntly in his book *The Way*: "Don't say: 'That's the way I'm made... It's my character.' It's your lack of character. Be a man – *Esto vir*" (n. 4). How do we change, then?

First, we should know that patience is a little daughter of the virtue of fortitude, or will power. We need will power to control our temper. This is not easy, but certainly the stronger our will, the easier it will be. How do we grow in will power? By doing things that we find difficult: getting up on time in the morning, tackling jobs we have been putting off, doing what we ought to do and not what we feel like doing at the time, controlling our disordered appetite for food and entertainment, fighting against our tendency to laziness and wasting time, going to bed on time...

Second, we will be more patient with others if we have more love for God. The more we love God, the more reserve of love we will be able to draw on when we are getting angry with someone. The saints were much more able to control their temper than the rest of us. Naturally, we grow in love for God through such means as prayer, penance, reading of Scripture and other spiritual books, reception of the sacraments, especially the Eucharist and Penance, etc.

Third, we grow in patience by growing in love for those who try our patience, whether students in the classroom, our own children, our spouse, our in-laws. Yes, growing in actual love for them, no matter how difficult or annoying they may be at times. To do this we should always focus on their good points, not only on what annoys us.

They are God's children and he loves them more than we ever will. If God loves them, there must be something good in them that we can love too. St John Bosco, founder of the Salesians, gives teachers some wise advice, which is applicable to parents and to all of us: "If we want to be thought of as men who have the real happiness of our pupils at heart and who help each to fulfil his role in life, you must never forget that you are taking the place of parents who love their children. I have always worked, studied, and exercised my priesthood out of love for them... My sons, how often in my long career has this great truth come home to me! It is so much easier to get angry than to be patient, to threaten a boy rather than persuade him. I would even say that usually it is so much more convenient for our own impatience and pride to punish them than to correct them patiently with firmness and gentleness" (*Letters* 4, 201-205).

St Angela Merici, sixteenth-century founder of the Ursulines, in her *Spiritual Testament* gives similar advice to teachers: "I ask you to be concerned with all your daughters individually, having each and every one deeply fixed in your hearts and minds; and not just their names, but their background and character, and everything concerning them. This will not be difficult, if you enfold them in real love. You can see that mothers of families, even if they had a thousand sons and daughters, would still find room for every single one in their hearts, because that is how true love works."

Finally, a big help in being patient with others is to remember how patient God is with us. We offend him time and again, yet he still loves us and is always ready to forgive us. Let us ask him to grant us that same patience with those we find difficult. And don't forget that wise advice of St Josemaría in *The Way*: "Don't say: 'That person gets on my nerves.' Think: 'That person sanctifies me'" (n. 174).

837 Abortion and Excommunication

Someone told me that if a woman used an IUD or took the oral contraceptive pill, she could be excommunicated because of the possibility of having a spontaneous abortion as a result. Is this true?

It is not true, as I will explain, but an understanding of the background is important. The reason you ask the question is undoubtedly because the penalty of excommunication does apply to a person who has been involved in an abortion. Canon 1398 of the *Code of Canon Law* reads: "A person who actually procures an abortion incurs a *latae sententiae* excommunication." A latae sententiae penalty is one which is incurred as soon as the offence is committed. The law itself applies the penalty, so that it does not need to be declared by a bishop, although a bishop may choose to declare it to make it publicly known. The reason the Church applies this severe penalty is, of course, to emphasise the seriousness of the sin of ending the life of the most innocent and vulnerable of human beings, the unborn child.

Who actually incurs the penalty? Is it just the woman who has the abortion? The question is answered in general terms in Canon 1329, which says: "In the case of a *latae sententiae* penalty attached to an offence, accomplices, even though not mentioned in the law or precept, incur the same penalty if, without their assistance, the crime would not have been committed, and if the penalty is of such a nature as to be able to affect them; otherwise, they can be punished with *ferendae sententiae* penalties." A *ferendae sententiae* penalty is one which is imposed by a bishop or other lawful superior when a person has been found guilty of an offence.

Among the accomplices in an abortion would be the abortionist and any others who assist in the theatre, as well as anyone close to the woman having the abortion who has urged her to go ahead with it and has assisted her in having it carried out.

Nonetheless, in the case of both the woman and any accomplices, the law establishes certain conditions in which the person would not be excommunicated. These include a person who habitually lacked the use of reason (Can. 1322), was under the age of sixteen when committing the offence (Can. 1323, 1), was ignorant of violating the law (Can. 1322, 2), or acted under physical force (Can. 1322, 3). If any of these conditions was present, the person would not be excommunicated.

What is more, if the person acted out of grave fear or by reason of necessity or grave inconvenience (Can. 1324, 5), or through no personal fault was unaware of the penalty of excommunication attached to the offence of abortion (Can. 1324, 9), the excommunication would not apply, but the person should be punished with a lesser penalty (Can. 1324 §1).

In view of these conditions and, given the widespread ignorance on these matters at the present time, including among many Catholics, it is likely that many people involved in an abortion would not in fact be excommunicated. Of course, they would still be guilty of grave sin.

The effect of an excommunication of a lay person is that the person is forbidden to receive any of the sacraments. However, once the person has truly repented of the offence and has made, or at least seriously promised to make, reparation for the damage and scandal caused by the offence, the excommunication must be remitted and the person absolved of the sin (cf. Can. 1347 §2, Can. 1358 §2).

Returning to your question, the reason that a person using an intrauterine device (IUD) or oral contraceptive pill, which can cause an abortion, does not incur the penalty of excommunication is that there is no certainty that an abortion has taken place. As we saw in Canon 1398, only a person "who actually procures an abortion" is excommunicated. The Latin text is more clear, with the phrase *effectu secuto*, (the effect having followed). So only when an abortion can be proven to have taken place does the excommunication apply. In view of this, a woman who ends a pregnancy by taking the RU-486 (mifepristone) pill, which is designed to cause an abortion up to about seven weeks of a confirmed pregnancy, would incur the penalty, provided the other conditions are fulfilled, because here there is certainty about the abortion.

838 Kinesiology and the faith

A friend said she has been suggested to see a kinesiologist for help with some medical issues and she asked me what I thought about it. I don't know anything about this form of treatment and wondered what you thought.

The first question we should ask is, what is kinesiology? In simple terms, kinesiology is the study of the body's movement. Kinesiologists use their knowledge of human physiology and movement to help recover patients' mobility and improve their lives through exercise.

The Australian Kinesiology Association (AKA) website says about it: "Kinesiology encompasses holistic health disciplines which use the gentle art of muscle monitoring to access information about a person's well being. Originating in the 1970s, it combines Western techniques and Eastern wisdom to promote physical, emotional, mental and spiritual health. Kinesiology identifies the elements which inhibit the body's natural internal energies and accessing the life enhancing potential within the individual."

The website goes on to say that initial research in the area began in the 1960s when Dr George Goodheart discovered that muscle testing could be used to gather information from the body. The system was called "applied kinesiology" and it saw chiropractors embracing Chinese medicine techniques of acupressure and meridian systems. Professional kinesiology practitioners undertake years of training to be able to access the movement of energy – or what the Chinese call 'Chi' – throughout the body.

Although Chinese medicine, which uses acupuncture among other forms of treatment, is regarded as a complementary or alternative form of medicine in Australia, it is a highly regarded and successful treatment for many conditions. Similarly, chiropractic medicine is considered complementary, but it too is widely practised and successful.

The AKA website describes how the treatment works: "Blocks or stresses prevent smooth energetic transmission, thus affecting functioning of our bio-systems, resulting in changes in energy. Muscle monitoring involves challenging the bio-feedback mechanism present in all muscles to reveal imbalances within the body. The 'read out', or findings, may present as physical pain, mental discomfort and the many expressions of disease. These can include allergies, depression, postural problems, poor performance levels, learning and relationship difficulties, digestive and nervous disorders – whatever the presenting problem, the system is saying it is malfunctioning. The real goal of any kinesiology 'balance' is to identify the bottom line cause of any imbalance and then resolve it."

Another kinesiology website says: "Kinesiology is concerned with imbalances in the body's energy. In this respect, kinesiology has close links with the acupuncture concept of energy flow." Since acupuncture has been found to be a very successful treatment for some conditions, kinesiology too may very well prove effective.

Has the Church said anything about kinesiology? The Vatican's document on the New Age, "Jesus Christ, the Bearer of the Water of Life" (2003) mentions kinesiology, but only as one of a number of forms of treatment advertised in New Age literature: "Advertising connected with *New Age* covers a wide range of practices as acupuncture, biofeedback, chiropractic, kinesiology, homeopathy, iridology, massage…" (n. 2.2.3). The Vatican document does not pass judgment on these forms of treatment, limiting itself merely to mentioning them. And since such practices as acupuncture, chiropractic and massage have obvious benefits, the Vatican is not ruling against them but merely stating that New Age literature advertises them.

I personally have met several people who say that kinesiology has helped them significantly in dealing with various medical issues. One said that the kinesiologist was a Catholic who actually prayed during the session.

All in all, it would seem that there is no moral objection to kinesiology in itself. Whether it actually works, or works for all people, would be another matter.

839 Children with same-sex attraction

Pope Francis recently said that parents of children with a different sexual orientation should accompany their children and not condemn them. In saying this is he possibly condoning what is in fact a sinful lifestyle?

In his weekly audience address on 26 January 2022, Pope Francis was considering the difficulty faced by St Joseph when, having fled to Egypt with Mary and Jesus, he received a message in a dream to return to Israel, but not to go to Judea, where Archelaus now reigned in place of his father King Herod. In that context, the Pope spoke of St Joseph's fear, but also of the power of prayer, which brings light into situations of darkness.

In this context the Pope reflected on the various problems parents may face with their children. Speaking "off the cuff", he mentioned children who are sick, who have accidents, who leave home, or who have a different sexual orientation… With reference to the latter, he said that parents should always accompany them, not condemn them.

This is a situation faced by many parents today. The Holy Father's words reflect his own deep sense of compassion, and most parents would find them reassuring and comforting. After all, no matter what their children may have done, or what they think or how they live, they are still their beloved children.

If the children have committed crimes and are sent to prison, if they have conceived a child out of wedlock, if they are living with their boyfriend or girlfriend, if they say they no longer believe in God, the parents will naturally be disappointed but they cannot forget that these are their children, whom they brought into the world and educated, whom they love and whom they want to see go to heaven one day. It is a new and unexpected situation for the parents, as was the flight into Egypt and the return to Galilee for St Joseph and Our Lady, but they accept the fact that God has allowed it and he will give them the strength to get through it.

The parents will pray more for these children, they will speak with them and try to help them see the errors of their ways and the consequences of their choices… But at the same time they will always love and respect them. They will accompany them and not condemn them. They will hate the sin but love the sinner.

After all, God loves these children, as he does all of us, who are sinners too in different ways. Christ died on the cross for every single human being, and he wants all to be saved and come to the knowledge of the truth. He has a place in heaven for everyone and he will give everyone sufficient grace to reach that place.

In urging parents to accompany these children, Pope Francis is not condoning a sinful lifestyle. On the contrary, on 22 February 2021 he approved a statement of the Congregation for the Doctrine of the Faith forbidding priests to bless same-sex couples. The statement was a response to the question of whether the Church has the power to give a blessing to unions of persons of the same sex, and the answer was in the negative.

The response explained that "it is not licit to impart a blessing on relationships, or partnerships, even stable, that involve sexual activity outside of marriage (i.e., outside the indissoluble union of a man and a woman open in itself to the transmission of life), as is the case of the unions between persons of the same sex. The presence in such relationships of positive elements, which are in themselves to be valued and appreciated, cannot justify these relationships and render them legitimate objects of an ecclesial blessing, since the positive elements exist within the context of a union not ordered to the Creator's plan."

This is not to discriminate unjustly against these persons: "The Christian community and its Pastors are called to welcome with respect and sensitivity persons with homosexual inclinations, and will know how to find the most appropriate ways, consistent with Church teaching, to proclaim to them the Gospel in its fullness. At the same time, they should recognise the genuine nearness of the Church – which prays for them, accompanies them and shares their journey of Christian faith – and receive the teachings with sincere openness."

840 Pope Francis and civil unions

Pope Francis has said he is in favour of civil unions for homosexual couples. I thought the Church was opposed to these. Can you please explain what this is all about?

The first thing to say is that the Pope's remarks, which made headlines around the world, were made in a newly-released documentary on Pope Francis, titled Francesco. There the Pope is speaking "off the cuff" in answer to questions, so his words do not form part of official Church teaching as they would if they were made, for example, in an encyclical or an official address.

What did the Pope actually say? First he said that persons with same-sex attraction "are children of God and have a right to a family. Nobody should be thrown out, or be made miserable because of it." We would all agree with that. The Catechism teaches that people with homosexual tendencies "must be accepted with respect, compassion, and sensitivity. Every sign of unjust discrimination in their regard should be avoided" (*CCC* 2358). So, just as homosexual people are accepted in their natural families, so they are welcome in the family of the Church, even if those in a sexual relationship with their partner are not able to receive Communion. They can attend Mass, raise their children in the faith and have them receive the sacraments, etc.

The controversy arose when Pope Francis went on to say: "What we have to create is a civil union law. That way they are legally covered. I stood up for that." The reason for the controversy is that in 2003 the Congregation for the Doctrine of the Faith, with the approval of Pope John Paul II, issued a declaration entitled *Considerations regarding proposals to give legal recognition to unions between homosexual persons*. The Considerations state that "respect for homosexual persons cannot lead in any way to approval of homosexual behaviour or to legal recognition of homosexual unions" (n. 11), since the recognition of such unions "would obscure certain basic moral values and cause a devaluation of the institution of marriage" (n. 6).

When Pope Francis said "I stood up for that" he was undoubtedly referring to his proposal to his brother bishops, during a debate in Argentina in 2010 over same-sex marriage, that accepting civil unions might be a compromise solution to prevent the passage of same-sex marriage laws. The Pope has frequently stated his opposition to same-sex marriage, affirming that marriage is a lifelong partnership between one man and one woman.

It now seems clear that the statements about homosexual persons and civil unions came from an interview with Pope Francis by Mexican journalist Valentina Alazraki in 2019, and that his brief statements in *Francesco* were excerpted from longer answers given in that interview to two different questions. Without knowing what else the Pope said in answer to those questions, it is unfair to criticise him without knowing his explanations for those statements.

Pope Francis said he was in favour of legal recognition for same-sex couples so that they would be "legally covered." It is reasonable that these couples, like any others in long-term relationships, such as those in *de facto* relationships, flatmates, etc., should have some legal protection. This is already provided for, for example, in the New South Wales Relationships Register, which went into effect in 2010 and which provides legal recognition for any couple, regardless of their marital status or sex, when they register their relationship. Were homosexual couples not able to register their relationship, they might consider that they are being unjustly discriminated against. This all-encompassing civil recognition is preferable to specific legislation recognising civil unions for homosexual couples, which would thereby seem to condone the homosexual lifestyle.

In summary, Pope Francis did not deny or call into question any doctrinal truth on marriage or sexuality that Catholics must believe.

841 *Amoris Laetitia* and the Year of the Family

Pope Francis has called for a Year of the Family in which his document Amoris Laetitia can be studied. I thought this was the controversial document that allowed divorced and remarried people to receive Holy Communion. Should we still study it?

You raise two issues. The first is that in his Apostolic Exhortation *Amoris Laetitia*, Chapter 8, Pope Francis does seem to open the door for Holy Communion to be given in some cases to people who have been divorced and remarried civilly. I say "in some cases" because the Pope is not opening the door to all people in this situation. In my book *Question Time 4*, question 511, I clarified the meaning of what the Pope said.

And, as you say, this did create confusion and controversy. Four senior Cardinals wrote to the Pope with their Dubia, or doubts, seeking clarification of the implications of what he wrote. I dealt with this too in *Question Time 4*, question 529.

Should we still study *Amoris Laetitia*? Absolutely. It is a wonderful document, dealing with a wide range of issues concerning love and marriage, and I highly recommend it. This Year of the Family and the study of *Amoris Laetitia* are especially important at the present time, when the family is under attack, perhaps as never before, besieged with such issues as same-sex "marriage", parents being prevented from guiding their children through gender dysphoria, the decline in the number of people marrying before a minister of religion, the increasing rate of marriage breakup and divorce, etc.

The Year of the Family commenced on 19 March 2021, the feast of St Joseph and the fifth anniversary of the publication of *Amoris Laetitia*, and it concluded on 26 June 2022, with the beginning of the Tenth World Meeting of Families in Rome.

Pope Francis launched the year on the feast of St Joseph with a message to participants in a webinar on the theme "Our Daily Love". Referring to *Amoris Laetitia*, he said that "the main intention of the document is to communicate…that today a new look at the family is necessary on the part of the Church." He stressed that reiterating the value of doctrine is not enough. Rather, we must become "custodians" of the beauty of the family, and take care of its fragilities and wounds "with compassion".

Amoris Laetitia is a very practical document. As is known, it reflects on the deliberations of the Synod of Bishops meetings at the Vatican in October 2014 and 2015. After considering numerous quotes from the Bible on love and marriage in Chapter 1, the Pope looks at the many experiences and challenges faced by families today in Chapter 2. Chapter 3 considers the vocation of the family in the world and in the Church, and Chapter 4 is a beautiful reflection on love in marriage, beginning with a long study of St Paul's hymn to love in 1 Corinthians 13. Chapter 5 deals with the fruitfulness of love in bringing children into the world, and with the various relationships within the family.

Chapter 6, entitled "Some pastoral perspectives", speaks of the family's mission in proclaiming to others the gospel of the family, of helping engaged couples prepare for marriage, of accompanying couples in the first years of their marriage, of assisting couples in facing the various crises they may encounter, and of accompaniment after marriage breakdown and divorce and after the death of one of the spouses.

Chapter 7 deals with the parents' role in the education of their children, including sex education and formation in the faith. Chapter 8, intended primarily for pastors, deals with how to help couples going through various irregular situations, including divorce and remarriage. Finally, Chapter 9 deals with the spirituality of marriage and the family. As I say, it is a beautiful document.

Ideally, parishes and individual couples could form groups to study *Amoris Laetitia* during this fifteen-month Year of the Family. Participants could read and then discuss the document chapter by chapter. It would give them a much richer understanding of marriage and it would undoubtedly help them improve their own married life and the life of their children.

842 Parental rights in education

A friend told me there is a bill before the New South Wales parliament to protect the rights of parents in the education of their children, and she asked me to support it. Can you tell me what this is all about?

The bill is the Education Legislation Amendment (Parental Rights) Bill 2020, introduced into the NSW Legislative Council last year and to be debated and voted on in coming months. It is an extremely important bill as it touches upon a fundamental principle of Catholic teaching: the rights of parents in the education of their children. I say Catholic teaching, but it is really a right of all parents, of whatever religion, since parents are naturally the first educators of their children.

An Overview of Bill sets out its object, the first paragraph saying that the bill proposes "to clarify that parents and not schools are primarily responsible for the development and formation of their children in relation to core values such as ethical and moral standards, social and political values and an understanding of personal identity, including in relation to gender and sexuality".

The matter of gender and sexuality is of primary concern among the core values to be protected as indicated in the second paragraph: "to prohibit the teaching of the ideology of gender fluidity to children in schools."

In one sense this bill shouldn't be necessary. Many years ago I heard the NSW Minister for Education say in a radio interview that the state's public schools existed to educate children on behalf of the parents. This is the way it should be. After all, governments are formed by citizens, many of them parents, to provide for needs that the citizens cannot carry out by themselves, needs such as education, defence, health care, police protection, means of communication, etc. But in many places today the education system is dictating the curriculum without reference to parents' wishes.

The Church has always insisted on the rights of parents in the education of their children. The Second Vatican Council's Declaration on Christian Education *Gravissimum educationis* (1965) was clear: "As it is the parents who have given life to their children, on them lies the gravest obligation of educating their family. They must therefore be recognised as being primarily and principally responsible for their education. The role of parents in education is of such importance that it is almost impossible to provide an adequate substitute" (*GE* n. 3).

The Declaration goes on to clarify the role of the state in education: "It should recognise the duties and rights of parents, and of those others who play a part in education, and provide them with the requisite assistance. In accordance with the principle of subsidiarity, when the efforts of parents and of other organisations are inadequate it should itself undertake the duty of education, with due consideration, however, for the wishes of the parents" (*ibid.*).

Moreover, the Church insists that the state should not provide only one system of education which does not allow parents to choose a school that respects their rights and interests: "Parents, who have a primary and inalienable duty and right in regard to the education of their children, should enjoy the fullest liberty in their choice of school. The public authority, therefore, whose duty it is to protect and defend the liberty of the citizens, is bound according to the principles of distributive justice to ensure that public subsidies to schools are so allocated that parents are truly free to select schools for their children in accordance with their conscience... In this, however, the principle of subsidiarity must be borne in mind, and therefore there must be no monopoly of schools which would be prejudicial to the natural rights of the human person and militate against the progress and extension of education, and the peaceful coexistence of citizens" (*GE* n. 6).

The principles are clear. But they are not always respected by state educational authorities.

Since, as we have seen, the state and its institutions, including the system of education, exist to provide for the needs of parents and other citizens, they should always be responsive to their wishes.

The present bill is designed to ensure that this is lived out in practice. It is of fundamental importance.

843 Using human remains as compost

I recently read that in the U.S. they are converting human remains into compost. I was astonished and want to ask whether this is permissible on moral grounds.

I too was astonished. If we thought the world was going crazy, this is just one more piece of evidence to justify that thought. It is a denial of the great respect with which we, at least we Christians, have always treated the body, both in life and in death.

But first, what are the facts? The latest piece of news was that on 18 September 2022 California's Governor Gavin Newsom signed legislation authorising the "composting" of human remains for soil. The Cemetery and Funeral Act will implement regulatory methods for that state to approve so-called "reduction facilities," in which human bodies are broken down in a process similar to a household composting system. The measure will take effect in January 2027.

California has thus become the fifth U.S. state to legalise the practice, joining Oregon, Washington State, Colorado and Vermont. Unlike Colorado's legislation, the California law does not forbid the sale of composted human remains or the use of the "soil" for growing fruit and vegetables for human consumption.

Behind the law was – you guessed it – concern for the environment. Cristina Garcia, the California politician who authored the bill, said the legislation was meant to help address "climate change and sea-level rise" by giving California residents "an alternative method of final disposition that won't contribute emissions into our atmosphere." She said that since trees are important carbon breaks for the environment, she looks forward to "continuing my legacy to fight for clean air by using my reduced remains to plant a tree."

The practice of composting the remains of human beings in order to enrich the soil is known by the euphemism Natural Organic Reduction (NOR). In 2020, NOR company and activist organisation Recompose became the first organisation in the U.S. to open a human composting funeral home. The facility in Kent, Washington, has ten hexagonal cylinders in which deceased human bodies are stored and their decomposition process is hastened. According to Recompose, the so-called "reduction" process involves placing the body in a reusable vessel, covering it with wood chips and aerating it, thus creating an environment for microbes and essential bacteria. A human body will be "fully transformed into soil" after about thirty days, the organisation says. "Soil" derived from the bodies can then be used "to enrich garden beds, planted with a tree, divided across multiple locations, or donated to conservation efforts."

Recompose's website leaves no secrets about the ideology behind the NOR movement, stating that employees must advocate for climate healing, soil health, and environmental justice, be anti-racist and committed to advocating for and protecting the rights of BIPOC [Black, Indigenous and People of Colour], religious minorities, and undocumented people, as well as engage with the work of queer feminist practices of inclusion and equity.

Is this practice admissible from a moral point of view? Certainly not. Our body is that of a human person, composed of body and soul, and it is destined to be reunited with the soul on the Last Day. It is not the body of an animal or a plant, which decomposes, never to rise again, and it is therefore to be treated with the utmost respect, even in death.

On 15 August 2016 the Congregation for the Doctrine of the Faith issued an Instruction on burial and cremation entitled *Ad resurgendum cum Christo*. It says with respect to burial: "By burying the bodies of the faithful, the Church confirms her faith in the resurrection of the body, and intends to show the great dignity of the human body as an integral part of the human person whose body forms part of their identity. She cannot, therefore, condone attitudes or permit rites that involve erroneous ideas about death, such as considering death as the definitive annihilation of the person, or the moment of fusion with Mother Nature or the universe, or as a stage in the cycle of regeneration, or as the definitive liberation from the 'prison' of the body" (*AR* 3).

Natural Organic Reduction is precisely a practice of fusing the body with Mother Nature. It is completely unacceptable.

Gender issues

844 Treating gender dysphoria

We are hearing more and more about children suffering from anxiety over their gender identity. I find this alarming and fear it might happen in my own family. What is the best way to help these children?

As you say, the number of these cases is increasing dramatically. A recent article published online by Family Life International reports that the number of children referred for transitioning treatment in the UK increased by 1,000% among males and 4,400% among females between 2009 and 2019. And in the United States, a Centers for Disease Control and Prevention report found that the number of young people identifying as transgender had nearly doubled since 2017.

What is to be done to help these children? There are essentially two approaches. A very common one, known as the gender-affirmative approach, has been followed by many schools with the agreement of health authorities. This approach regards the children as suffering from a mental condition known as gender dysphoria, and it seeks to alleviate their distress by assisting them to transition to the opposite sex. At a basic social level, this includes allowing them to dress according to their new-found identity, call themselves by a new name, use the appropriate toilet and dressing room facilities, etc. At a more radical, medical, level, if they are pre-pubescent they may be given puberty blockers to delay the onset of puberty, then cross-sex hormone treatment and finally gender-reassignment surgery.

The other approach also regards these children as suffering from a mental illness, but it consists in counselling them against making hasty judgments, helping them to accept their biological sex. After all, they are only children and most of them will grow out of their dysphoria. In fact, the *Diagnostic and Statistical Manual* (DSM-5) of the American Psychiatric Association, reports that as many as 98 per cent of gender-confused boys and 88 per cent of girls will accept their biological sex by late adolescence.

There is a growing awareness around the world that it is unwise to affirm children unquestioningly in their gender dysphoria. The United Kingdom's National Health Service (NHS) recently warned doctors not to encourage children who believe they are transgender to change their names and pronouns, finding that most of them are only going through a "phase". The NHS also warned that social transition – in which a child wears the clothes of the opposite sex and takes on a new name – "should not be viewed as a neutral act", as it could have "significant effects" on the child's "psychological functioning". Significantly, the NHS announced that the UK's Tavistock gender identity clinic, where most of the gender reassignment therapy was conducted, would be shut down early in 2023, following a review which found staff felt under pressure to adopt an unquestioning affirmative approach.

The closure was related to a High Court case brought against the clinic by Keira Bell, 25, who had been given puberty blockers at age 16 and later changed her mind about transitioning to male. "I went through a lot of distress as a teenager", she said. "Really, I just needed some mental health support and therapy from everything that I've been through. There needs to be mental health support first and foremost."

England wasn't the only country. In February 2022, the French National Academy of Medicine warned that "great medical caution must be taken in children and adolescents, given the vulnerability, particularly psychological, of this population and the many undesirable effects, and even serious complications, that some of the available therapies can cause." The press release stated that "there is no test to distinguish a 'structural' gender dysphoria from transient dysphoria in adolescence" and it highlighted the negative side effects of puberty blockers and hormone therapy, including "impact on growth, bone fragility, risk of sterility, emotional and intellectual consequences and, for girls, symptoms reminiscent of menopause."

Similar concerns were raised by Sweden's National Board of Health and Welfare in February 2022, after a review found "the evidence base for hormonal interventions for gender-dysphoric youth is of low quality, and ... hormonal treatments may carry risks."

845 The Church and gender variance

You wrote in an earlier column about various countries becoming alarmed about indiscriminate treatment of children suffering from gender dysphoria. Has the Church given any guidelines that might help parents and schools deal with this issue?

The Church, at both the universal and the local levels, has issued documents that can be very helpful for both parents and schools. In 2019 the Vatican's Congregation for Catholic Education brought out *"Male and female he created them" – towards a path of dialogue on the question of gender theory in education*. It gives a comprehensive set of criteria intended primarily for schools, but at the same time emphasising the primary role of parents and the family in this matter.

With regard to the family, it insists that two fundamental rights must always be respected. "Firstly, the family's right to be recognised as the primary pedagogical environment for the educational formation of children. This primary right finds its most concrete expression in the most grave duty of parents to take responsibility for the well-rounded personal and social education of their children, including their sexual and affective education..." (n. 37). The second right is that of children to "grow up in a family with a father and a mother capable of creating a suitable environment for the child's development and emotional maturity and continuing to grow up and mature in a correct relationship represented by the masculinity and femininity of a father and a mother and thus preparing for affective maturity" (n. 38).

At the local level, the Australian Catholic Bishops Conference (ACBC) released a document on 6 September 2022 entitled *Created and Loved – a guide for Catholic schools on identity and gender*. It follows similar lines to the Vatican document. It states, for example:

"Popular rhetoric around gender variance sometimes accepts perceptions of sex and gender that are inconsistent with a Christian understanding: that gender is something entirely separate from biological sex; that gender is arbitrarily assigned rather than (usually) a given aspect of the gift of life; and the concept that gender can be fluid and oscillate between a male or female gender identity according to a subjective personal choice."

The document makes a very important point: "Research data strongly suggests that for the vast majority of children and adolescents, gender incongruence is a psychological condition through which they will pass safely and naturally with supportive psychological care: studies quote between 80-90% of prepubescent children who do not seem to fit social gender expectations are not gender incongruent in the long term."

For this reason, parents should not become alarmed if a young child manifests some degree of gender variance. In most cases this is just a passing phase, and so the child should be calmly and compassionately helped to accept their biological sex.

The ACBC document cautions Catholic schools against indiscriminate affirming of children who experience gender variance: "If it is suggested to a school that the only pathway forward is simply to affirm the student's chosen gender, school leadership should be careful to be guided by the Christian anthropology described below." Among the elements of this anthropology is this important one: "A human being's sex is a physical, biological reality. Sex is how human beings' bodies are organised with respect to reproductive function. Each person's biological sex unfolds in the womb from conception onward as complex genetic and hormonal processes combine to give each person a unique set of male or female characteristics. Apart from rare cases of people born with a combination of both male and female biological characteristics, every human being is born either biologically male or biologically female."

The ACBC document gives comprehensive guidelines for schools to help them deal with this growing issue. It is well worth reading by all.

846 Assisting transgender children

My daughter is in fifth class in a state school and she came home telling me that a boy in her class now wants to be a girl and the school allows her to wear the girls' uniform and to use the girls' toilets. My daughter is very upset and so am I. What should I think about this?

Unfortunately, this is an increasingly common phenomenon in schools. It was exceedingly rare until recent years, when the theory of gender fluidity suddenly burst into the public domain. I wrote extensively about this topic in my book *Question Time 5*, questions 690-697.

The percentage of transgender people in the most liberal and accepting parts of the world was always very low, estimated to be somewhere between 0.1 and 0.5 per cent of the population. This is based on a very broad definition of transgender, which includes cross-dressers, gender-fluid persons, etc.

One possible reason for the increase in the number of children suffering from gender dysphoria – where a child believes he or she is of the opposite sex to that of their birth – is the popularity of programs like Safe Schools, which are designed to promote sexual and gender diversity and the theory of gender fluidity. When a school actually supports and even celebrates children transitioning from one gender to another, it is only natural to expect that the numbers will increase.

In fact, more and more schools are assisting children to transition. South Australia already has a mandatory policy for all state schools to allow students to choose the bathroom, uniform, sporting team and sleeping quarters which correspond to their chosen gender identity, without the consent, consultation or even notification of their parents. This is dangerous. Parents, after all, are the ones who know their children best and who are in the best position to make decisions about their well-being. They should not be excluded from this process.

What is more, assisting children to transition is not in their best interests for a number of reasons.

First, children, especially in primary school, are not old enough to make decisions which will so radically affect their future well-being. It is ironic that there is currently a debate about raising the age of criminal responsibility from 10 to 14 for this very reason. A research paper on this issue by the Australia Institute in July 2020 includes statements like the following: "The medical evidence is that the brains of young children are not sufficiently developed for them to be held criminally responsible... Higher function, like planning, reasoning, judgement and impulse control, is only fully developed in a person's third decade (their 20s)... Children in grades four, five and six do not have the cognitive development to be held criminally responsible for their actions."

Why can't we apply sound reasoning like this to children's judgment in wanting to transition in their gender, which affects their future far more fundamentally than does committing a crime and being held in a detention centre?

Second, the *Diagnostic and Statistical Manual* (DSM-5) of the American Psychiatric Association reports that as many as 98 per cent of gender-confused boys and 88 per cent of girls will accept their biological sex by late adolescence. To encourage them to change their gender when they are young would thus make it harder for them to accept their biological sex later.

Third, a report by the American College of Pediatricians in June 2017 says that the effects of taking cross-sex hormones (testosterone for girls and oestrogen for boys) and sex reassignment surgery to aid gender transition can be severe. The rate of suicide in Swedish adults who used these means was nearly twenty times higher than in the rest of the population and 62 per cent of male-to female transgender persons and 55 per cent of female-to-male persons suffered from depression, much higher than in the rest of the population. In the U.S., a survey conducted by the National Gay and Lesbian Task Force and National Center for Transgender Equality found that 41 per cent of transgender persons had attempted suicide, vastly exceeding the 4.6 per cent in the overall U.S. population.

Fourth, pre-pubescent children with gender dysphoria will often be given puberty blockers and they will require cross-sex hormones in later adolescence to continue to live in accordance with the opposite sex. As a result they may become sterile and never able to conceive any genetically-related children even via artificial reproductive technology. What is more, cross-sex hormones are associated with such dangerous health risks as cardiac disease, high blood pressure, blood clots, stroke, diabetes and cancer. To give these treatments to children who are too young to give valid informed consent, is nothing short of child abuse.

What these children needs is counselling and psychological or psychiatric help, not encouragement to change their sex. If a child is suffering from anorexia or depression, we don't encourage them to eat less or end their life, and we shouldn't encourage someone suffering from gender dysphoria to change their sex, but rather counsel them to accept it. American left-wing comedian Bill Maher puts it humorously: "Gender-fluid kids are fluid about everything. If kids knew what they wanted to be at age eight the world would be filled with cowboys and princesses. I wanted to be a pirate. Thank God nobody took me seriously and scheduled me for eye removal and peg leg surgery."

847 Conversion therapy legislation

With legislation in several Australian states prohibiting therapy to help people who wish to change their sexual orientation, is this not a violation of a fundamental human right? I am disturbed by this development.

The development is indeed disturbing. It reeks of the Marxist program where the state decides what is best for the individual and the family. It is totalitarianism at its worst. But let me explain.

Queensland, the Australian Capital Territory and Victoria have all passed legislation banning so-called "conversion therapy", defined in the Queensland legislation as "a treatment or other practice that attempts to change or suppress a person's sexual orientation or gender identity." Other jurisdictions are planning to enact similar laws. Proponents of the legislation argue, rightly, that extreme practices to get someone to change their gender identity like torture, electroshock or forced medication should be prohibited.

We would all agree with that. But the new legislation goes well beyond that. Under it, if a person wishes to get help to change their gender or express their same-sex attraction, that is acceptable, but if they wish to be counselled to overcome unwanted same-sex attraction or gender dysphoria, it would be an offence in law.

Thus, if a girl in primary school wanted to live and dress as a boy, she could get counselling to assist her in the transition. But if her parents wanted to get counselling to help her accept her female sex, they could not do so. Nor could an adult with unwanted same-sex attraction or gender dysphoria get help to remain as they are. We should remember that gender dysphoria is recognised as a mental disorder in the *Diagnostic and Statistical Manual* (DSM-5) of the American Psychiatric Association. When someone suffers from a mental disorder they should be free to get help to overcome it. Their basic human right to get this help is denied by the new legislation.

In effect, the state is telling us that it is perfectly acceptable to be gay, lesbian or transgender, etc., but it is a crime to want to change these unwanted orientations or tendencies. The legislation is a blatant attack on patient autonomy, the professional independence and judgment of general practitioners, psychiatrists, psychologists, counsellors and pastors, and on the rights of parents to decide what is best for their children.

The most extreme legislation is that of Victoria, which prohibits not only health practitioners but also family members and religious counsellors from attempting to help someone overcome gender dysphoria. Former Deputy Prime Minister John Anderson AO said of this legislation, which was then under discussion: "A law before the Victorian parliament seeking to outlaw parental, therapeutic or religious discussions on issues of sexuality and gender is the biggest threat to our democratic freedoms in Australia's entire legislative history" (Twitter, 14 December 2020).

In Victoria it would even be an offence to pray for someone to overcome their gender dysphoria. In an article titled "Prohibiting prayer in Australia", Carl R. Trueman wrote: "It is an ominous sign when such a basic religious practice as prayer is now the target of hostile legislation in a democratic country. We may not yet be at the point where thought is a crime, but we seem to be at the point where the expression of certain thoughts, even in prayer, could be considered criminal behaviour" (*First Things*, 8 February 2021).

A few days before Victoria's legislation was passed, Leah Gray, a former lesbian who is now married with a young son, testified: "Ten years ago I voluntarily sought counsel from Christian psychologists, ministries, support networks and people who had walked before me. It was difficult, but I found relief and happiness. Every step of my journey will become illegal under the Victorian government's *Change or Suppression (Conversion) Practices Prohibition Bill.*

"For the record, none of these avenues of support were ever harmful or coercive. In fact, the counselling I received saved my life. Ex-LGBT people like me are living proof that real and lasting change is possible, that suicides have been prevented, and that it is good for people to have the freedom to choose the type of help and support they want – including (shock horror) the religious kind" (*MercatorNet*, 2 February 2021).

848 A conversion therapy testimony

I have heard that some people who have reversed their unwanted gay or transgender lifestyle are angry with new legislation in some Australian jurisdictions which would prevent them from getting the help they needed. Is this true?

It is indeed true and these people feel betrayed by the legislation. One such person is Erin, whose story appears on the website "freetochange.

org". She relates that between kindergarten and first grade she and her brother were abducted by two men and taken to a public toilet, where she was brutally sexually assaulted and her brother was not. Although she did not make the connection at the time, that led her to think that if she were a boy, this would not happen again. She hated her female body and dressing as a girl, and already in grade one she identified as a boy.

Her first-grade teacher was concerned and referred her to the school psychologist, who met with her mother, teacher and principal to suggest ways she could feel more comfortable as a girl. Some of the recommendations included putting her in girls' organisations like Bluebirds or Brownies so that she would be around other girls, encouraging her to stop wearing her brother's old clothes, and exposing her to strong women who would be good role models.

Referring to recent conversion therapy legislation Erin writes: "If I were a child today, 'conversion therapy' bans would require my school psychologist to report to my teacher, principal, and mother that I was a 'trans' kid. The school would allow me to dress like a boy, be called by the boy's name [I'd picked out 'Timothy'] and use male pronouns. The school psychologist would likely insist that I be allowed to use the boys' bathrooms at school and play on the boys' teams. The school psychologist would 'affirm' my belief that I was born in the wrong body and that my self-hatred was valid...

"Not my mother, not my school teacher, not my school psychologist knew that my trans identity was based upon my desire to keep my body from being sexually violated again. It took years of therapy before I understood the connection. If therapists had not been allowed to question my gender identity, I never would have made the connection. I never would have understood that my hatred of my female body was the result of it being violently violated. I never would have realised that my transgender identity was a coping mechanism.

"The talk therapy that helped me and many others is now illegal in many states. Children are being denied appropriate mental health services and therapists are required by law to 'affirm' a child's transgender identity or same-sex attraction. Transgender activists have adopted a philosophy regarding children with gender identity issues; children should be transitioned to the gender they identify with, first socially, and as they reach puberty, medically. These activists deny that talk therapy is helpful in managing and resolving gender dysphoria, and assert, without any proof, that it is harmful.

"No evidence supports transgender advocates' contention that transitioning children is beneficial in any way, but there is strong evidence proving that transitioning can be harmful. A Swedish study shows that those who transition have a higher suicide rate. Transgender advocates scare parents, telling them that if they do not allow their children to transition, their child is at risk of depression, anxiety, drug use, homelessness, and suicide. This fear-mongering convinces parents to allow children to dictate name changes, preferred pronouns, and medical interventions even though we recognise that children are not capable of making these kinds of life-altering decisions in any other situation.

"There is no other situation in which therapists are encouraged, required, or legislated to affirm a child who has inaccurate perceptions about themselves. A child who suffers from anorexia is not 'affirmed' in her perception that she is fat. A child who suffers from bi-polar disorder is not 'affirmed' in a belief that he will rule the world when he is manic. A child who is crippled by anxiety is not 'affirmed' that her anxiety is a healthy coping mechanism."

Erin's story, like that of many others, rings loud alarm bells warning against affirming children's desire to transition in their gender. And against conversion therapy legislation which would prevent people like Erin receiving the counselling they need.

849 Gender terminology

I am increasingly disturbed by attempts to change our language so as to use gender-inclusive terminology and do away altogether with words like woman and man, father and mother, etc. Where is this coming from and is there anything we can do about it?

The push to change the language is coming from a tiny proportion of the population in some countries, but they wield an influence completely out of proportion to their numbers. They dominate the agenda of the national discourse and they insist on the rest of the population respecting their agenda. Often referred to as the "woke" element, they include radical feminists, Marxists, transgender advocates and others. They do not speak for the immense majority of the population, who are ordinary people like you and me, who have no problem recognising that we are men or women, with a father and a mother, and brothers and sisters. For practically everyone, even the woke, when a baby is born the first question that is still asked is: "Is it a boy or a girl?"

The danger of this agenda is that by changing the meaning and use of words, we change our perception of reality, our whole way of thinking. This is dangerous. Let me cite a few examples of more recent developments, borrowing in part from an article by 91-year-old Babette Francis in the October 2021 issue of the Endeavour Forum Newsletter.

When you are introduced to someone, you are now supposed to ask what that person's preferred pronouns are. It used to be "he" or "she", but now that there are supposedly some 57 genders, it would be considered an insult to presume to call the person by the traditional pronouns. The irony of the situation is that, while gender ideologues reject the binary sex terminology of male and female, when they want to change their gender a boy only wants to become a girl and a girl only a boy, thus adopting the very binary model they claim to reject.

Likewise, when inviting people to a function, you should not invite them to bring their husband or wife, but rather their partner, so as not to offend people in same-sex or other irregular relationships. While the number of people in these irregular relationships is increasing, the immense majority of people are married and they have no problem referring to their husband or wife. In fact, they would feel insulted to call their spouse a partner.

The height of absurdity in this area comes in a recent directive of the Academy of Breastfeeding Medicine that discourages any mention of women or mothers. The ABM, an international body of physicians and other health professionals who promote breastfeeding, wants health professionals to use gender-neutral terms like "birthing people" and "persons who breastfeed"! In a document dated 1 August 2021, the ABM declared that this new terminology should be used in order to avoid discriminating unfairly against "vulnerable populations". Could it not equally be said that the new terminology discriminates unfairly against the majority of breastfeeding mothers, who would feel insulted by being referred to as "birthing persons"?

The new terminology is being promoted right from the top. The ABM issued its directive after the U.S. Biden administration released a budget health proposal that used the phrase "birthing people" rather than "mothers". As would be expected, critics denounced the use of this phrase as effectively reducing women to their reproductive capabilities. Likewise, the U.S. Centers for Disease Control (CDC) issued its guidelines on COVID vaccinations for what it called "pregnant and recently pregnant people." American bioethicist and writer Dr Christine Rosen commented: "The use of 'people' deliberately erases motherhood and devalues women. 'People' can't get pregnant. Only those who are born biologically female can have babies."

One can go on and on with examples like these, which are worrisome in the extreme. What can we do? First, continue to use the traditional terms, which are based on nature, not on ideology. Second, protest when we hear people using the new terminology, and point out to them that this offends our sensitivity, demeaning the very dignity of women and mothers. At a time when antidiscrimination legislation is in vogue, point out that this terminology discriminates against us. Third, write letters to the editor and get involved in talk-back radio to make our position known on this issue. A lot is at stake.

Covid-19 and vaccinations

850 The morality of Covid vaccinations

I am in my 70s and have some questions about Covid-19 vaccinations that perhaps you could answer for me. Can I take a vaccine derived from aborted foetuses, as I understand one of them is, and do I have a moral obligation to be vaccinated at all?

In December 2020 the Vatican's Congregation for the Doctrine of the Faith issued a *Note on the morality of using some anti-Covid-19 vaccines*, and I will draw on it to answer your questions.

As you say, at least one of the vaccines available in this country, the one produced by Astra-Zeneca, was derived from aborted foetuses. The Congregation for the Doctrine of the Faith issued the Instruction *Dignitas personae* back in 2008 on the morality of using vaccines derived from aborted foetuses to prevent children's illnesses. It concluded that, in the absence of any other vaccine, their use was acceptable. Since the cell lines used for the vaccines were derived from foetuses aborted back in the 1970s, the cooperation of the person using the vaccines is remote and there is a proportionate reason to use them, their use is morally justified.

Those same cell lines have now been used to produce at least one anti-Covid vaccine and the same criterion applies. The difference today, however, is that in many countries there are several different vaccines available, so that wherever possible the person should choose a vaccine whose origin is not ethically tainted. Nonetheless, there may be circumstances in which a person in fact cannot choose which vaccine to use. The *Note* explains that "when ethically irreproachable Covid-19 vaccines are not available (e.g. in countries where vaccines without ethical problems are not made available to physicians and patients, or where their distribution is more difficult due to special storage and transport conditions, or when various types of vaccines are distributed in the same country but health authorities do not allow citizens to choose the vaccine with which to be inoculated) *it is morally acceptable to receive Covid-19 vaccines that have used cell lines from aborted foetuses in their research and production process*" (n. 2).

In view of this, a person in these circumstances should have no qualms about receiving a vaccine derived from aborted foetuses. Another consideration to take into account is the relative effectiveness and the relative danger of harmful side effects, of one vaccine over another. This may argue in favour of receiving the vaccine from aborted foetuses even when another vaccine is available. Here the cooperation in the evil of abortion of the person receiving the vaccine is very remote and it is material, not formal cooperation, meaning that the person is opposed to abortion.

The *Note* explains: "The moral duty to avoid such passive material cooperation is not obligatory if there is a grave danger, such as the otherwise uncontainable spread of a serious pathological agent – in this case, the pandemic spread of the SARS-CoV-2 virus that causes Covid-19. It must therefore be considered that, in such a case, all vaccinations recognised as clinically safe and effective can be used in good conscience with *the certain knowledge that the use of such vaccines does not constitute formal cooperation with the abortion* from which the cells used in production of the vaccines derive" (n. 3).

Do you have an obligation to be vaccinated at all? The Note answers that "vaccination is not, as a rule, a moral obligation and that, therefore, it must be voluntary. In any case, from the ethical point of view, *the morality of vaccination depends not only on the duty to protect one's own health, but also on the duty to pursue the common good.* In the absence of other means to stop or even prevent the epidemic, the common good may recommend vaccination, especially to protect the weakest and most exposed. Those who, however, for reasons of conscience, refuse vaccines produced with cell lines from aborted foetuses, must do their utmost to avoid, by other prophylactic means and appropriate behaviour, becoming vehicles for the transmission of the infectious agent. In particular, they must avoid any risk to the health of those who cannot be vaccinated for medical or other reasons, and who are the most vulnerable" (n. 5).

In summary, there is no strict obligation to be vaccinated but, for the sake of the common good, especially of the health of vulnerable people, it would be recommended. Those who choose not to be vaccinated should take great care to avoid infecting vulnerable people.

851 Should vaccination be mandatory?

Because of personal health issues I am not planning to receive any Covid vaccination, but my employer has now made vaccination compulsory, so I may lose my job. Also, I fear I may not even be able to attend Mass, when it resumes. Should vaccination be compulsory?

The Vatican's Congregation for the Doctrine of the Faith, in December 2020, stated in a *Note on the morality of using some anti-Covid-19 vaccines*, that "vaccination is not, as a rule, a moral obligation and that, therefore, it must be voluntary. In any case, from the ethical point of view, *the morality of vaccination depends not only on the duty to protect one's own health, but also on the duty to pursue the common good*. In the absence of other means to stop or even prevent the epidemic, the common good may recommend vaccination, especially to protect the weakest and most exposed" (n. 5).

In view of this, Sydney Archbishop Anthony Fisher OP, in a letter dated 10 August 2021, urged his clergy and others to be vaccinated in order to protect not only themselves, but others, especially the most vulnerable.

Also, a letter from the Australian Catholic Medical Association, released in September 2021 and signed by its four chaplains, justifies conscientious objection to vaccination, either because the vaccine involves in some way cell lines derived from aborted foetuses, or because of its possible adverse side effects. At the same time, it mentions the duty to promote the common good by reducing the risk of transmitting the disease to others. In balancing these two objectives, the letter says: "Yet as the Congregation for the Doctrine of the Faith makes clear, there is no essential contradiction between upholding the legitimacy of conscientious objection and concern for the common good. In other words, there is no overriding moral obligation on the part of the common good to be vaccinated."

What then should those who choose not to be vaccinated do to prevent the spread of the illness? The Vatican Note goes on to say: "Those who, however, for reasons of conscience, refuse vaccines produced with cell lines from aborted foetuses, must do their utmost to avoid, by other prophylactic means and appropriate behaviour, becoming vehicles for the transmission of the infectious agent. In particular, they must avoid any risk to the health of those who cannot be vaccinated for medical or other reasons, and who are the most vulnerable" (n. 5).

What this means in practice is that those who do not wish to be vaccinated should use such means as restricting their movements, wearing face masks, and getting tested for Covid should they have any symptoms, to minimise the risk of contracting the illness and of infecting others.

As you say, some employers are insisting that their staff must be vaccinated or they will lose their jobs. This is unnecessary, and even unreasonable. What employers want is that their workplace be safe from Covid, as far as possible. Vaccination of staff, although a step in this direction, is no guarantee, since vaccinated people can still contract the illness and they can pass it on to others. For non-vaccinated staff they could simply ask them to stay home if they have Covid symptoms and get tested for the disease, and perhaps take a Covid test, including a rapid antigen test, on a regular basis. Naturally, if the government mandates vaccination for workers in certain sectors, employers will have no choice but to comply and demand the vaccination.

As regards attendance at Mass and other religious services, our religious leaders are adamant that church services should be open to all, and they are currently lobbying government officials to bring this about. We should pray that they are successful.

In summary, there is no need for vaccination to be mandatory for employment or for entry to various venues, including churches, restaurants, cinemas, etc., when current restrictions are lifted. The Australian Human Rights Commission reports on its website that in the EU, Great Britain and New York State, so-called "passports" for entry to venues and activities are given to people who have either been vaccinated or have had a recent negative Covid test. There is no need to go beyond this.

852 Life with Covid-19 restrictions

I try to be faithful to the restrictions the authorities have placed on us to prevent the spread of the coronavirus, but I know people who say these precautions are too extreme and they ignore them. What should we be doing?

We are now living through restrictions on many activities that the world has not seen since wartime or since the so-called Spanish flu ravaged the world in 1918-19. That flu, by the way, had truly devastating effects. Of the 1.5 billion people in the world at the time one third, or 500 million, contracted the illness and between 20 and 50 million died from it, more than the estimated 17 million who died in the First World War, which ended in 1918. The experience of different countries and cities in dealing with the Spanish flu showed clearly that where more restrictions were placed on people's movements, the number of those affected was lower.

The present coronavirus and the associated illness known as Covid-19 first appeared in China towards the end of 2019 but quickly spread throughout the world, acquiring the designation of a pandemic. Authorities everywhere have placed restrictions on their people to try to slow the rate of infections. In some places this has included total lockdown, where people cannot leave their homes except in cases of absolute necessity. One can always disagree with the severity of some of these restrictions, which may be excessive, but where they are in place it is best to observe them.

In some countries, particularly in Southeast Asia, these measures have been singularly successful because people have obeyed them faithfully, given their traditional respect for those in authority. In other places fewer restrictions have been made or the people have ignored them in greater numbers, leading to a higher rate of infection.

In Australia the authorities have seen what has happened overseas and they have put significant restrictions on people's movements and activities in an effort to keep the rate of infection down. They wanted to be ahead of the virus, not waiting until it had taken hold and then acting when it was too late. Even then, the number of new cases has continued to rise.

In the eyes of some, these restrictions have seemed excessive, among them closing churches and forbidding Masses and other acts of worship, drastically limiting the number of people at weddings and funerals, closing gyms, fitness centres and beaches as well as pubs, restaurants and cinemas, enforcing social distancing, etc.

If it were not for the rising toll of infections and deaths in other countries, some of these measures could indeed appear extreme, given that the numbers in Australia to date have been relatively small. But if we want to avoid experiencing the high rates we see elsewhere, we should be diligent in fulfilling whatever the authorities say.

If this costs us, as it already has in many of ways, sometimes severely, we should accept it as a necessary sacrifice to save the health and lives of others, and possibly our own. In this time of Lent we can unite our sacrifice with that of Christ on the cross. He suffered for us and we can offer our suffering in union with him for others.

If we cannot attend Mass or receive Communion, that too is a sacrifice we can offer to God, in union with the many people around the world who over the centuries and at the present time, cannot attend Mass.

853 The bright side of isolation

With the enforced isolation we have been enduring for some weeks due to the coronavirus outbreak, many people are constantly complaining while others see the bright side of it. How should we react in these circumstances?

It is always good to look on the bright side of any situation, to be optimistic, no matter how bad the situation is. As they say, when it is raining we can look for the rainbow and when it is dark we can look for the stars. To be positive is a healthier attitude than to be pessimistic, which only leads to sadness. And there have been many positive aspects in the present isolation.

One of the most frequently commented experiences has been the improvement of family life. Many people who have been working from home, or are out of work for that matter, have mentioned how spending more time with their family has led to improved relations. They have time just to be together, to talk, to play games, to have meals together, to watch films, etc. If it were only for this, the corona crisis would have already paid important dividends.

Another experience has been the improvement in family prayer. Before the isolation, a working parent might arrive home late and the children might be out at night for various activities, so that family prayer was difficult to arrange. Now, many families are finding that they can pray together, including longer prayers like the rosary, the chaplet of Divine Mercy, and so on. And of course they can participate in a live-streamed Mass, in many cases every day. Some parents have even found that their young children, who can't sit still for Mass in a church, now actually enjoy watching Mass on a screen, and they want more of it!

Another benefit has been the awareness of the suffering of others and the manifestation of concern for them. People, even children, are aware that around the world many people are sick and dying from the virus, and many others are having to observe even stricter isolation than they are. This helps to foster prayer for those who are suffering.

Many people have also been able to help the less fortunate in a material way. Some have returned to the various health professions to look after the sick and the dying, often risking their own health and life to do so. Others help out as volunteers in a variety of ways. And people with means have donated food or money to help those in need.

The enforced isolation has also led to contacting family members and friends by phone or video-conference simply to chat with them and ask how they are. This is turn strengthens family and social bonds, which is always a good thing. Many people are using the technology of video-conferencing for these gatherings, allowing people in different households, and even in different countries, to be together and enjoy one another's company.

The awareness of widespread suffering and death reminds people of their own mortality, that God might call them too. This in turn leads them to pray more, to entrust themselves to God's loving care, to examine their life, to be sorry for their sins, to rectify what is not proper, and in general to come closer to God.

With the limitations imposed by isolation, people are discovering that they don't really need much of what they so depended on before: travel overseas or around the country, going to the cinema, shopping for extra clothes, engaging in certain sports, etc. They have become more detached from the world and consequently more free, happy to live a simple lifestyle.

Being at home has helped many people do jobs around the house that they didn't have the time to do before, whether painting rooms or areas that needed it, cleaning up the garden, doing repairs, etc.

Not being able to attend Mass and receive Communion has been a great sacrifice for many, but it has reminded them of the many Catholics in various places who can practically never attend Mass, because the Church is persecuted where they are or there is simply a shortage of priests. This helps them to pray for those fellow Catholics and give thanks for their own situation.

And, in any case, people have offered up their confinement in union with Christ's Cross and so derived great supernatural benefit from it. Thank God for little blessings!

Euthanasia

854 The value of life

I work as a nurse in a palliative care ward and sometimes have to defend the Church's teaching on euthanasia before other nurses, who argue that it is better to let suffering people die than to keep them alive with their suffering. How can I convince them otherwise?

Apart from the usual arguments against euthanasia, some of which we find in the *Catechism of the Catholic Church* in paragraphs 2276-2279, the Letter *Samaritanus bonus* of the Vatican's Congregation for the Doctrine of the Faith, dated 22 September 2020, offers some very helpful reflections on the value of human life.

The tendency of many people is to say that it is better to die and thus end one's suffering than to stay alive in suffering. Yet life itself, even with suffering, is always a gift of inestimable value. As the Letter says, "Human life is a highest good, and society is called to acknowledge this. Life is a sacred and inviolable gift and every human person, created by God, has a transcendent vocation to a unique relationship with the One who gives life. The invisible God out of the abundance of his love offers to each and every human person a plan of salvation that allows the affirmation that life is always a good" (n. III).

God has given each person life and a certain time on earth during which to work out their eternal salvation. Only while they are alive on earth can they do this. When they die it is too late. In the last stages of life, many people come to believe in God or come back to the practice of their faith and receive the sacraments. And if they accept their suffering and offer it to God, their very suffering purifies them of the effects of sin and prepares them for heaven. Yes, as the Letter says, "life is always a good."

The Letter goes on to say: "God the Creator offers life and its dignity to man as a precious gift to safeguard and nurture, and ultimately to be accountable to Him." And later: "Life is the first good because it is the basis for the enjoyment of every other good including the transcendent vocation to share the trinitarian love of the living God to which every human being is called: The special love of the Creator for each human being confers upon him or her an infinite dignity" (ibid.). It is the dignity that only man, made in the image and likeness of God and called to eternal life with him, possesses.

Moreover, "The uninfringeable value of life is a fundamental principle of the natural moral law and an essential foundation of the legal order. Just as we cannot make another person our slave, even if they ask to be, so we cannot directly choose to take the life of another, even if they request it. Therefore, to end the life of a sick person who requests euthanasia is by no means to acknowledge and respect their autonomy, but on the contrary to disavow the value of both their freedom, now under the sway of suffering and illness, *and* of their life by excluding any further possibility of human relationship, of sensing the meaning of their existence, or of growth in the theologal life" (*ibid.*).

Thus, to end someone's life, even if they ask for it, is to exclude any further possibility of their relationship with others or, more importantly, with God, to whom they will have to render an account of their life in the judgment. This is what we mean when we say that the right to life is inalienable: it cannot be alienated, surrendered, given up.

"Moreover, it is to take the place of God in deciding the moment of death. For this reason, abortion, euthanasia and wilful self-destruction (…) poison human society, but they do more harm to those who practise them than those who suffer from the injury. Moreover, they are a supreme dishonour to the Creator" (*ibid.*).

Since it is God who has given life, it should be God who decides when it should end. He is all wise, all loving, all merciful. He knows what is best for us. When a person is suffering, they may think a good God wouldn't want them to suffer like this, and they may ask for their life to be ended. But, for all we know, when their earthly suffering has ended, they may very well now be suffering far more in purgatory.

God may have disposed that they should suffer a little longer on earth in order to go straight to heaven when they died. God knows what is best. Let us trust him.

855 Attending the dying

I am a palliative care specialist in a hospital and am happy to spend a lot of time with my patients and their families. Some of my colleagues criticise me and tell me to work more quickly. Do you have any advice for me?

Your work in palliative care is vital for the well-being of suffering and dying patients and, apart from being an expression of Christian charity, it is an important way to stave off the request for euthanasia. The recent Letter *Samaritanus bonus* (2020) of the Vatican's Congregation for the Doctrine of the Faith on the care of persons in the terminal phase of life answers your question in a beautiful way.

The Letter mentions the example of the Good Samaritan, who not only draws near to the man he finds half dead but takes responsibility for him. Similarly, "Every individual who cares for the sick (physician, nurse, relative, volunteer, pastor) has the moral responsibility to apprehend the fundamental and inalienable good that is the human person… At work here is *a contemplative gaze* that beholds in one's own existence and that of others a unique and unrepeatable wonder, received and welcomed as a gift. This is the gaze of the one who does not pretend to take possession of the reality of life but welcomes it as it is, with its difficulties and sufferings, and, guided by faith, finds in illness the readiness to abandon oneself to the Lord of life who is manifest therein" (n. I).

The Letter goes on to consider the suffering of Christ on the Cross, where he experienced scorn, abandonment, physical pain and anguish: "Christ's experience resonates with the sick who are often seen as a burden to society; their questions are not understood; they often undergo forms of affective desertion and the loss of connection with others" (n. II). In these circumstances the genuine care of those looking after them is vital: "Every sick person has the need not only to be heard, but to understand that their interlocutor 'knows' what it means to feel alone, neglected, and tormented by the prospect of physical pain. Added to this is the suffering caused when society equates their value as persons to their quality of life and makes them feel like a burden to others" (*ibid.*).

In the face of terminal illness and the pain associated with it, "one must necessarily know how to speak a word of comfort drawn from the compassion of Jesus on the Cross. It is full of hope – a sincere hope, like Christ's on the Cross, capable of facing the moment of trial and the challenge of death" (*ibid.*). Those who remain beside the sick, dying person "not only betoken but also embody affections, connections, along with a profound readiness to love. In all this, the suffering person can discern the human gaze that lends meaning to the time of illness. For, in the experience of being loved, all of life finds its justification" (*ibid.*).

The Letter goes on to stress the importance of truly "remaining", with love and compassion, beside the dying person: "While essential and invaluable, palliative care in itself is not enough unless there is someone who 'remains' at the bedside of the sick to bear witness to their unique and unrepeatable value. For the believer, to look upon the Crucified means to trust in the compassionate love of God ... Nearby the Cross there are also the functionaries of the Roman state, there are the curious, there are the distracted, there are the indifferent and the resentful: they are at the Cross, but they do not 'remain' with the Crucified. In intensive care units or centres for chronic illness care, one can be present merely as a functionary, or as someone who 'remains' with the sick.

"The experience of the Cross enables us to be present to the suffering person as a genuine interlocutor with whom to speak a word or express a thought, or entrust the anguish and fear one feels. To those who care for the sick, the scene of the Cross provides a way of understanding that even when it seems that there is nothing more to do there remains much to do, because 'remaining' by the side of the sick is a sign of love and of the hope that it contains" (*ibid.*).

So yes, your extra time spent with the sick and dying is invaluable. You are truly "remaining" with them, comforting them, showing them the love of Christ, giving them hope. You are their Good Samaritan.

856 Why the call for euthanasia

I come from Africa, where the health system is nowhere near as good as it is here, so that consequently more people die in pain and suffering, and yet there is no widespread call for euthanasia. Why do you think there is such a call for it here and in other developed countries?

You touch upon a very important question and perhaps, having lived in both worlds, you could answer it better than I can. I have been pondering the same question for many years and have come up with several answers. Actually, the recent Letter *Samaritanus bonus* of the Vatican's Congregation for the Doctrine of the Faith offers some useful reflections which answer your question. It lists three obstacles that diminish our sense of the intrinsic value of every human life.

The first is the notion of a "dignified death" as measured by the standard of the "quality of life". Quoting an address of Pope Francis to Italian physicians in 2014, the Letter says that this quality of life is seen today in a utilitarian perspective, "primarily related to economic means, to 'well-being', to the beauty and enjoyment of physical life, forgetting the other, more profound, interpersonal, spiritual and religious dimensions of existence" (n. IV).

That is, in the developed world people tend to think life is worth living only when they have a maximum of comfort and material means, of freedom from pain and suffering. When these are lacking people no longer want to go on living and they ask for euthanasia or assisted suicide.

In Africa and many other parts of the world, on the contrary, the material aspect is given much less importance, since a majority of people live without anything like our standards of comfort and abundance of material things. They value much more family bonds, their relationship with God, what the Letter refers to as the "interpersonal, spiritual and religious dimensions of existence". When someone is sick or suffering in any way, the family surrounds them with love and affection, accompanying them with great generosity. They have "quality of life" in the true sense and they don't think of ending their life.

The second obstacle that obscures our understanding of the sacredness of life is a false understanding of "compassion". When a person is suffering greatly, the termination of their life is justified in the name of compassion, thinking that it is better to die than to suffer and that it would be more compassionate to help them die to end their suffering.

But by its very etymology, the word "compassion" means "to suffer with" another. What most people want when they are suffering is someone to stay with them, showing them that they are loved and valued. They don't want to die but rather to know they are loved. As the Letter says, "human compassion consists not in causing death, but in embracing the sick, in supporting them in their difficulties, in offering them affection, attention, and the means to alleviate their suffering" (*ibid.*). I think Africans and other peoples understand this much better than we do.

The third obstacle is "growing individualism within interpersonal relationships, where the other is viewed as a limitation or a threat to one's freedom" (*ibid.*). This can be seen both from the point of view of the family and others caring for the suffering person, and also from that of the sick person himself.

Individualism, an exaggerated selfishness on the part of family members or carers, sees the suffering person as an obstacle to their own comfort and way of life, as a burden to be carried, and they are very happy to be rid of the burden by getting the sick person "out of the way". They may naturally find it difficult to see someone suffering greatly, or to visit them frequently, and they think more about their own comfort than about the needs of the other. This attitude leads to what Pope Francis has called the "throw-away" culture, where people are "discarded" when they no longer serve others' purpose (cf. *ibid.*).

On the other hand, the individualism may be on the part of the suffering person himself, who experiences a lack of independence, of self-sufficiency, of autonomy, and wants to end his life so as not to be reliant on others. But this too can be a lack of charity for their loved ones, who want to have the person with them as long as possible.

857 Is euthanasia legal in many countries?

Now that there is a bill before the parliament of New South Wales to legalise euthanasia, my work colleagues argue that we should not be behind the rest of Australia and the world, but should do what everyone else is doing and legalise it. Is legalised euthanasia really that widespread?

Before I answer your question, an interesting observation is that Australia, like other prosperous countries, has a well-developed health system, with excellent hospitals and good palliative care. One would think that in a country like ours we would not need, or want, euthanasia, since we can help people die with a minimum of pain and discomfort. At the same time, we might logically think that in less developed countries, where the health system and palliative care are not as good, there would be a big push for euthanasia. The opposite is true.

The push for euthanasia comes from wealthy countries, not poor ones. In fact, it comes from very few countries. We might think here in New South Wales, where we are the only state in Australia not to have legalised it, that euthanasia is a reality practically everywhere in the developed world. That is not so. Euthanasia is legal in only ten of the 195 countries recognised by the UN: Belgium, Canada, Colombia, Luxembourg, the Netherlands, New Zealand, Spain, Switzerland, a few states in the U.S. and all states in Australia except New South Wales. The immense majority of the countries of the world do not have it.

This has to tell us something. Do we really need to legalise assisted suicide, as it is called in the laws of some countries? We deplore suicide and yet we want to legalise it for certain suffering people. In so doing we are making a distinction between people whose lives are "worth living", who therefore should not commit suicide, and others whose lives are "not worth living", who may do so. On that basis, the fundamental principle of a democracy that all are equal before the law is not respected. Incidentally, it was in part for that reason that the British House of Lords rejected the legalisation of euthanasia in the 1990s. All lives are worth living. Suffering is part and parcel of the life of man on earth. We all have it in varying degrees and at different times.

As we see in the list of countries where euthanasia is legal, there is not one African or Asian country. In view of this, Pope St John Paul II's observation in his encyclical *Evangelium vitae* is very relevant: "Here we are faced with one of the more alarming symptoms of the 'culture of death', which is advancing above all in prosperous societies, marked by an attitude of excessive preoccupation with efficiency and which sees the growing number of elderly and disabled people as intolerable and too burdensome" (*EV* 64).

I think we would agree that in a prosperous country like ours, many people can tend to see the sick, the elderly and people with disabilities as a burden, as a threat to their comfort and desire to get on with life. We are not used to seeing suffering and we would prefer not to have to deal with it. If we legalise euthanasia and let suffering people die, it will be easier for us.

When a good friend of mine in Melbourne was dying of cancer some years ago, his wife told me that several younger women had asked her if she was going to have her husband "put away". She loved her husband, visited him every day and had no such thoughts. She said these young women were all well-to-do and "just selfish". Perhaps so.

Another comment on this comes from Dr Brian Pollard, who established the first palliative care unit in New South Wales and wrote two books on euthanasia. He said that in all his years of giving palliative care to dying people he had never had a request for euthanasia from a patient. He did have requests from family members who, he says, seemed to be saying, "Could you please put him/her out of our misery?"

What suffering people most want is good care from medical staff, as well as compassion, love, and the presence of their loved ones, not a quick end to their suffering. As St John Paul II put it: "True 'compassion' leads to sharing another's pain; it does not kill the person whose suffering we cannot bear" (*EV* 66). If we were more compassionate and generous, we would not need or want euthanasia.

858 Medical care at the end of life

When my grandmother was dying, our family was confused about the morality of giving or withholding certain treatments suggested by the doctors. Does the Church have any teaching on this question?

The *Catechism of the Catholic Church* gives the general criterion: "Discontinuing medical procedures that are burdensome, dangerous, extraordinary or disproportionate to the expected outcome can be legitimate; it is the refusal of 'over-zealous' treatment" (*CCC* 2278).

This criterion is made more specific in the Letter *Samaritanus bonus* (2020) of the Vatican's Congregation for the Doctrine of the Faith. The document stresses the importance of always respecting human dignity, saying that "the dignity of the human person entails the right to die with the greatest possible serenity and with one's proper human and Christian dignity intact. To precipitate death or delay it through 'aggressive medical treatments' deprives death of its due dignity" (V.2)

While it is clear that nothing should be done to precipitate death, aggressive treatments to prolong life may also be problematic: "Medicine today can artificially delay death, often without real benefit to the patient. When death is imminent, and without interruption of the normal care the patient requires in such cases, it is lawful according to science and conscience to renounce treatments that provide only a precarious or painful extension of life" (*ibid.*).

Nonetheless, basic ordinary care must always be given: "It is not lawful to suspend treatments that are required to maintain essential physiological functions, as long as the body can benefit from them (such as hydration, nutrition, thermoregulation, proportionate respiratory support, and the other types of assistance needed to maintain bodily homeostasis and manage systemic and organic pain)" (*ibid.*).

When the person is critically ill but not in a terminal phase, futile treatments may be discontinued, but this *"must not involve the withdrawal of therapeutic care*. This clarification is now indispensable in light of the numerous court cases in recent years that have led to the withdrawal of care from – and to the early death of – critically but not terminally ill patients, for whom it was decided to suspend life-sustaining care which would not improve the quality of life" (*ibid.*). That is, this care might not improve the quality of life of the patient but it would at least keep them alive a little longer and perhaps even cure their underlying condition.

To put family members at ease, the Letter makes clear that "the renunciation of extraordinary and/or disproportionate means 'is not the equivalent of suicide or euthanasia; it rather expresses acceptance of the human condition in the face of death' or a deliberate decision to waive medical treatments which have little hope of positive results" (*ibid.*).

Although nutrition and hydration must generally be provided, "When the provision of nutrition and hydration no longer benefits the patient, because the patient's organism either cannot absorb them or cannot metabolise them, their administration should be suspended. In this way, one does not unlawfully hasten death through the deprivation of the hydration and nutrition vital for bodily function, but nonetheless respects the natural course of the critical or terminal illness" (ibid.). The patient will then die, not from dehydration or starvation, but from the underlying condition which prevents them from benefitting from nutrition and hydration.

What about the use of morphine which might render the person unconscious? The Church "affirms the moral liceity of sedation as part of patient care in order to ensure that the end of life arrives with the greatest possible peace and in the best internal conditions. This holds also for treatments that hasten the moment of death (deep palliative sedation in the terminal stage), always, to the extent possible, with the patient's informed consent" (V.7). Naturally the patient should receive spiritual preparation beforehand, and the morphine must not be given with the intention of causing death, even though it might shorten their life.

This criterion is most welcome and it can help to allay the fears of family members that some treatments might be immoral when in fact they are good medical practice.

859 Sharing the suffering of others

I have been looking after my elderly mother, who has been suffering from cancer for several years. She is still with me at home and is now in considerable discomfort and pain. It is not easy for me and I know of others in the same situation. Do you have any advice for us?

First, at a time when many people are arguing that the solution for your difficult situation is euthanasia, or voluntary assisted dying, it is good to see that you obviously would not think of doing anything to end your mother's life. She is your mother. She loves you and you love her; you are showing how much you love her by your sacrifice.

One helpful thought in your situation is to think of how much your mother loved you and sacrificed herself for you when she brought you into the world. First, there was the pregnancy, when she suffered morning sickness for some months and became increasingly tired and aching as the time drew near for your delivery. Then came all the pain of labour and childbirth, which only a mother can know. This was followed by feeding you every few hours for months, including throughout the night, so that she suffered from chronic sleep deprivation. And so much more, as you gradually grew from infancy to childhood to adolescence and adulthood.

If she did all this for you when you were young and unaware, you now have an opportunity to return her love and sacrifice by looking after her in her old age and sickness. Whatever sacrifice you make for her now will be only a small repayment for what she did for you. Your kindness and care will show her that you truly love her, which is what she most wants and needs at this time.

Another thought is to remember that whatever you do for her, you are doing for Jesus Christ himself. He said so, and he promised you an eternal reward for it: "Come, O blessed of my Father, inherit the kingdom prepared for you from the foundation of the world; for I was hungry and you gave me food, I was thirsty and you gave me drink, … I was sick and you visited me… Truly, I say to you, as you did it to one of the least of these my brethren, you did it to me" (*Mt* 25:34-40).

With these words, Our Lord is telling us that not only you, who are looking after your own mother, but all those who care for others with compassion, regardless of their relationship with them, are doing it for Christ and are storing up for themselves treasure in heaven. This can be a great help to nurses and doctors, to those working in aged care facilities, those looking after the handicapped, the poor and the homeless, and so many more.

The Letter *Samaritanus bonus* of the Congregation for the Doctrine of the Faith has much to tell us in this regard: "Every individual who cares for the sick (physician, nurse, relative, volunteer, pastor) has the moral responsibility to apprehend the fundamental and inalienable good that is the human person… At work here is a contemplative gaze that beholds in one's own existence and that of others a unique and unrepeatable wonder, received and welcomed as a gift. This is the gaze of the one who does not pretend to take possession of the reality of life but welcomes it as it is, with its difficulties and sufferings, and, guided by faith, finds in illness the readiness to abandon oneself to the Lord of life who is manifest therein" (n. I).

Speaking of Christ's suffering on the cross, the letter says: "Christ's experience resonates with the sick who are often seen as a burden to society; their questions are not understood; they often undergo forms of affective desertion and the loss of connection with others... Every sick person has the need not only to be heard, but to understand that their interlocutor 'knows' what it means to feel alone, neglected, and tormented by the prospect of physical pain. Added to this is the suffering caused when society equates their value as persons to their quality of life and makes them feel like a burden to others" (n. II).

If everyone treated their loved ones who are dying with this spirit, with as much love and kindness as you are showing your mother, there would be no great push for euthanasia.

860 Finding meaning in suffering

I am totally opposed to euthanasia but when someone is suffering greatly both they and their carers can find it difficult to bear. What can we do to help them cope with their pain and find meaning in it?

When someone is experiencing great pain, as many do, the first thing, of course, is to use all the available means to relieve the pain. These days drugs such as morphine can be very effective in reducing pain to a point where it is at least bearable. It is the role of palliative care to help those people, especially at the end of their life, to be as comfortable as possible, and this care is now widely available. It is in this area where money and effort should be put, rather than in finding better ways to end the life of those who are suffering. We should kill the pain of the person, not the person with the pain.

Nonetheless, I suspect we have all been with people who were experiencing great pain or discomfort, and the best efforts of medicine were not enough to alleviate it. It is then that we can help them find meaning and purpose in their suffering. Some considerations can be of help.

First, we can remind those suffering that they can unite their suffering with that of Christ on the Cross. He suffered more than we ever will and, because he loves us, he sometimes shares his cross with us. A Canberra mother of six expressed this eloquently when she was dying with cancer some years ago and wrote in her diary: "The pain in my chest is crushing me. As the pain crushed You as You struggled to breathe while you hung on the Cross. You are in my pain. I am in Yours. We are one – my God and I! What else can I ever ask for? In this You have given me proof of your love."

Second, just as Christ's suffering and death on the Cross redeemed us, so our suffering, borne with love, helps to redeem us and make up for our sins. It can be our "purgatory on earth" and hopefully enable us to go straight to heaven when we die. It is better to do our purgatory here rather than hereafter, since all agree that the slightest pain of purgatory is greater than the greatest pain on earth. It would be a great waste if we didn't take advantage of suffering in this way.

In this regard, Pope St John Paul II writes in his Apostolic Letter *Salvifici doloris* on the Christian meaning of suffering: "Human suffering has reached its culmination in the Passion of Christ. And at the same time it has entered into a completely new dimension and a new order: it has been linked to love, to that love of which Christ spoke to Nicodemus, to that love which creates good, drawing it out by means of suffering, just as the supreme good of Redemption of the world was drawn from the Cross of Christ, and from that Cross constantly takes its beginning" (n. 18).

Third, it is important to remember that our earthly suffering lasts only for a time whereas the happiness of heaven is forever. And our suffering on earth is little compared with the happiness which awaits us in heaven. The Old Testament Book of Wisdom, speaking of people of faith, says: "The world sees nothing but the pains they endure; they themselves have eyes only for what is immortal; so light their suffering, so great the gain they win!" (*Wis* 3:4-5). And St Paul writes: "We are . . . fellow heirs with Christ, provided we suffer with him in order that we may also be glorified with him. I consider that the sufferings of this present time are not worth comparing with the glory that is to be revealed in us." (*Rom* 8:17-18). When we are suffering, we can lift our thoughts above and think of the great joy that awaits us in heaven, where God will wipe away every tear from our eyes (cf. *Rev* 7:17).

Fourth, and very importantly, we can offer our suffering for others: for the souls in purgatory, for the Pope and the Church, for members of our family, for anyone with special needs... Since suffering is a sacrifice, it has special value because it costs us more. If we do this, the suffering benefits us greatly and it helps others too, through the communion of saints.

All in all, suffering has great value. It is a treasure. Anyone who bears it with love and offers it for others is sanctified by it and helps many others.

861 Euthanasia and financial pressure

I have heard that where euthanasia is legal some health insurance companies are refusing to pay for expensive treatments like chemotherapy, and will only pay for assisted dying. This sounds horrific. Is it true?

You highlight one of the many reasons why euthanasia, or voluntary assisted dying, as it is often euphemistically called, should not be legalised. And you are right, some health insurance companies are doing exactly what you say. Let me give you one example. In 2015, just weeks after California legalised physician-assisted suicide, 29-year-old Stephanie Packer, suffering from terminal Scleroderma, was informed by her insurance company that they would not pay for the chemotherapy she needed, but would only make a $1.20 co-payment for life-ending drugs.

If we consider that insurance companies are not philanthropic organisations dedicated to helping people in need, but rather businesses which exist to make money while providing health care, that decision made sense. Always looking for ways to contain their costs, it also made lots of cents for the insurance company. Stephanie had been told that she had three years to live, so perhaps the insurance company was daunted by the prospect of funding her treatment for that length of time. In any case, without their help, four years later she was still alive, defying the predictions of medical specialists.

Most voluntary assisted dying (VAD) laws require that, in the judgment of two medical specialists, the person must have less than six months, or sometimes a year, to live. We all know that that judgment in many cases is no more than guesswork. I suspect you, like me, know a good number of terminally ill people who were given only months to live and who were still alive years later. In some cases they recovered, or went into remission, and lived a normal life for decades. If VAD is legalised and, all the more, if insurance companies refuse to pay for expensive treatment, there will be many people who will choose to die prematurely and unnecessarily, when they might have lived for many more years. This is tragic.

What is more, VAD legislation selectively hurts the poor. Those with financial means usually have health insurance which may pay for their treatment, or they can afford to pay for it themselves. Hence, they will be more likely to draw on those resources in order to live longer, and sometimes they will recover completely. But those with fewer means cannot afford to do this. The cheapest, and sometimes the only, alternative is to choose to die. This is very sad.

But the financial pressure to choose death rather than life can come not only from insurance companies. It can come too from family members and others who stand to benefit from the inheritance they will receive from the dying person. The longer that person lives, the more money that will be spent on their treatment and their hospitalisation or nursing home care. Family members then see their own inheritance gradually dwindling away and they may be moved, out of "compassion" of course, to suggest to their relative to end their suffering by choosing VAD. The ones that will be particularly vulnerable in this situation are those with disabilities, the mentally ill, the elderly and the poor, especially if their family members see them as a financial burden.

It can also be the sick persons themselves who see the financial and human burden they are placing on their relatives by staying alive, and who therefore choose to "do the right thing" and end their life. Remember that the phrase "do the right thing" is used in this country to refer to tossing your rubbish in the bin. To apply it to human beings is absolutely abhorrent. Yet, without necessarily using those words, this is what is happening.

A 2015 report from the Oregon Health Department revealed that the percentage of Oregon VAD deaths attributed to a patient's reluctance to "burden" their families had risen from 12% in 1998 to 40% in 2014, essentially making the right to die option for some vulnerable people more like a duty to die. The lethal drugs used for VAD normally cost less than $100, making VAD the cheapest "treatment option" and one that also saves insurance companies money. This is not the most important reason for rejecting VAD legislation, but it should not be overlooked. Such legislation leads us into uncharted and very dangerous waters.

862 Cooperation in euthanasia

I recently read that a Catholic organisation that operates several hospitals has declared that it will close its hospitals if they are forced to provide euthanasia or assisted suicide for any patient who requests it. Is this going too far or is it good ethics?

It is sad that the situation has come to this in our country, but what this organisation has said is completely justified. Just as Catholic hospitals cannot perform abortions, which are the killing of the innocent in the womb of their mother, neither can they cooperate in euthanasia, the killing of innocent people at the end of their life. Thus far, to my knowledge, no Catholic hospital has been forced to close because they refused to perform abortions, and we pray that they will not have to close over euthanasia. After all, we are a pluralist society and there are many other institutions prepared to carry out these unfortunate procedures, so Catholic institutions should not be forced to do so.

The Vatican's recent Letter *Samaritanus Bonus* sets out the criterion for cooperation in euthanasia. It says that formal cooperation, where the person agrees with the wrong that others are doing, and immediate material cooperation, where the person does not agree but nonetheless cooperates with it in an immediate, close, way, are to be excluded. This would of course apply to Catholic hospitals allowing euthanasia to be done on their premises.

"Such situations offer specific occasions for Christian witness where 'we must obey God rather than men' (*Acts* 5:29). There is no right to suicide nor to euthanasia: laws exist, not to cause death, but to protect life and to facilitate co-existence among human beings. It is therefore never morally lawful to collaborate with such immoral actions or to imply collusion in word, action or omission. The one authentic right is that the sick person be accompanied and cared for with genuine humanity. Only in this way can the patient's dignity be preserved until the moment of natural death. No health care worker, therefore, can become the defender of a non-existing right, even if euthanasia were requested by the subject in question when he was fully conscious" (V, 9).

Even though the law permits euthanasia or assisted suicide, it should not require those who have a conscientious objection to cooperate in it. If they were asked to cooperate, they would have to refuse. The Letter says: "Governments must acknowledge the right to conscientious objection in the medical and healthcare field, where the principles of the natural moral law are involved and especially where in the service to life the voice of conscience is daily invoked. Where this is not recognised, one may be confronted with the obligation to disobey human law, in order to avoid adding one wrong to another, thereby conditioning one's conscience. Healthcare workers should not hesitate to ask for this right as a specific contribution to the common good" (*ibid.*).

Any individuals or heads of institutions will have to answer to God for whatever cooperation they provide: "This cooperation can never be justified, neither by invoking respect for the freedom of others, nor by relying on the fact that civil law provides for it and requires it: for the acts that each person personally performs, there is, in fact, a moral responsibility that no one can ever escape and on which each one will be judged by God himself (cf. *Rom* 2:6; 14:12)" (*ibid.*).

What should a Catholic institution do if the failure to cooperate in euthanasia and assisted suicide results in government funding being withdrawn? The Letter answers that "healthcare institutions must resist the strong economic pressures that may sometimes induce them to accept the practice of euthanasia. If the difficulty in finding necessary operating funds creates an enormous burden for these public institutions, then the whole society must accept an additional liability in order to ensure that the incurably ill are not left to their own or their families' resources. All of this requires that episcopal conferences and local churches, as well as Catholic communities and institutions, adopt a clear and unified position to safeguard the right of conscientious objection in regulatory contexts where euthanasia and suicide are sanctioned" (*ibid.*).

So the battle lines are drawn. Let us pray that this strong position of Catholic healthcare providers will be respected.

863 Advanced directives and euthanasia

I work in palliative care where euthanasia is legal and we sometimes have patients leave an advanced directive to have their life ended if they are suffering greatly and can't communicate, or they ask for it directly. What should we do in these cases?

Some advanced directives can be quite acceptable. For example, if a patient has a severe cardiac condition and suffers a cardiac arrest, the directive can be not to resuscitate. This is acceptable since the person's heart is not functioning properly and, even if resuscitated, he is likely to die reasonably soon after, perhaps from another cardiac arrest. The same can be said about a patient dying from cancer and in great pain who does not wish to be resuscitated after a cardiac arrest. A doctor will have no problems of conscience in implementing such a directive.

But other directives can be tantamount to a request for euthanasia. For example, that if the patient becomes unconscious, he is no longer to be given nutrition or hydration, or his life is to be terminated through an excessive dose of morphine or a lethal injection.

Fortunately, the Congregation for the Doctrine of the Faith's Letter *Samaritanus bonus* (2020) gives some criteria to answer your question. It says that "the dissemination of medical end-of-life protocols such as the *Do Not Resuscitate Order* or the *Physician Orders for Life Sustaining Treatment* – with all of their variations depending on national laws and contexts – were thought of as instruments to avoid aggressive medical treatment in the terminal phases of life. Today these protocols cause serious problems regarding the duty to protect the life of patients in the most critical stages of sickness. On the one hand, medical staff feel increasingly bound by the self-determination expressed in patient declarations that deprive physicians of their freedom and duty to safeguard life even where they could do so" (V, 1).

In these circumstances, "the Church is convinced of the necessity to reaffirm as definitive teaching that euthanasia is a *crime against human life* because, in this act, one chooses directly to cause the death of another innocent human being. The correct definition of euthanasia depends, not on a consideration of the goods or values at stake, but on the *moral object* properly specified by the choice of 'an action or an omission which of itself or by intention causes death, in order that all pain may in this way be eliminated' (*ibid.*).

The Letter clarifies that even when the patient has requested that his life be terminated, there are higher goods at stake which must be respected: "The moral evaluation of euthanasia and its consequences does not depend on a balance of principles that the situation and the pain of the patient could, according to some, justify the termination of the sick person. Values of life, autonomy, and decision-making ability are not on the same level as the quality of life as such. Euthanasia, therefore, is an intrinsically evil act, in every situation or circumstance" (*ibid.*). That is, even the autonomy of the patient, expressed through an advanced directive or a direct request to the doctor, cannot take precedence over the higher good of life itself, which may never be terminated, even to end the person's suffering.

In summary, as the document says, "No authority can legitimately recommend or permit such an action. For it is a question of the violation of the divine law, an offence against the dignity of the human person, a crime against life, and an attack on humanity. Therefore, euthanasia is an act of homicide that no end can justify and that does not tolerate any form of complicity or active or passive collaboration" (*ibid.*).

Euthanasia and assisted suicide are always the wrong choice: "the medical personnel and the other health care workers – faithful to the task 'always to be at the service of life and to assist it up until the very end' – cannot give themselves to any euthanistic practice, neither at the request of the interested party, and much less that of the family. In fact, since there is no right to dispose of one's life arbitrarily, no health care worker can be compelled to execute a non-existent right" (*ibid.*).

These indications from the Vatican should put all healthcare workers at ease. Medical personnel cannot cooperate in ending the life of a person, even if the person requests it.

864 Pastoral care of the dying

If someone has asked for euthanasia or assisted suicide, is a priest allowed to give them the last sacraments before they die?

This is a very important question and one which, unfortunately, priests will face increasingly now that more and more states and territories are legislating for euthanasia and assisted suicide. It is to be hoped that Catholics, at least practising ones, will not request euthanasia so that priests will not face this question, but we have to be prepared. Fortunately, the Congregation for the Doctrine of the Faith, in the Letter *Samaritanus bonus*, has given us some criterion.

The Letter stresses the importance of pastoral care for all people at the end of life, which can be of great assistance in discouraging someone from asking for euthanasia: "The quality of love and care for persons in critical and terminal stages of life contributes to assuaging the terrible, desperate desire to end one's life" (n. V, 10). To be sure, if dying people receive considerable love and support, they are much less likely to think of ending their own life.

If, however, someone does ask for euthanasia and requests the sacraments before they die, the criterion is clear. The person is asking for absolution for their sins, but this would necessarily include the sin of intending to end their life, either through the hand of someone else who gives them a lethal injection or by themselves when they swallow a lethal substance. How can they be sorry for this sin when they fully intend to carry it out?

The Letter explains: "With respect to the Sacrament of Penance and Reconciliation, the confessor must be assured of the presence of the true contrition *necessary for the validity of absolution* which consists in 'sorrow of mind and a detestation for sin committed, with the purpose of not sinning for the future.' In this situation, we find ourselves before a person who, whatever their subjective dispositions may be, has decided upon a gravely immoral act and willingly persists in this decision. Such a state involves a manifest absence of the proper disposition for the reception of the Sacraments of Penance, with absolution, and Anointing, with Viaticum" (n. V, 11).

Due to the lack of genuine contrition, the priest cannot grant absolution of the sin, nor the sacrament of Anointing of the Sick. Is there a circumstance in which he might be able to confer these sacraments? The answer is yes, but only if the person resolves not to proceed with the euthanasia or assisted suicide: "Such a penitent can receive these sacraments only when the minister discerns his or her readiness to take concrete steps that indicate he or she has modified their decision in this regard. Thus, a person who may be registered in an association to receive euthanasia or assisted suicide must manifest the intention of cancelling such a registration before receiving the sacraments" (*ibid.*).

If the person is not in these dispositions, family members and carers can, and should, continue to look after him in the hope that they may help him change his mind. "It is necessary to remain close to a person who may not be in the objective condition to receive the sacraments, for this nearness is an invitation to conversion, especially when euthanasia, requested or accepted, will not take place immediately or imminently. Here it remains possible to accompany the person whose hope may be revived and whose erroneous decision may be modified, thus opening the way to admission to the sacraments" (*ibid.*).

As regards someone who has taken the lethal substance and is now unconscious, "The priest could administer the sacraments to an unconscious person sub condicione if, on the basis of some signal given by the patient beforehand, he can presume his or her repentance" (ibid.).

Finally, "those who spiritually assist these persons should avoid any gesture, such as remaining until the euthanasia is performed, that could be interpreted as approval of this action. Such a presence could imply complicity in this act. This principle applies in a particular way, but is not limited to, chaplains in the healthcare systems where euthanasia is practised, for they must not give scandal by behaving in a manner that makes them complicit in the termination of human life" (*ibid.*).

IV CHRISTIAN PRAYER

Prayer and Devotions

865 Holy Hour before the Blessed Sacrament

I have heard that Archbishop Fulton Sheen made a holy hour before the Blessed Sacrament every day. Can you tell me more about this devotion, and whether it must be done in a church?

First, in answer to your second question, Archbishop Sheen always did his holy hour before the tabernacle in a church or chapel. Obviously, the best place to do a holy hour is before the Blessed Sacrament. But if you cannot pray before a tabernacle, but can pray for an hour in some other place, by all means do it. It will help you greatly and it will be very pleasing to God.

For anyone not familiar with Archbishop Fulton Sheen, he was an American bishop who, in addition to his prolific writings, had an average audience of over 30 million viewers on his weekly television program *Life is Worth Living* in the 1950s. Billy Graham called him "the great communicator" and Pope Pius XII "a prophet of the times".

In his autobiography, *Treasure in Clay*, published shortly before his death in 1979, Archbishop Sheen says that on the day of his priestly ordination he made two resolutions: to offer the Mass every Saturday in honour of Our Lady to ask her protection on his priesthood, and to spend a continuous Holy Hour every day in the presence of our Lord in the Blessed Sacrament.

He goes on to say that in the course of his priesthood, he kept both of these resolutions. As regards the Holy Hour: "The Holy Hour had its origin in a practice I developed a year before I was ordained. The big chapel in St. Paul's Seminary would be locked by six o'clock; there were still private chapels available for private devotions and evening prayers. This particular evening during recreation, I walked up and down outside the closed major chapel for almost an hour. The thought struck me – why not make a Holy Hour of adoration in the presence of the Blessed Sacrament? The next day I began, and the practice is now well over sixty years old."

He goes on to explain why he kept up the practice and encouraged others to do the same: "First, the Holy Hour is not a devotion; it is a sharing in the work of redemption. Our Blessed Lord used the words 'hour' and 'day' in two totally different connotations in the Gospel of John. 'Day' belongs to God; the 'hour' belongs to evil. Seven times in the Gospel of John, the word 'hour' is used, and in each instance it refers to the demonic, and to the moments when Christ is no longer in the Father's Hands, but in the hands of men. In the Garden, our Lord contrasted two 'hours' – one was the evil hour: 'this is your hour' – with which Judas could turn out the lights of the world. In contrast, our Lord asked: 'Could you not watch one hour with Me?' In other words, he asked for an hour of reparation to combat the hour of evil; an hour of victimal union with the Cross to overcome the anti-love of sin.

"Secondly, the only time Our Lord asked the Apostles for anything was the night he went into his agony. Then he did not ask all of them ... perhaps because he knew he could not count on their fidelity. But at least he expected three to be faithful to him: Peter, James and John. As often in the history of the Church since that time, evil was awake, but the disciples were asleep. That is why there came out of His anguished and lonely Heart the sigh: 'Could you not watch one hour with me?' Not for an hour of activity did He plead, but for an hour of companionship.

"The third reason I keep up the Holy Hour is to grow more and more into his likeness. As Paul puts it: 'We are transfigured into his likeness, from splendor to splendor.' We become like that which we gaze upon. Looking into a sunset, the face takes on a golden glow. Looking at the Eucharistic Lord for an hour transforms the heart in a mysterious way as the face of Moses was transformed after his companionship with God on the mountain."

To encourage us to persevere in this practice, he says: "The Holy Hour. Is it difficult? Sometimes it seemed to be hard; it might mean having to forgo a social engagement, or rise an hour earlier, but on the whole it has never been a burden, only a joy."

What should one do in this hour? It can be any spiritual activity: engaging in a loving conversation with Our Lord or simply contemplating him, saying the rosary or other vocal prayers, reading the Scriptures or spiritual books… For those who can take up this admirable practice, it will do them the world of good, and through them it will help many souls.

866 Priests and the Holy Hour

Our parish priest is very holy and I often see him praying before the Blessed Sacrament. I know that Archbishop Fulton Sheen made a holy hour before the Blessed Sacrament every day and I would like to pass on some of his ideas to our priest. What can I tell him?

Over the years Archbishop Sheen, or simply Fulton Sheen as he is more commonly known, encouraged thousands of priests, laity and even Protestant ministers to do a continuous hour of prayer every day. He writes of the benefits in his autobiography *Treasure in Clay*.

Given that priests are very busy, especially with the shortage of priests in recent times, the first difficulty is finding time for the holy hour. Fulton Sheen explains how he resolved this himself. "At the beginning of my priesthood I would make the Holy Hour during the day or the evening. As the years mounted and I became busier, I made the Hour early in the morning, generally before Holy Mass." He did this even when he had to rise very early on particular occasions: "One difficult Holy Hour I remember occurred when I took a train from Jerusalem to Cairo. The train left at four o'clock in the morning; that meant very early rising."

As regards the benefit for priests, he writes: "The purpose of the Holy Hour is to encourage deep personal encounter with Christ. The holy and glorious God is constantly inviting us to come to Him, to hold converse with Him, to ask for such things as we need and to experience what a blessing there is in fellowship with Him. When we are first ordained it is easy to give self entirely to Christ, for the Lord fills us then with sweetness, just as a mother gives candy to her baby to encourage her child to take the first step. This exhilaration, however, does not last long; we quickly learn the cost of discipleship, which means leaving nets and boats and counting tables. The honeymoon soon ends, and so does our self-importance at first hearing the stirring title of 'Father.'

"Sensitive love or human love declines with time, but divine love does not. The first is concerned with the body which becomes less and less responsive to stimulation, but in the order of grace, the responsiveness of the divine to tiny, human acts of love intensifies. Neither theological knowledge nor social action alone is enough to keep us in love with Christ unless both are preceded by a personal encounter with him."

In answer to why spending a whole hour is so valuable, he writes: "I have found that it takes some time to catch fire in prayer. This has been one of the advantages of the daily Hour. It is not so brief as to prevent the soul from collecting itself and shaking off the multitudinous distractions of the world. Sitting before the Presence is like a body exposing itself before the sun to absorb its rays. Silence in the Hour is a tête-à-tête with the Lord. In those moments, one does not so much pour out written prayers, but listening takes its place. We do not say: 'Listen, Lord, for Thy servant speaketh,' but 'Speak, Lord, for Thy servant heareth.'"

Fulton Sheen writes too of how important the holy hour is for a priest's fidelity to his vocation. "It is impossible for me to explain how helpful the Holy Hour has been in preserving my vocation. Scripture gives considerable evidence to prove that a priest begins to fail his priesthood when he fails in his love of the Eucharist."

Another way the holy hour helps the priest is in keeping him away from the attractions of the world. "So the Holy Hour, quite apart from all its positive spiritual benefits, kept my feet from wandering too far. Being tethered to a tabernacle, one's rope for finding other pastures is not so long. That dim tabernacle lamp, however pale and faint, had some mysterious luminosity to darken the brightness of 'bright lights.' The Holy Hour became like an oxygen tank to revive the breath of the Holy Spirit in the midst of the foul and fetid atmosphere of the world. Even when it seemed so unprofitable and lacking in spiritual intimacy, I still had the sensation of being at least like a dog at the master's door, ready in case he called me."

As is clear, the holy hour is an extremely valuable practice for all, not only for priests. Let us do all we can to take it up ourselves and to encourage others, especially priests, to do so.

867 Promises of the rosary

Someone recently gave me a leaflet with fifteen promises, supposedly from Our Lady, for those who say the rosary. Are these really from Our Lady and can you please comment on them?

The promises were supposedly given by Our Lady to St Dominic, founder of the Dominicans, in the thirteenth century, although none of the early sources of St Dominic's life mentions them. It seems that the fifteenth-century Dominican preacher Blessed Alain de la Roche claimed to have had a vision in which it was revealed to him that Our Lady had appeared to St Dominic, giving him the rosary as a means of converting the Albigensian heretics of his day.

While it now seems certain that Our Lady did not give St Dominic the rosary itself, since the rosary had gradually been taking shape through Christian piety for a century or two before that, she did urge him to use it in his efforts of conversion and she apparently gave him the fifteen mysteries of the life of Christ on which to meditate while saying the Hail Marys. In any case he did begin to use the rosary and to urge others to say it for that intention, and he was singularly successful in bringing the heretics back to the faith (cf. J. Flader, *Question Time 1*, q. 131).

Our Lady would supposedly have communicated the fifteen promises to St Dominic when she appeared to him at some time. The sources on this question are very vague and therefore uncertain. Comprehensive books on the rosary, with an extensive treatment of its history, like Fr Donald Calloway's recent *Champions of the Rosary* (Marian Press, 2016), say nothing about the promises. So we cannot safely say that Our Lady gave the promises directly to St Dominic.

Wherever they came from, the promises are consistent with Catholic belief and are benefits that anyone praying the rosary with faith and love would hope to receive. A leaflet listing the promises was given the *Imprimatur*, let it be printed, by Patrick J. Hayes, Archbishop of New York from 1919 to 1938. It had previously been given the *Nihil obstat*, nothing stands in the way, a declaration that there is nothing against the Catholic faith in the promises. The promises fall under the category of private revelation, which a person is free to accept and believe or not.

What then are the promises? Our Lady promises to someone who recites the rosary, that they "will receive significant graces" and that she will give them "her special protection and the greatest graces".

She promises that the rosary "will be a powerful armour against hell, it will destroy vice, decrease sin and defeat heresies". It will "cause virtue and good works to flourish; it will obtain for souls the abundant mercy of God; it will withdraw the heart of men from the love of the world and its vanities, and will lift them to the desire of eternal things".

The soul which commends itself to Mary by the recitation of the rosary "shall not perish". Moreover, "whoever shall recite the rosary devoutly, applying himself to the consideration of its sacred mysteries, shall never be conquered and never overwhelmed by misfortune. God will not chastise him in his justice, he shall not perish by an unprovided death (unprepared for heaven). The sinner shall convert. The just shall grow in grace and become worthy of eternal life".

A person with true devotion to the rosary "shall not die without the sacraments of the Church" and "will have during their life and at their death, the light of God and the plenitude of his graces; at the moment of death they shall participate in the merits of the saints in paradise".

Our Lady will "deliver them from Purgatory" and they will "merit a high degree of glory in heaven". People will "obtain all they ask of Our Lady by the recitation of the rosary". Those who spread devotion to the rosary "will be aided by Mary in their necessities" and they will "have for intercessors the entire celestial court during their life and at the hour of death".

Those who recite the rosary "are Mary's sons, and brothers of her only son Jesus Christ" and "devotion to the rosary is a great sign of predestination".

All of these promises are eminently reasonable and consistent with what we know of God's mercy and the power of Our Lady's intercession. Naturally, people have to correspond freely to the graces God gives them. The more people pray the rosary, the more they can look forward to being blessed by God on earth and being with him forever in heaven.

868 The Memorare

I am a recent convert and a friend taught me to say the Memorare, which I find very beautiful. Can you tell me anything about the background of this prayer?

For those unfamiliar with the Memorare, these are the words: "Remember, O most gracious Virgin Mary, that never was it known that anyone who fled to thy protection, implored thy help, or sought thy intercession was left unaided. Inspired by this confidence, I fly unto thee, O Virgin of virgins, my mother; to thee do I come, before thee I stand, sinful and sorrowful. O Mother of the Word Incarnate, despise not my petitions, but in thy mercy hear and answer me. Amen."

As you say, it is a very beautiful prayer, a prayer of complete trust in Our Lady's powerful intercession. It is only right to have complete trust in Our Lady because, after all, she is the Mother, Daughter and Spouse of God, and God will answer her every request. The one who says the prayer comes before Our Lady with humility, "sinful and sorrowful", and, trusting in her mercy, begs her for some favour. The name Memorare, by the way, is the Latin rendering of the prayer's first word, Remember.

The origin of the prayer is uncertain. It has often been attributed to St Bernard of Clairvaux, a twelfth-century Cistercian monk who had great devotion to Our Lady, but this is now regarded as unlikely. The prayer first appeared as part of a longer fifteenth-century prayer, "Ad sanctitatis tuae pedes, dulcissima Virgo Maria", "At the feet of your sanctity, O most sweet Virgin Mary."

There is a touching story of the power of the Memorare in the life of St Francis de Sales, the seventeenth-century bishop of Geneva and author of the popular *Introduction to the Devout Life*. At the age of eighteen, while a student at the University of Paris, he was influenced by the Calvinist teaching on predestination to a point where he believed he was destined to be damned. He was so convinced of his damnation that he lost his appetite, was unable to sleep and began to waste away. His tutor and director asked him why he was so dejected, but he was unable to answer. He was in that state for a month and lost all the divine love he had enjoyed before.

He then entered the church of Saint Etienne des Grès, knelt before a statue of Our Lady and said the Memorare, entrusting himself to Our Lady with sighs and tears. As he later wrote in a letter, "The torment of despair came to a sudden end". He credited Our Lady with saving him "from falling into despair or heresy." After that, he recited the Memorare every day.

A great figure in promoting the Memorare was the seventeenth-century French priest Fr Claude Bernard, who learned the prayer from his father. Fr Herbert Thurston SJ, in his book *Familiar Prayers: Their Origin and History* (1953), writes of him: "Fr Claude Bernard, known as the 'Poor Priest', zealously dedicated himself to the preaching and aiding of prisoners and criminals condemned to death. Trusting his charges to the care and intercession of the Blessed Virgin Mary, Fr Bernard employed the Memorare extensively in his work of evangelisation to great effect. Many a criminal was reconciled to God through his efforts. At one time he had more than 200,000 leaflets printed with the Memorare in various languages so he could distribute the leaflets wherever he felt they would do some good."

Part of the reason Fr Bernard had such high regard for the Memorare was that he felt he had been miraculously cured through saying it. In a letter to Queen Anne of Austria, wife of King Louis XIII, he wrote that he had once been seriously ill and, fearing for his life, had prayed the Memorare and immediately began to recover. Feeling himself unworthy of such a miracle he attributed the cure to some unknown natural cause.

Sometime later, an Augustinian Brother visited Fr Bernard and told him that Our Lady had appeared to him in a vision and told him it was she who had cured Fr Bernard of his illness, and that he was to assure him of that fact. Fr Bernard went on to say in the letter that he was ashamed of his lack of gratitude and asked God to forgive him.

Another person who received a great favour through the Memorare was the Frenchman Alphonse Ratisbonne. Born in 1814, he was a nominal Jew but when his older brother converted to the Catholic faith and became a priest, Alphonse came to hate both him and the Catholic Church. He also became a rabid atheist. One day, on a visit to Rome, Alphonse met a Catholic convert who knew his priest-brother. The convert challenged Alphonse to wear the Miraculous Medal and to say the Memorare every morning and night. Alphonse accepted, thinking it would show up the ridiculous nature of the Catholic religion. Sometime later, when the two entered a Catholic church in Rome, Alphonse saw a bright light and in it Our Lady as she appeared on the medal. Several days later he was received into the Catholic Church and became a Jesuit priest.

The Memorare became popular in England by way of France and it was included in the 1856 edition of Bishop Richard Challoner's *The*

Garden of the Soul. Fr Herbert Thurston SJ considered the Memorare one of the prayers most of the faithful knew by heart. It is a beautiful and powerful prayer, one we would do well to say every day.

869 The "Hymn of the Three Young Men"

I have a friend who suggests reciting the "Hymn of the Three Young Men" for thanksgiving after Mass. I hadn't heard of it before but am now saying it and I find it helpful. What is the background to this prayer?

For those who may be unfamiliar with the hymn, it is found in the Old Testament book of Daniel, Chapter 3, verses 57-88. Because the hymn appears only in the Greek Septuagint version of the Bible, it is sometimes italicised and has special verse numbers, following verse 23.

It is the hymn sung by three Hebrew boys, Ananiah, Azariah and Mishael, during the Babylonian captivity in the sixth century BC. King Nebuchadnezzar II, who ruled from 605 to 562 BC, had erected a huge golden statue, some 27 metres high, and required all his subjects to worship it. The three Hebrews, faithful to their Jewish religion, refused to do so and were thrown into a fiery furnace, where they sang the hymn.

Even though the flames burned some of the Chaldeans who were close to the furnace, it did not harm the Hebrews, because an angel came down and protected them from the flames. This moved the king to declare that anyone who spoke against the God of the Hebrews was to be punished severely, and he promoted the three young men to positions in his court. The fidelity of the three young men inspired the Jews in the second century BC to be loyal to their faith during the persecution of that time, narrated in the two books of the Maccabees.

The early Christians saw in the liberation of the Hebrews from the fire a figure of the death and resurrection of Christ and they represented the scene in art in the catacombs, on tombs and on reliquaries. What gave the hymn great importance was its introduction in the liturgy of the Easter Vigil and in other ceremonies. Also, beginning in the eighth century its popularity was such that it was translated into various national languages.

In the ninth century the hymn was included in the Mass, and in the missal of Pope Pius V in 1570 it was added to the rites at the end of Mass. It is not clear, however, who recited it and when. Some sources say it was recited by all those who took part in the procession to the sacristy, while others say it was said by the priest as he took off his vestments. What is certain is that in the missal of 1920 the priest recited the hymn as an act of thanksgiving as he left the altar. This was the case until 1962, when it was no longer required but it was included among the prayers recommended to be said, if considered opportune, after Mass. Recent editions of the Roman Missal do not include it among the proposed prayers of thanksgiving after Mass.

Among the saints who recommended the custom was St Josemaría Escrivá. In 1932 he wrote that it would be good to recite in thanksgiving after Mass the *Trium puerorum* (Hymn of the Three Young Men) with two psalms and prayers as found in the Breviary at the time. In 1947 he recommended that in the centres of Opus Dei those present should recite the hymn at the end of their thanksgiving after Mass.

The current Divine Office, or Liturgy of the Hours, often includes the hymn in the office of Morning Prayer, especially on Sundays and feast days.

The hymn, as a hymn of praise to God, prolongs the liturgical praise of the Eucharistic Prayer, which begins with the "Holy, Holy, Holy" and ends with praise of the Father through the Son: "Through Him, with Him and in Him".

The hymn itself calls upon all of creation to praise God. It begins: "Bless the Lord, all you works of the Lord, sing praise to him and highly exalt him for ever." The subsequent verses call upon the heavens, the angels, the waters above the heaven, the sun and moon, the stars, the rain and dew, the winds, the cold and heat, the earth, the mountains and hills, the whales and creatures that move in the waters, the birds, the beasts and cattle, etc., to bless the Lord. Towards the end, the hymn asks Ananiah, Azariah and Mishael to bless the Lord, to "sing praise to him and highly exalt him for ever." The hymn is customarily followed by Psalm 150, the last of the psalms, which continues the theme of praise of God. The devotion concludes with a series of prayers.

870 Devotion to the angels

We don't hear much about angels anymore, even though the Church celebrates two feasts in their honour. Is devotion to the angels still important?

Devotion to the angels is very important. It has always been. As you say, the Church celebrates two feasts in their honour: on September 29 the feast of the Archangels Michael, Gabriel and Raphael, and on October 2 the feast of the Guardian Angels. Those feasts can be an occasion for priests to preach on the importance of the angels in our lives, for parents to teach their children about them, and for all of us to grow in devotion to them.

The angels appear throughout the Scriptures. To mention just a few, already in the first book of the Bible, angels are placed at the entrance of the garden of Eden to guard the tree of life (*Gen* 3:24), and an angel appears to Jacob, telling him to return to the land of his birth (cf. *Gen* 31:11-13). Also in the Old Testament, an angel appears to Manoah's wife announcing the birth of Samson (cf. *Judg* 13:3) and the Archangel Raphael accompanies the young Tobias on a journey in the book of Tobit. In the New Testament an angel appears to St Joseph in a dream to tell him that the child Mary is carrying is of the Holy Spirit (cf. *Mt* 1:20); and the Archangel Gabriel appears both to Zechariah to announce the birth of John the Baptist (cf. *Lk* 1:11) and to Mary to announce the birth of Jesus (cf. *Lk* 1:26-31). Finally, in the last book of the Bible, the book of Revelation, angels appear numerous times giving glory to God.

Angels are real, and they were created by God to give him glory in heaven as well as to perform various roles on earth, including looking after human beings as guardian angels. I don't know how much the average person hears about angels these days, but I suspect, as you say, that it is not much. This is sad. Why is devotion to the angels so important?

A first reason is quite general but fundamental. In recent times mankind has tended to focus more and more on the visible world, on the here below, and to forget the spiritual, the supernatural. But it is in the realm of the spiritual where God himself is, and where our ultimate destiny, heaven, is. And it is in that realm too where angels, who are invisible, are. Remembering the angels and having devotion to them thus helps to lift our thoughts above and to be heavenly minded, not earthly minded (cf. *Col* 3:1-2).

What is more, all the angels, not only the guardian angels, are with us in the Church. St Thomas Aquinas writes: "It is manifest that both men and angels are ordained to one end, which is the glory of the divine fruition. Hence the Mystical Body of the Church consists not only of men but also of angels" (*STh* III, q. 8, art. 4). So angels too form part of the Church. We can call on them to help us be the saints God wants us to be and so build up the body of Christ, the Church, helping others too to grow in holiness.

We should not forget either that the angels constantly adore Our Lord in the Tabernacle, where Christ is truly present. When we go into a church we can ask the angels to help us adore Our Lord as they do. We don't see the angels but they are truly there, day and night. When we can't be there ourselves, we can ask them to keep Our Lord company on our behalf. And, of course, during the celebration of Mass, the angels surround Our Lord when he becomes present in the host and in the chalice. Awareness of this helps us to be more supernatural, more spiritually minded.

Awareness of the existence of our guardian angel is also very helpful. When we are tempted to sin or are in any difficult set of circumstances we can ask our angel to help us get through the situation successfully. And being aware that our angel is always there watching us can be an added help to avoid doing things that we wouldn't want our angel to see. St John Vianney, the Curé of Ars, writes: "If we did like St Remigius, we would never be angry. See, this saint, being questioned by a Father of the desert how he managed to be always in an even temper, replied: 'I often consider that my guardian angel is always by my side'". He also says: "The devil writes down our sins, our guardian angel all our merits. Labour so that guardian angel's book may be full, and the devil's empty."

So yes, devotion to the angels is very important. Let us do all we can to foster it.

871 The Seven Sundays of St Joseph

I have heard that there is a devotion honouring St Joseph on the seven Sundays preceding his feast on March 19. Can you tell me something about it?

The devotion was instituted by Pope Gregory XVI, who was Pope from 1831 to 1846. Pope Gregory encouraged the custom of dedicating the seven Sundays before 19 March to Saint Joseph in memory of his seven sorrows and joys, and he attached many indulgences to the devotion. His successor, Blessed Pope Pius IX, asked the faithful to petition Saint Joseph to alleviate the afflictions of the universal Church at that time. We would do very well to go to St Joseph in our own time, begging him to alleviate the many afflictions of the Church today.

There is a story associated with this devotion. It seems that two Franciscan friars were in a ship sailing along the coast of Flanders when a terrible storm arose, sinking the vessel with three hundred passengers aboard. The two friars seized hold of a plank and managed to survive for three days and nights. Fearing for their lives, they prayed to St Joseph to save them. It seems that a young man with beautiful features appeared to them, encouraging them to confide in his assistance, and he guided them safely to a harbor. When they asked him who he was, he told them he was St Joseph, and he advised them to recite the Our Father and Hail Mary seven times each day in memory of his seven sorrows and seven joys. Then he disappeared.

What are the seven sorrows and joys? The first sorrow came when St Joseph saw that Mary, his betrothed, was carrying a child which was not his and he decided to send her away informally. The joy came when an angel revealed to him in a dream that the child was by the Holy Spirit and he should take Mary as his wife (cf. *Mt* 1:18-25).

St Joseph experienced the second sorrow in Bethlehem when there was no place in an inn for Jesus' birth, but this was followed by the great joy of Jesus' birth in a stable, a birth announced to the shepherds by an angel (cf. *Lk* 2:6-11).

The third sorrow came when St Joseph saw Jesus shedding blood in his circumcision (cf. *Lk* 2:21), followed by the great joy of giving him the holy name of Jesus (cf. *Mt* 1:25).

The fourth sorrow was when Jesus was presented in the temple forty days after his birth and Simeon told Mary, "Behold, this child is set for the fall and rising of many in Israel, and for a sign that is spoken against (and a sword will pierce through your own soul also), that thoughts out of many hearts may be revealed" (*Lk* 2:34-35). The fourth joy was hearing Simeon announce that Jesus was to be the Saviour of all mankind: "Lord, now let your servant depart in peace, according to your word; for my eyes have seen your salvation which you have prepared in the presence of all peoples, a light for revelation to the Gentiles, and for glory to your people Israel" (*Lk* 2:29-32).

The fifth sorrow came some days later when an angel announced to Joseph in a dream that Herod wanted to kill Jesus and he must take the child and his mother and flee into Egypt (cf. *Mt* 2:13-15). This was followed by the joy of arriving safely and knowing that the prophecy of Hosea was to be fulfilled: "Out of Egypt I have called my son" (cf. *Hos* 11:1; *Mt* 2:15). Some versions give as the fifth joy the fulfilment of the prophecy of Isaiah: "Behold, the Lord is riding on a swift cloud and comes to Egypt; and the idols of Egypt will tremble at his presence, and the heart of the Egyptians will melt within them" (*Is* 19:1).

St Joseph experienced the sixth sorrow when he was told by an angel that Herod had died, "but when he heard that Archelaus reigned over Judea in place of his father Herod, he was afraid to go there, and being warned in a dream he withdrew to the district of Galilee" (*Mt* 2:22). The joy came when "he went and dwelt in a city called Nazareth, that what was spoken by the prophets might be fulfilled, 'He shall be called a Nazarene'" (*Mt* 2:23).

St Joseph had the seventh sorrow when he and Mary could not find Jesus a day after leaving Jerusalem for the Passover. They were overjoyed when "they found him in the temple, sitting among the teachers, listening to them and asking them questions" (*Lk* 2:46).

After meditating on these sorrows and joys, the person is encouraged to recite one Our Father, Hail Mary and Glory be, along with other prayers that are listed in each version of the devotion.

872 A crucifix and an icon of Our Lady

Along with my wife I watched Pope Francis' wonderful hour of prayer at St Peter's Basilica on 27 March 2020 and was struck by the beautiful crucifix and image of Our Lady behind him. Do they have any special significance?

The crucifix and image of Our Lady, apart from being beautiful, are in fact very old and have great significance in the context of the worldwide coronavirus pandemic.

The crucifix was that of San Marcello. It is of the Sienese school and dates to the fourteenth century. It normally hangs above the tabernacle in the church of San Marcello al Corso in Rome and is considered by many to be the most realistic model of the crucifixion in Rome. A number of miracles have been attributed to it.

The first miracle dates to 1519 when the church of San Marcello caught fire on the night of May 22 to 23 and was completely destroyed. At dawn the people rushed to the church to find only the outer walls standing and everything inside destroyed except the crucifix, which was still hanging above the altar with an oil lamp burning beneath it, although deformed by the heat. Soon some of the people began to gather every Friday night at dusk to pray and light lamps at the feet of the cross. This gave rise to the Confraternity of the Holy Crucifix, which still exists today.

Another miraculous event took place three years later and relates to a health crisis not unlike our present one. In 1522 a great plague struck Rome, so severe that it was feared no one would survive. Mindful of the miracle of the crucifix saved in the fire, the friars of the Servants of Mary decided to take the crucifix in a penitential procession from the church of San Marcello to St Peter's Basilica to pray for an end to the plague. It was led by Spanish Cardinal Raimondo Vich, bishop of Valencia and Barcelona.

The authorities, fearing the risk of contagion, tried to stop the religious procession, but the people did not accept the warning and accompanied the crucifix through the streets of the city in large numbers. The chronicles of the time relate that the procession lasted from August 4 to 20, more than two weeks. The reason it took so long is that, as the procession advanced, the plague receded so that each district tried to hold on to the sacred image as long as possible. When it returned to San Marcello, the plague had completely ceased and Rome was saved. Since 1650, the miraculous crucifix has been taken to St Peter's on the occasion of each Holy Year.

The image of Our Lady used by Pope Francis was the ancient and much loved icon of Our Lady, *Salus Populi Romani*, which is kept in the Lady Chapel of the Basilica of St Mary Major in Rome. The title *Salus Populi Romani* means literally "health" or "salvation" or "protectress" of the Roman people.

The actual origin of the image is uncertain. One tradition has it that it was taken to Rome by St Helena, the mother of the emperor Constantine in the fourth century. It is said that it was Pope Liberius

(352-366) who hung the image in the newly completed Basilica of St Mary Major.

According to a pious tradition, the icon was instrumental in saving Rome from the ravages of a devastating plague during the pontificate of Pope St Gregory the Great (590-604). Pope Gregory carried the image in a solemn penitential procession through the streets of the city during the Easter season, praying for an end to the plague. When the procession reached the Mausoleum of Hadrian, a choir of angels was heard singing the Resurrection hymn "Queen of Heaven, rejoice". The Pope immediately added, "Pray for us to God, alleluia". At that point an angel, believed to be St Michael, appeared above the Mausoleum, putting his sword back in its scabbard, as if indicating that the plague would cease, as in fact it did. The Mausoleum is now known as the Castel Sant'Angelo, the Castle of the Holy Angel. It is located along the Tiber River, very near St Peter's Basilica.

Since both the crucifix and the icon of Our Lady were instrumental in ending plagues many centuries ago, Pope Francis undoubtedly chose to use them in the hour of prayer for an end to the pandemic.

Our Lady and the Saints

873 Our Lady of the Snows

I attended Mass in my parish on August 5 and the priest said something about this feast having been called Our Lady of the Snows. Can you tell me the background to this title?

The feast, which is celebrated as an optional memorial on August 5, is more properly called the anniversary of the Dedication of the basilica of St Mary Major. The basilica is one of the four major basilicas in Rome, along with St Peter's, St Paul Outside the Walls, and St John Lateran. The basilica has an interesting history, in two stages.

In the fourth century, according to an ancient tradition, a Roman patrician named John and his wife, who were childless, decided to leave their estate to Our Lady. They prayed assiduously, asking Mary to make known to them what work they should undertake in her honour. One night on August 4 during the pontificate of Pope Liberius (352-366), Our Lady appeared to each of them in a dream and asked that a church be built in her honour at a place where snow would fall. It should be remembered that August is an extremely hot month in Rome and it never snows then.

The following day, August 5, snow appeared on the Esquiline hill, one of the seven hills of Rome. The couple reported their dream to Pope Liberius who, it turns out, had had a similar dream. According to the story, the Pope then went to the site and traced the outlines of the church, which was later built there. It was the first church in Rome dedicated to Our Lady. According to some accounts, the site was that of the large palace where John lived with his wife, and the new church was added on to the palace.

In view of this, it is understandable that the feast was for a time called Our Lady of the Snows. It was originally called *Dedicatio Sanctae Mariae,* Dedication of Saint Mary's, and was celebrated only in

Rome until it was inserted for the first time in the General Roman Calendar in 1568. From then on, until 1969, its official name was Dedicatio Sanctae Mariae ad Nives, Dedication of Saint Mary of the Snows. To commemorate the tradition of the snow, every year on August 5 a cascade of white rose petals is dropped from the dome of the basilica during Mass.

In the fifth century, after the Council of Ephesus in 431 declared Our Lady the Mother of God, Pope Sixtus III (432-440) rebuilt the church and dedicated it to Our Lady on 5 August 434. He decorated the apse and walls with mosaics of Our Lord and Our Lady. The mosaics, which now adorn the present basilica, completed centuries later, are some of the oldest in existence.

As early as the end of the fourth century a replica of the nativity grotto in Bethlehem was placed in the church, and for this reason the church has also been called St Mary of the Crib. Other names for the basilica are the Basilica of Liberius, St Mary Major, because it is the largest church in Rome dedicated to Our Lady, and Our Lady of the Snows.

It was in this Basilica that St Ignatius of Loyola celebrated his first Mass and that Pope St Pius V said the rosary, praying for the success of the Christian navy over the Turks in what was to be the Battle of Lepanto in 1570. St Pius is buried in the basilica.

Another important feature in St Mary Major is the ancient image of Our Lady entitled *Salus Populi Romani*, meaning literally "health", "salvation" or "protectress" of the Roman people. The actual origin of the image is uncertain although, according to some, it was painted by St Luke himself. One tradition has it that the image was taken to Rome by St Helena, mother of the emperor Constantine, in the fourth century. It is said that it was Pope Liberius who hung the image in the newly completed church of Our Lady. According to a pious tradition, the icon was instrumental in saving Rome from the ravages of a devastating plague during the pontificate of Pope St Gregory the Great (590-604).

Pope Francis used this image in the prayer vigil at St Peter's on 27 March 2020 for an end to the coronavirus pandemic. Before his trips overseas, Pope Francis visits St Mary Major and entrusts the fruits of the trip to Our Lady. Upon returning he again goes to the basilica to thank Our Lady for the fruits.

874 The Desert Fathers

I am enjoying learning about the Desert Fathers, who are very often venerated as saints in Eastern Catholic and Eastern Orthodox Churches. Can a Roman Catholic too enjoy their writings and teachings?

In saying that these Fathers are venerated in the Eastern Catholic Churches, you are in effect answering your own question. The Eastern Churches are fully part of the one Catholic Church and therefore all the faithful may venerate these saints. What is more, most of these saints lived in the first four centuries, when the Church was still united. Only after the Council of Chalcedon in 451 was there a substantial rupture of this unity, when those who are now the Coptic Orthodox separated from Rome along with the Syriac Orthodox and others.

But who were the Desert Fathers? They were hermits and other ascetics who lived primarily in the desert regions of Egypt, beginning around the third century. They included both men and women.

The first of them was St Paul of Thebes (ca. 227-341), commonly known as St Paul the First Hermit. He went to the desert around 250AD, during the persecution of Decius and Valerian, and lived there in a cave until his death around 341, at the age of 113. He is venerated as a saint in both the Catholic and Orthodox traditions. His feast is celebrated on January 15 in the Catholic Church.

The most well-known of the Desert Fathers was undoubtedly St Anthony the Great, or St Anthony Abbott, who moved to the desert around 270AD. St Anthony is venerated as a saint in the Roman Catholic tradition, and his feast is celebrated on January 17. In spite of the hardship of life in the desert, he died at the age of 105. St Anthony became known as both the father and founder of desert monasticism. By the time he died, in 356AD, thousands of monks and nuns had been drawn to the desert. This moved his biographer, St Athanasius of Alexandria, who also spent some time in the desert, to write that "the desert had become a city."

Although at the beginning the hermits tended to live on their own, little by little they gathered together in groups of two or three. Then informal larger groups were gradually formed until the monk St Pachomius (292-348), who is celebrated as a saint in both the Catholic and Orthodox traditions, saw the need for a more formal structure. He established a monastery where the monks lived together and had rules which included obedience, manual labour, silence, fasting and long periods of prayer.

The first fully organised monastery under St Pachomius had men and women living in separate quarters, with up to three in a room. They supported themselves by weaving cloth and baskets and by other tasks. All property was held in common, meals were eaten together in silence, and they fasted twice a week. They came together several times a day for prayer and readings, and they wore simple peasant clothing with a hood to cover their head.

The movement grew to a point where, within decades of Pachomius' death, there were tens of thousands of monks and nuns in these monasteries. One of the early pilgrims to the desert monasteries was St Basil the Great, who took the rule of St Pachomius to other places in the East. St Basil's rule had the monks and nuns under the authority of a bishop and serving the poor and needy.

St John Cassian played an important role in taking this rule to the West, where it developed especially under St Benedict of Nursia in Italy (480-547). He urged his monks to read the writings of St John Cassian on the Desert Fathers. It was also from the Egyptian monasteries that the rule passed to the Eastern monastic tradition at Mount Athos in Greece.

The Desert Fathers had a major influence on the development of Christianity. It was largely due to their staunch defence of the faith that Egypt retained a strong Christian presence when the Muslims swept across North Africa in the seventh century, practically wiping out Christians in the other countries. Much later, religious renewals such as the *Devotio Moderna* movement in 14th-century Europe, the German evangelicals and Pietists in Pennsylvania in the seventeenth and eighteenth centuries, and the Methodist Revival in England in the eighteenth century are considered by modern scholars to have been inspired by the Desert Fathers.

875 St Corona

With the coronavirus sweeping through the world. I understand that, coincidently, there is a Saint Corona. Who was she and might we pray to her for an end to the pandemic?

St Corona was a second-century martyr who died in Syria along with St Victor, and she can most certainly be invoked to end the coronavirus pandemic. Her remains, along with those of St Victor, have been preserved in the northern Italian city of Feltre, which has been so ravaged by the virus.

Little is known with certainty about St Corona, but she and St Victor are listed in the Roman martyrology of the Church. It is not certain exactly where they died, with most sources saying it was in Syria, then under Roman rule, in either Damascus, Antioch or Alexandria.

There is some disagreement about whether they were put to death during the reign of emperor Antoninus Pius (138-161 AD) or that of his successor Marcus Aurelius (161-180 AD).

According to the most common tradition the Romans discovered that one of their soldiers named Victor was a Christian. They brought him before a prefect named Sebastian, who despised Christians and decided to make an example out of him. He ordered Victor to be subjected to horrendous tortures and finally to have his eyes gouged out. Through it all, he never denied Christ.

Witnessing this was a sixteen-year-old girl name Corona. She was the wife of one of the Roman soldiers and was also a Christian, although her husband did not know it. As Victor was being tortured Corona, moved with compassion, decided to help the slowly dying man. She announced her Christianity to all those present and hurried over to Victor, kneeling and praying for him, and letting him know she was there for him. Very soon the soldiers took her too before the prefect.

Sebastian was furious that this young woman had so disrespected his authority and he had her put in prison and tortured. Then he ordered her to be tied to the tops of two palm trees, which had been bent down to the ground toward each other. At his signal, the ropes holding the trees were cut, causing them to spring up with so much force that Corona's body was torn apart. Sebastian ordered Victor to be beheaded.

The remains of Saints Corona and Victor have been in the town of Feltre since the ninth century. At the end of the eleventh century the crusaders built a basilica there in their honour which now houses their remains. In 1943 and again in 1981 the remains were examined, and the bones were confirmed to be those of a male and a female, born around the second century in the East. A Latin inscription found in the tomb in 1943 attested to the transferring of the bodies of the martyrs Victor and Corona to Cyprus in the year 205. In the 1981 examination scientists from the University of Padua discovered cedar pollen, from a typical plant from the Mediterranean basin during the time in question. Archaeologists confirm that this pollen would have been present in Syria and Cyprus.

The two martyrs are patron saints of numerous Italian cities, including Feltre. Their feast day is May 14. We can ask them to pray for the coronavirus pandemic to subside quickly.

876 St Tarcisius, patron saint of altar servers

My son is an altar server and our parish priest told the servers to pray to St Tarcisius, their patron saint, for a love of the Blessed Sacrament. What do we know about this saint?

We do not have much certain knowledge of St Tarcisius, but it seems he died in the third century, defending the Eucharist while taking it to Christians in prison. Pope Benedict XVI gave a moving account of this saint in an address to altar servers from all over Europe in Rome on 4 August 2010. What follows is taken largely from that address.

When Emperor Valerian (253-260) was persecuting Christians, including ordering the execution of the bishops of Carthage and Rome, Christians were forced to meet secretly in private houses or underground in the catacombs to hear the word of God, pray and celebrate Holy Mass. It is said that St Tarcisius was a boy who went regularly to the catacombs of St Calixtus in Rome and took his Christian duties very seriously. He had great love for the Eucharist and was presumably an acolyte, or altar server.

At that time the custom of taking the Eucharist to prisoners and the sick was very dangerous. One day, when the priest asked who was prepared to take the Eucharist to those who were waiting for it, young Tarcisius stood up and said: "Send me!" The boy seemed too young for such a demanding service, but he argued: "My youth will be the best shield for the Eucharist". Convinced, the priest entrusted the Blessed Sacrament to him, saying: "Tarcisius, remember that a heavenly treasure has been entrusted to your weak hands. Avoid crowded streets and do not forget that holy things must never be thrown to dogs, nor pearls to swine. Will you guard the Sacred Mysteries faithfully and safely?". "I would die", Tarcisius answered with determination, "rather than let go of them".

As he went on his way, he met some friends who approached him and asked him to join them. When he refused, these pagan boys became suspicious and they realised he was clasping something to his chest that he appeared to be protecting. They tried to prize it away from him, but in vain. The struggle became ever more fierce, especially when they realised that Tarcisius was a Christian. They kicked him and threw stones at him, but he did not surrender. While Tarcisius was dying, a Pretorian guard called Quadratus, who was also a Christian, picked him up and carried him to the priest. Tarcisius was already dead when they arrived, but he was still clutching a small linen bag containing the Eucharist.

Tarcisius was buried in the catacombs of St Calixtus. In the following century, Pope Damasus (366-384) had an inscription carved on St Tarcisius' tomb, saying that he died in the year 257. The Roman Martyrology fixed the date as 15 August, and in the same Martyrology a beautiful oral tradition is recorded. It claims that the Blessed Sacrament was not found on St Tarcisius' body, either in his hands or in his clothing. It explains that the consecrated Host which the little martyr had defended with his life had become flesh of his flesh, thereby forming, together with his body, a single immaculate Host offered to God.

Pope Benedict told the altar servers that St Tarcisius' witness and this beautiful tradition teach us the deep love and great veneration that we must have for the Eucharist. "It is a precious good, a treasure of incomparable value. It is the Bread of life, Jesus himself, who becomes our nourishment, support and strength on our daily journey and on the open road that leads to eternal life. The Eucharist is the greatest gift that Jesus has given us.

"Serve Jesus present in the Eucharist generously. It is an important task that enables you to be particularly close to the Lord and to grow in true and profound friendship with him. Guard this friendship in your hearts jealously, like St Tarcisius, ready to commit yourselves, to fight and to give your lives so that Jesus may reach all peoples. May you too communicate to your peers the gift of this friendship with joy, with enthusiasm, without fear, so that they may feel that you know this Mystery, that it is true and that you love it! Every time that you approach the altar, you have the good fortune to assist in God's great loving gesture as he continues to want to give himself to each one of us, to be close to us, to help us, to give us strength to live in the right way."

877 St Januarius

A friend told me that the blood of an Italian saint from the early centuries liquefies from time to time and that it has done so again recently. Is this true and, if so, can you please tell me what it is all about?

A reliquary with the blood of the early Church martyr St Januarius is one of the treasures of Naples, Italy. The blood is said to liquefy miraculously on certain days of the year, including on the Saturday before the first Sunday of May. Despite the lockdown due to the coronavirus pandemic in Italy in 2020, Cardinal Crescenzio Sepe, Archbishop of Naples, reported that the miracle had occurred again on May 2 that year, and he blessed the city with the reliquary via livestream. He said: "How many times our saint has intervened to save us from the plague, from cholera. St Januarius is the true soul of Naples."

According to the tradition, St Januarius was bishop of Naples, or possibly Benevento, in the early fourth century. Although no contemporary records of his life remain, tradition holds that he hid other Christians to save their lives during the fierce persecution of Christians under the Roman emperor Diocletian at the beginning of the fourth century. When the authorities found out that he was doing this they sentenced him to death. He was beheaded in Pozzuoli, near Naples on 19 September 305. His name is mentioned as a "holy martyr" in writings from the fifth century.

After St Januarius' public execution, a faithful woman named Eusebia collected his blood in two flasks to keep as a relic, and they arrived in Naples in the fifth century. They are now kept in the cathedral there. Although the reddish blood has now dried up and adheres to one side of the vial, it miraculously liquefies from time to time, covering the glass from side to side.

The first recorded liquefaction was on 17 August 1389. Since then, the blood has liquefied numerous times, usually on any of three days. The most common one is the saint's feast day on September 19, the day of his martyrdom and the day when his feast is celebrated in the liturgical calendar. On this day in Naples there is a great festival with a procession. Because of the presence of the blood there, Naples is called the "City of Blood".

Another day is December 16, the day of the eruption of Mt Vesuvius in 1631, when St Januarius' intercession was invoked and Naples was spared the effects of the eruption. The third is the Saturday before the first Sunday in May, in commemoration of the transfer of St Januarius' relics to Naples.

The blood also liquefied in the presence of Pope Francis during his visit to Naples on 21 March 2015. It was the first time the miracle had occurred in the presence of a Pope since 1848, when Blessed Pius IX visited the city.

When the blood liquefies, the reliquary with the vials remains on view for the faithful to venerate it for eight days, during which they can kiss it. A priest turns it to show that the blood is still liquid. Then it is returned to the safety vault and locked away in the Chapel of the Treasury of the cathedral.

Investigations have been conducted to find a scientific explanation for the liquefaction of the blood but none has been successful thus far. The Church believes that the miracle takes place in response to the dedication and prayers of the faithful. When the blood doesn't liquefy, the people take it as an omen of some misfortune. There has been no official Church approval of the miracle.

St Januarius is venerated as a saint and martyr not only in the Catholic tradition but also in that of the Eastern Orthodox Churches. He is considered the patron saint of blood donors, goldsmiths and people who have suffered heart attacks.

878 St Lydwine of Schiedam

A friend of mine who is very sick has been praying to St Lydwine of Schiedam. I never heard of her. Who was she?

St Lydwine (1380-1433) was a Dutch saint who was very sick, more sick than can be imagined, as we shall see. If her suffering seems too great to be real, it is well documented. The mayor and other authorities of Schiedam issued a formal declaration in 1421 detailing many of her ailments, and biographies were written by people who were very close to her. One of them was by her confessor and another was edited by Thomas à Kempis, a contemporary of hers. I will draw largely on the work of à Kempis in what follows.

Lydwine, or Lydia, was the fifth child, and the only girl of the nine children of Peter and Petronilla, of Schiedam in the Netherlands. Having gone to Palm Sunday Mass in the local church, Petronilla rushed home to give birth to Lydwine while the Passion was being sung, an omen of the suffering Lydwine was to endure. The family was poor and Peter worked as a night watchman over the city to support his family.

At the age of seven or eight, Lydwine already had great devotion to the image of Our Lady in the church of Schiedam. She was a beautiful and intelligent girl. When she was twelve many men wanted to marry her, but she declared her intention to remain a virgin. Early in her fifteenth year she became very sick but recovered at least partially. Later that year, while ice skating with friends, someone bumped into her, throwing her onto the ice. She suffered a broken rib on her right side, developing into an abscess which gave her much pain.

Early in her sixteenth year the abscess burst and fluids came up through her mouth with vomiting. From then on she had constant infirmities. Soon she was unable to walk except with a stick or crutch and her body began to waste away.

When she was about eighteen her confessor taught Lydwine how to meditate on the Passion of Christ. She found this very difficult at first, but with persevering effort she acquired great recollection and soon began to feel happiness in her pains, recognising in them God's will and her special vocation. At the time she was receiving Communion twice a year.

From the age of twenty Lydwine was confined to bed, where she remained until her death at the age of fifty-three. She ate almost nothing except for an occasional piece of apple, a little bread, some milk or wine, a little sugar or grapes. When her body could no longer tolerate even these, she drank only a little water from the Meuse River each week and she survived on the Eucharist. Another of her maladies was that for long periods of time she was completely unable to sleep.

Lydwine had three large open wounds on her body and maggots began to eat into her rotting flesh. The maggots came out of the wound on her stomach and so a plaster of fresh wheat and honey was placed over the wound so that the maggots would feed on it rather than on her. The smell given off was surprisingly sweet. At around the age of thirty-two Lydwine vomited small pieces of organs, including bits of her lungs, liver and intestines. During her last years she could not move her limbs except for her head and left arm, and she always lay on her back.

As if this weren't enough, Lydwine also had intense headaches, toothaches, fevers and dropsy. She could hardly speak because of a cleft in her lower lip and chin. She could not see out of her right eye and her left eye was so weak that it was painful for her to see any light, requiring her to remain in darkness all the time. She accepted all her ailments with great love for God and offered them up for the conversion of sinners and for the souls in purgatory.

Around the age of twenty-five she began to experience ecstasies which continued until her death. She was taken in spirit to purgatory where she saw the suffering of souls, including some of her friends, and she was also given visions of hell and heaven. At around forty she was happy to be able to receive Communion several times a week.

In April, 1433, God finally ended her suffering and took her to heaven. She was canonised by Pope Leo XIII in 1890 and her body lies in the Basilica of St Lydwine in Schiedam.

879 Thomas à Kempis

I have been reading and enjoying Thomas à Kempis' book The Imitation of Christ but don't know anything about the writer. Can you tell me something about him? Is he a saint?

The name Thomas à Kempis means Thomas from Kempen, a town in Rhineland in western Germany. Thomas was born in Kempen around

1380 but spent most of his life in the Netherlands, where he died in 1471. He is best known for *The Imitation of Christ*, one of the most popular classics of spiritual literature, but he wrote a good number of other works.

Thomas' father Johann was a blacksmith and his mother, Gertrud, a schoolmistress. It seems they had two children: Johann and Thomas, who was born some fourteen years later. In 1392 Thomas followed his brother to Deventer in the Netherlands to attend the famous Latin school located there.

There he met the Brothers of the Common Life, a religious community who were followers of the spiritual movement known as *Devotio Moderna*, or Modern Devotion. The movement began in the Netherlands with Geert Groote (1340-1384), who founded the Brothers and the Sisters of the Common Life. It emphasised spiritual renewal through such practices as humility, obedience, and simplicity of life. The members took no vows but lived poverty, chastity and obedience in keeping with their state of life, usually living in their own homes. They earned their living through their work and contributed to a common fund at the disposal of the superior. *The Imitation of Christ* is a classic expression of their spirituality.

When Thomas arrived in Deventer he found that his brother Johann had left two years earlier with five other Brothers of the Common Life to found a new congregation of Canons Regular at Windesheim, near Zwolle in the Netherlands. While the Brothers and Sisters lived in the world, the Canons Regular were a monastic community. Both practised the Devotio Moderna. In Deventer Thomas was taken in by Florentius Radewyn, one of the founders of the Brothers of the Common Life, and he joined the Brothers himself.

Thomas was known throughout his life for his neatness and skill in transcribing manuscripts, among them numerous treatises of the Fathers of the Church and of St Bernard. Especially noteworthy were his four large volumes of the whole Bible, which are still in existence. He also produced a missal for the use of his community.

After completing his studies in humanities in Deventer, in the autumn of 1399 Thomas left for Windesheim to join the Canons Regular, where his brother Johann was then prior. The house had been established only the previous year and there were no buildings with a proper cloister, no garden, no benefactors and no funds. Over the next eight years Johann would build the priory and commence building the church. Given the circumstances of the fledgling foundation, Thomas did not become a novice until 1406, when the cloister was completed, and he was not ordained a priest until 1413, when the church was consecrated. He chronicled the history of the priory until shortly before his death.

Over the following years Thomas was twice elected subprior and once procurator, this latter office in view of his love for the poor. After some time he was relieved of the job in order to devote himself to literary work and contemplation. Among the duties of the subprior was to train the young religious, and most of his minor treatises were written for that purpose, especially his "Sermons to the Novices Regular". Thomas frequently preached in the church attached to the priory and two volumes of these sermons are extant: "Prayers and Meditations on the Life of Christ" and "The Incarnation and Life of Our Lord". Among his other writings are biographies of Geert Groote and St Lydwine of Schiedam.

Thomas was known as kind and affable towards all, especially the sorrowful and afflicted. His favourite occupations were reading, writing and prayer. He showed little interest in the affairs of the world but was eloquent when speaking about God and the soul. His body now lies in St Michael's Church in Zwolle, with a magnificent monument erected in 1897 from contributions from all over the world. Thomas à Kempis is not a canonised saint.

880 St Nicholas of Flüe

In paragraph 226 of the Catechism of the Catholic Church there is a prayer attributed to St Nicholas of Flüe. I had never heard of him. Who was he?

The prayer you mention is very beautiful: "My Lord and my God, take from me everything that distances me from you. My Lord and my

God, give me everything that brings me closer to you. My Lord and my God, detach me from myself to give my all to you."

St Nicholas of Flüe is undoubtedly little known in most of the world, but he is well known in Switzerland, where he lived and died. Indeed, he is the patron saint of the country and of the Swiss Guards.

St Nicholas was born in 1417 in Flüeli, near Sachseln, in the Swiss canton of Obwalden. He was the oldest son of wealthy parents. In 1439, at the age of 21, he enrolled in the army and fought in the war against the canton of Zurich waged by the rest of the Swiss confederacy, distinguishing himself as a soldier. He took up arms again in the so-called Thurgau war against Archduke Sigismund of Austria in 1460. It was thanks to his influence that a convent of Dominican nuns in Katharinental escaped destruction by the Swiss confederates when many Austrians fled to it after the capture of Diessenhofen.

At around the age of 30 Nicholas married Dorothea Wyss, the daughter of a farmer. They farmed in the municipality of Flüeli, in the foothills of the Alps, and had ten children. At the same time he continued to serve in the army until the age of 37, rising to the rank of captain. There is a tradition that he fought with a sword in one hand and a rosary in the other.

After leaving the army he became a councillor for his canton and then, in 1459, he was made a magistrate, serving for nine years in that role. Several times he declined an opportunity to serve as the governor of his canton. He was highly respected in his civic life and service to his country.

After receiving a vision of a horse pulling a plough and eating a lily, he was led to understand that the horse in some way symbolised the cares of his worldly life, which were swallowing up his spiritual life, symbolised by the lily, a symbol of purity. He then decided to devote himself entirely to the contemplative life. In 1467, at the age of 50, with the consent of his wife and children, he embraced the life of a hermit, living in a little cell near Ranft and giving up any aspirations to political activity. There he built a chapel with his own funds and engaged a priest to celebrate Mass for him each day.

Nicholas continued to have visions in his prayer and he was renowned for his holiness and wisdom. He became a spiritual guide to many civic leaders and high-ranking persons, as well as simple men and women who sought his advice. His reputation was such that people from all over Europe went to seek his counsel. To all he was known simply as "Bruder Klaus", Brother Klaus.

In 1470 Pope Paul II granted an indulgence to the chapel at Ranft, which became a place of pilgrimage for many, since it lay on the route of the Way of St James to Santiago de Compostela in northwest Spain.

Through his counsel and success in bringing about the inclusion of Fribourg and Soleure in the Swiss Confederation in 1481, he helped prevent the eruption of a civil war between the rural and urban cantons of the Confederation, which were meeting at the Diet of Stans. Despite having had little formal education, he is honoured by Protestants and Catholics alike for contributing to permanent national unity in Switzerland. Letters of thanksgiving to him from Berne and Soleure still survive. For his efforts at Stans he is regarded in Switzerland as one of the earliest champions of arbitration as a method for resolving disputes.

St Nicholas died on 21 March 1487, at the age of 70, surrounded by his wife and children. He was beatified in 1669, after which the municipality of Sachseln built a church in his honour. His body was interred there. He was canonised in 1947 by Pope Pius XII. His feast day is 21 March, except in Switzerland and Germany, where it is 25 September.

As a layman with family responsibilities who took his civic duties seriously, St Nicholas of Flüe is a model of manhood and fatherhood, as well as of involvement in civic life.

881 St Camillus de Lellis

Our parish priest belongs to the Camillians, who are chaplains in the nearby hospital, and I am interested in knowing something of their founder, St Camillus. I have heard that he had had a problem with gambling. Is this true?

St Camillus was one of the many great saints and founders of religious institutes in the sixteenth century. And yes, he had a problem with gambling.

St Camillus was born in Bucchianico, Italy, in 1550. His mother Camilla was nearly fifty years old when she gave birth to him, and his father, Giovanni de Lellis, was an army officer. Camillus had his father's strong temper, and his mother, due to her age and retiring nature, felt unable to control him as he grew up. She died when he was only twelve. Camillus was taken in by relatives and, at the age of thirteen, began to accompany his father from one military camp to another. At sixteen he joined his father in the Venetian army and fought in a war against the Turks.

When his regiment was disbanded in 1575, he entered Rome's San Giacomo degli Incurabili Hospital for the treatment of injuries to his leg suffered while in the army. He was eventually sent away because of his bad temper and quarrelsome attitude. At that time he had already gambled away all his possessions and he took work as a labourer in the Capuchin friary in Manfredonia. One of the friars there saw his better side and this helped him have a religious conversion in 1575. He entered the novitiate of the Capuchins but because his leg wound was declared incurable by the doctors, he was denied admission to the Order.

Camillus then returned to St Giacomo Hospital in Rome and worked there as a caregiver to pay for his stay, eventually becoming superintendent. He lived a very ascetical life, doing many penances, including wearing a hairshirt. He took as his spiritual director St Philip Neri, the founder of the Oratorians. Seeing the poor attention the sick received in the hospital, he invited a group of pious men to help care for them. This led him in due course to establish a religious community for this purpose and to seek ordination as a priest. St Philip gave his approval and Camillus was ordained a priest on Pentecost Sunday, 1584, at the age of thirty-four by Lord Thomas Goldwell, the last surviving Catholic bishop of Great Britain.

St Camillus established the Order of Clerks Regular, Ministers of the Infirm (MI are their initials), better known as the Camillians. In 1585 his friends hired a large house for the group, where he taught them the basics of health care. In 1586 Pope Sixtus V gave the group formal recognition as a Congregation and assigned them the church of St Mary Magdalene in Rome, which they look after to this day. They wore a large red cross on their soutanes.

In 1588 St Camillus, along with twelve companions, founded a new house in Naples. When some galleys with men suffering from the plague were refused entry into the harbour there, his men went on board and attended to them, two of them dying of the plague as a result. St Camillus showed similar charity in Rome, when a plague killed great numbers, and again when the city suffered from a great famine. The Camillians began work in Milan in 1594.

In 1591 Pope Gregory XV raised the Congregation to the status of an Order, equivalent to the Mendicant Orders like the Franciscans, Dominicans and Carmelites, and they took a fourth vow to serve the sick, even with danger to their own life. Thoughout his life, St Camillus' wounds caused him great suffering, but he allowed no one to wait on him and, when he could no longer walk, he would crawl to attend to the sick. When he resigned as Superior General in 1607, communities of the Camillians had been established all over Italy and in Hungary.

In the course of an inspection of the hospitals of the Order in Italy, he fell ill and died in Rome on 14 July 1614. His body was laid to rest in the church of St Mary Magdalene. St Camillus was beatified by Pope Benedict XIV in 1742 and canonised by him in 1746. In 1886

Pope Leo XIII proclaimed him patron saint of all hospitals and of the sick. In 1930 Pope Pius XI named him co-patron, along with St John of God, of nurses and nursing associations, and he is also invoked against the habit of gambling. His feast is celebrated as an optional memorial on July 14, the day of his death.

882 St Philip Neri

In a recent visit to Brisbane I met some of the priests of the Oratory founded by St Philip Neri. Can you tell me something about the saint and the origins of the Oratory?

St Philip was born in Florence, Italy, on 21 July 1515, one of the four children of Francesco and Lucrezia di Neri. His father was a lawyer and his mother came from a noble family. Already from a very young age he was known for his cheerfulness and obedience, becoming known as "good little Phil". He received his early education from the Dominican friars in Florence.

When he was eighteen, Philip was sent to live with a wealthy relative in San Germano, near Naples, to work in and possibly inherit the family business. However, soon after his arrival he had a mystical vision which radically changed his life. He lost all interest in engaging in business and felt a call to live a simple life in the service of the Church.

Philip then went to Rome, where he tutored the sons of a family from Florence, helping them grow in virtue and faith. During his first two years in Rome, Philip lived an ascetical life, dedicated to prayer and eating only small meals of bread, water and a few vegetables.

In 1535 he began studying theology and philosophy and, although he was considered a promising scholar, after three years of study he gave up all thought of priestly ordination. He then went to help the poor people of Rome and to evangelise the city. He encouraged his listeners to consider the Christian way of life and to practise good deeds, taking them to hospitals to care for the sick, or to church to pray and develop a relationship with Jesus Christ. At night he would go to pray in the church or in the catacombs along the Appian Way.

On the eve of Pentecost in 1544, Philip saw what appeared to be a globe of fire, which entered his mouth and made him feel as if his heart was dilating. It filled him with such love for God that he screamed out, "Enough, enough, Lord, I can't bear any more." In 1548, with the help of his confessor, he founded the Confraternity of the Most Holy Trinity, a group of laymen dedicated to the service of poor pilgrims in Rome and of the sick in their convalescence.

With his appealing nature, Philip made friends at all levels of society, among them St Ignatius of Loyola, Pope St Pius V and St Charles Borromeo. Even though at the age of thirty-four he had already achieved a great deal, his confessor, Fr Persiano Rossa, was determined that he would be more effective if he were ordained a priest. Following this advice and after finishing his studies, he was ordained on 23 May 1551. After that he went to live with Fr Rossa and other priests at the hospital of San Girolamo, where he carried on his mission, spending long hours in the confessional and helping people of all ages to lead a better life.

They built a large hall, the oratory, at San Girolamo for the growing number of pilgrims, leading them in prayer, hymns, Scripture readings and giving them talks. Soon this group of priests were called the Oratorians, because they would ring a bell to call the faithful to the oratory. A few years later the Congregation of the Priests of the Oratory was founded, with priests dedicating themselves to help others deepen their faith. They lived a simple rule, sharing a common table and performing spiritual exercises together. They did not take vows or renounce their property. The Congregation was officially approved by Pope Gregory XIII in 1575.

The Congregation was given the church of Santa Maria in Vallicella, but Fr Philip found it necessary to demolish it and build a larger one. Donations came from all over, including from St Charles Borromeo and Pope Gregory. In 1577 the Chiesa Nuova, the New Church, was ready for the Oratorians to move there, although Fr Philip remained at San Girolamo for another seven years. Fr Philip became a trusted advisor to popes, kings and cardinals as well as to the poor. He soon earned the title of "Apostle of Rome."

On the feast of Corpus Christi, 25 May 1595, Fr Philip became ill and he realised that his life was ending. He spent the day hearing confessions and receiving visitors and, before going to bed, he said, "Last of all, we must die." Around midnight he suffered a haemorrhage and died. He was eighty years old. His body lies in the Chiesa Nuova, where the Oratorians still serve, and he was canonised by Pope Gregory XV in 1622. His feast is celebrated on May 26.

883 St Joseph Calasanz

I recently attended a weekday Mass in honour of St Joseph Calasanz. I know nothing of him. Who was he?

St Joseph Calasanz is certainly a lesser known saint but nonetheless an important one. He was born into a noble family in 1557 at the castle of Calasanz, near Peralta de la Sal, in Aragon, Spain, the youngest of eight children. His father was a minor nobleman and mayor of the town. Joseph was educated first at home and then in the elementary school of Peralta. When he was twelve his parents sent him for classical studies to a college in Estadilla run by the friars of the Trinitarian Order. While there, at the age of fourteen, he felt the call to the priesthood, although his parents were not happy with his decision.

After secondary school Joseph studied philosophy and law in university, obtaining a Doctorate in Law. Then came studies of theology at two universities. His mother and brother having died, his father wanted him to marry and look after the family, but a serious illness in 1582 brought Joseph to the point of death, after which his father relented. Joseph was ordained a priest in 1583 and served in important posts in several dioceses.

In 1592, at the age of 35, St Joseph moved to Rome, where he spent most of his remaining fifty-six years. There he found a protector in

Cardinal Colonna, who appointed him his theologian and put him in charge of the spiritual direction of his staff. He joined the Confraternity of Christian Doctrine and gathered boys from the streets to bring them to school. In 1597, with the help of two other priests, he opened the first free public school in Europe.

After a devastating flood on Christmas Day in 1598 which caused thousands of deaths and left many people homeless and without food, St Joseph dedicated himself to helping the poor and assisting in the recovery. In 1600 he opened his "Pious School" in the centre of Rome to provide free education for all, at a time when only the children of the elite received schooling. In a short time there were some one thousand students in his care.

In 1602 St Joseph rented a house at Sant'Andrea della Valle in Rome and commenced community life with his assistants, laying the foundation for what was to be the Order of the Pious Schools. In 1617 Pope Paul V approved the new order, the first religious institute dedicated exclusively to the education of youth. St Joseph and fourteen other priests received the habit as the first members of the institute on 25 March 1617.

In 1621 Pope Gregory XV approved the Order of Poor Clerics Regular of the Mother of God of the Pious Schools as a religious order with solemn vows. It is more commonly known as the Piarists. In addition to the traditional vows of poverty, chastity and obedience, the Piarists take a fourth vow to dedicate their lives to the education of youth.

In 1610 St Joseph wrote a document setting out the fundamental principles of his educational philosophy, including regulations for teachers and students. In 1616, at his initiative, the first public and free school was opened in Frascati, outside of Rome, and in the following years Pious Schools were established all over Europe.

St Joseph accepted not only the poor but also Jews and Protestants into his schools. Such was his fame that even the Ottoman Empire asked him to establish schools in their territory, something he could not do for lack of teachers. He was concerned not only with the minds of his students but also with their physical education and health. The students were taught to read Latin and the vernacular, and great emphasis was placed on mathematics and science.

But St Joseph's main concern was for the moral and religious education of the students, considering education as the best way to change society. He was the first educator to advocate the preventive method of anticipating and preventing mischievous behaviour, rather than punishing it when it had already taken place. He favoured the mildest punishment possible. St John Bosco would later take up this method.

St Joseph died on 25 August 1648 at the age of 90. He was beatified in 1748 and canonised in 1767. His feast day is August 25, the day of his death. In 1948 Pope Pius XII declared him "Universal Patron of all Christian popular schools in the world."

884 St Peter Claver

I am interested in current efforts to abolish slavery in its various forms and heard that St Peter Claver might be someone to whom to entrust this work. What did he do that would make this appropriate?

St Peter Claver would be a great saint to whom to entrust efforts to abolish slavery, since he dedicated most of his life to helping slaves. He was born Pedro Claver y Corberó in 1580 in Verdú, a village in the region of Catalonia, Spain. His parents, devout Catholics, were farmers. Peter went on to study at the University of Barcelona, where he was known for his intelligence and piety. After two years of study there he wrote in his notebook: "I must dedicate myself to the service of God until death, on the understanding that I am like a slave."

After completing his university studies, Peter entered the Society of Jesus, the Jesuits, in Tarragona at the age of twenty. Upon completing the novitiate, he went to study philosophy in Palma, on the Mediterranean island of Mallorca. While there he came to know St Alphonsus Rodriguez, a lay brother known for his holiness and gift of prophecy. Rodriguez felt that God was calling Peter to spend his life in the Spanish colonies of the Americas and he urged him to accept that calling.

St Peter did volunteer to serve in the Spanish colonies and he arrived in Cartagena, Colombia, in 1610. Not yet a priest, he lived in Jesuit houses in Tunja and Bogotá while completing his six years of theology. During those years he became deeply disturbed on learning of the harsh treatment given to the black slaves arriving from Africa.

At that time the slave trade had been established in the Americas for about a century, bringing Africans from Angola and the Congo to work in mines and on plantations. Cartagena was a hub where some ten thousand slaves arrived each year. The conditions on the ships were so bad that an estimated one third died in transit. Although the slave trade had been condemned by Popes Paul III and Urban VIII, it was a lucrative business and it continued to flourish.

St Peter set out to minister to the slaves, boarding the ships and entering the filthy holds to treat the frightened slaves, who had managed to survive several months at sea in horrendous, crowded conditions. When the slaves were taken from the ships to penned yards to be scrutinised by crowds of buyers, St Peter would take them food and medicine and treat them with great kindness. With the help of African interpreters and catechists, he would give them basic instructions in the faith. When St Peter was solemnly professed in 1622, he signed his final profession document in Latin, "Peter Claver, ever the servant [or slave] of the Africans".

During the season when the ships did not arrive, St Peter would go through the countryside where the slaves worked, giving them spiritual consolation, urging their masters to treat them humanely and ensuring that their Christian and human rights were respected. During those country missions he would, as far as possible, avoid the hospitality of planters and overseers and lodge instead with the slaves in their own quarters.

During his forty years of ministry to the slaves, it is estimated that he personally catechised and baptised some 300,000 slaves. He worked for the abolition of slavery, and through his work the condition of the slaves slowly improved.

St Peter's work went beyond caring for the slaves themselves. He would preach in the city square and minister to well-to-do members of society as well as sailors, traders, visitors and condemned criminals, often preparing them for death. He was a frequent visitor to the hospitals.

Four years of ill health prevented him from leaving his room, where he was largely neglected and badly treated, and he finally died on 8 September 1654. Such was his fame of sanctity that people took away from his room anything that might serve as a relic.

St Peter Claver was canonised in 1888 by Pope Leo XIII, along with St Alphonsus Rodriguez. On that occasion Pope Leo said, "No life, except the life of Christ, has moved me as deeply as that of Peter Claver." In 1896 Pope Leo declared him the patron of missionary work among African peoples.

885 St Joseph of Cupertino

A friend said St Joseph Cupertino was famous for flying, without an airplane of course. I found that hard to believe. Is this true and, in any case, who was this saint?

It is true that St Joseph of Cupertino had a reputation for a certain type of "flying". But first, let us see who this saint was and when he lived.

St Joseph was born in 1603 at Cupertino in the Region of Apulia, then in the Kingdom of Naples, Italy. His father died before Joseph was born and the family home was seized to pay off the large debts he had left. As a result, Joseph's mother gave birth to him in a stable.

When he was still a child, Joseph began to experience visions while in ecstasy and these continued throughout his life. Unfortunately, they made him an object of scorn. Soon his uncle, who was looking after him, apprenticed him to a shoemaker. Feeling drawn to the religious life, in 1620 he applied to the Conventual Franciscan friars but was rejected due to his lack of education. He then applied to the Capuchin friars in Martino, near Taranto, and was accepted in 1620 as a lay brother. But since his frequent ecstasies and a certain clumsiness made him unfit for the duties required of him, he was dismissed.

He then returned home, where his family treated him with scorn. He pleaded with the Conventual friars near Cupertino to be allowed to work in their stables. They accepted this and, after several years working there, he so impressed the friars with his devotion and simplicity of life that they admitted him to the Order. After the necessary studies, with which he struggled, he was ordained a priest on 28 March 1628. After ordination he was sent to the friary at the shrine of Madonna delle Grazie in Gravina, Puglia.

From then on, his ecstasies increased and there are more than seventy accounts of people seeing him levitate, or rise up inexplicably from the floor, while participating in the Mass or praying the Divine Office with the community. Hence his reputation for "flying". In his ecstasies he would be caught up in talking with God and he fell so deeply in love with him that everything he saw only drew him into deeper union. He said that all the troubles of this world were nothing but the "play battles" children have with their popguns. St Joseph also became famous for his many miracles.

These events led to his widespread reputation for holiness among the people of the region and further afield. Unfortunately, in his community he was deemed disruptive, and so he was confined to a small cell and forbidden to join in any public gatherings. This only made him all the happier, since it gave him more time to be alone with God.

People flocked to him in great numbers, seeking help and advice in the confessional, and he helped many to live a truly devout Christian life. St Joseph was consecrated to the Blessed Virgin Mary and he promoted devotion to her among all sorts of people as a path to a deeper Christian life and love for Jesus Christ.

Since levitation at that time was widely believed to be associated with witchcraft, St Joseph was denounced to the Inquisition. At their command he was transferred from one Franciscan friary in the region to another for observation. He first went to Assisi (1639-1653), then briefly to Pietrarubbia and finally to Fossombrone, where he lived under the supervision of the Capuchin friars from 1653 to 1657.

Finally, in July 1657, St Joseph was allowed to return to the Conventual community of Osimo, where he died on 18 September 1663. His last thirty-five years were lived in severe asceticism, usually consisting in eating solid food only twice a week and adding bitter powders to his meals.

He was beatified in 1753 and canonised in 1767. St Joseph is the patron saint of air travellers, pilots and those with learning difficulties.

886 St Kateri Tekakwitha

I have a friend named Kateri, who says she is named after an American Indian saint. I had never heard of this saint. Who was she?

St Kateri is the first native North American to be recognised as a saint by the Church. She was of the Mohawk tribe and was born around 1656 in the village of Ossernenon, on the Mohawk River in northeastern New York state. Her father Kenneronkwa was a Mohawk chief and her mother Kahenta, of the Algonquin tribe, was baptised a Catholic and educated in the faith by French missionaries.

Kateri was the first of the couple's two children and she was followed by a brother. When she was around four, both of her parents and her baby brother died of smallpox and Kateri was left with scars on her face and impaired eyesight. After that she often covered much of her face with a blanket to hide the scars. Kateri was taken in by her father's sister and her husband, a Mohawk chief from the nearby village of Caughnawaga.

When she was eleven, she met the Jesuit missionaries who had come to the village, but her adoptive uncle objected because he didn't want her to convert to Christianity. Kateri was a modest girl who avoided social gatherings. She became skilled at the traditional women's arts of making clothing and belts from animal skins, weaving mats and baskets from reeds and grasses, and preparing food from game and crops. As was the custom, at the age of thirteen she was pressured to marry, but she refused.

When she was seventeen, Kateri's adoptive parents once again tried to arrange for her to marry a young Mohawk man, but again she refused and fled into a nearby field. They subjected her to ridicule, threats and harsh workloads, but she continued to resist, and at last they gave up.

In the spring of 1674, at the age of eighteen, Kateri met the Jesuit priest Jacques de Lamberville, who was visiting the village, and told him of her desire to become a Catholic. After that she began studying the catechism with him. Two years later, on Easter Sunday, 18 April 1676, she was baptised, taking the name Kateri, the Mohawk form of Catherine, after St Catherine of Siena. She remained in Caughnawaga for another six months, but some of the Mohawks opposed her conversion and accused her of sorcery. Fr de Lamberville then suggested that she go to the Jesuit mission of Kahnawake, on the St Lawrence River south of Montreal, where other native converts had gathered. She joined them in 1677 and spent the rest of her short life there.

Kateri continued to learn more about Christianity, helped by her mentor Anastasia, and she decided to dedicate herself completely to Christ in celibacy. One of the Jesuit priests recorded that she said: "I have deliberated enough. For a long time, my decision on what I will do has been made. I have consecrated myself entirely to Jesus, son of Mary, I have chosen him for a husband, and he alone will take me for a wife."

Kateri lived a holy, austere, life. She put thorns on her sleeping mat and lay on them, while praying for her relatives' conversion and forgiveness. That was her way of living a custom among some Native Americans of piercing themselves with thorns in thanksgiving for some benefit or as an offering for oneself or others' needs. She ate little and was said to add unpleasant tastes to her food. Having seen the terrible burns inflicted on prisoners, she burned herself.

In Holy Week of 1680, Kateri's health began to fail. When it became clear that she was dying, villagers gathered around her and she was given the last rites. She died on Wednesday of Holy Week, 17 April 1680, at the age of twenty-four. Her final words were "Jesus, Mary, I love you." Within some fifteen minutes of her death, the scars on her face had disappeared and her skin became smooth and beautiful. In the weeks after her death, she appeared to three different people, among them her mentor Anastasia and one of the priests. A chapel was built near her gravesite and by 1684 people were making pilgrimages to honour her there.

The American bishops initiated her cause of canonisation at the Third Plenary Council in Baltimore in 1885. After the approval of a miracle attributed to her intercession, Kateri was beatified by Pope St John Paul II in 1980, and she was canonised by Pope Benedict XVI in 2012.

887 St Elizabeth Ann Seton

An American friend recently told me that that day was the feast of St Elizabeth Ann Seton, an American saint. I had never heard of her. Can you tell me something about her?

St Elizabeth Ann Seton was the first American-born person to be canonised a saint. She was born on 28 August 1774, the second child of a prominent New York surgeon, Dr Richard Bayley, and his wife Catherine. Her parents' families were among the earliest European settlers in the New York area.

Dr Bayley was the Chief Health Officer for the port of New York and he looked after the immigrants disembarking from ships onto Staten Island. He later became professor of anatomy at Columbia College. His parents were of French Huguenot and English descent. His wife Catherine was the daughter of a Church of England priest, who was the rector of St Andrew's Church on Staten Island. Elizabeth was raised in what would later become the Episcopal Church.

When Elizabeth was only three her mother died, possibly from complications arising from the birth of her daughter Catherine, who herself died the following year. Elizabeth's father then married Charlotte Amelia Barclay, a member of the Jacobus Roosevelt family. Charlotte often took Elizabeth with her when she visited the poor to give them food and other necessary items. The new couple had five children, but the marriage ended in separation, leaving Elizabeth once again bereft at the loss of a mother. Elizabeth was fluent in French, was an accomplished musician and horsewoman, and she had deep religious aspirations, with a great love for the Bible.

In 1794 at the age of 19, she married William Seton, a wealthy businessman in the import business. They moved into a fashionable residence on Wall Street and attended Trinity Episcopal Church. Elizabeth was a devout communicant and had a spiritual director. She continued her stepmother's ministry of charity, looking after the sick and dying among her family, friends and neighbours. When her husband's father died, the couple took in William's six younger siblings, in addition to their own five children.

Through most of their married life, William suffered from tuberculosis and in 1803 his doctors sent him to Italy for the warmer climate. Elizabeth and their eldest daughter Anna Maria accompanied him but, unfortunately, he died there in December 1803. Elizabeth and Anna Maria were then taken in by William's Italian business partners, who introduced them to the Catholic faith. Returning to New York, Elizabeth was received into the Catholic Church in 1805. A year later she was confirmed by Bishop John Carroll, the only Catholic bishop in the country. She had a deep devotion to the Eucharist, Sacred Scripture, and the Virgin Mary, whom she regarded as her mother.

Then, at the invitation of the French Sulpician priest, Fr William Dubourg SS, Elizabeth established St Joseph's Academy and Free School, dedicated to the education of Catholic girls, in Emmitsburg, Maryland. It was the first free Catholic school in America and marked the beginning of the Catholic parochial school system in that country.

Elizabeth also established there a religious community dedicated to caring for the children of the poor, the first congregation of religious sisters founded in the United States. It was called the Sisters of Charity of St Joseph and it adopted the rule of the Daughters of Charity, founded in France by St Vincent de Paul and St Louise de Marillac. Taking her vows in 1809, Mother Elizabeth spent the rest of her life leading and developing the new congregation.

Having suffered for some time from tuberculosis, she died on 4 January 1821 at the young age of 46. Her body lies in the National Shrine of St Elizabeth Ann Seton in Emmitsburg.

Elizabeth was beatified by Pope St John XXIII in 1963 and canonised on 14 September 1975 by Pope St Paul VI. In his homily Pope Paul said: "Elizabeth Ann Seton is a saint. St Elizabeth Ann Seton is an American. All of us say this with special joy, and with the intention of honouring the land and the nation from which she sprang forth as the first flower in the calendar of the saints." Her feast day is January 4, the day of her death.

888 Blessed Anne Catherine Emmerich

I have read some of the revelations of Blessed Anne Catherine Emmerich and have liked them very much. Can you tell me something about who she was, and whether her revelations are trustworthy?

Anne Catherine, whose German name is Anna Katharina, was born in Flamschen, in Westphalia, Germany, on 8 September 1774. She was was one of ten children of very poor, pious farmers. Her schooling was brief and she felt drawn to prayer at an early age. She said that as a child she had visions in which she talked with Jesus on familiar terms, and she thought all children enjoyed these favours. At the age of twelve she began to work for three years on a large farm, followed by work as a seamstress. She applied for admission to several convents but was rejected because she could not afford a dowry. Eventually, in 1802 she was accepted by the Augustinian nuns in Dülmen at the age of 28.

There she was content to be regarded as the lowest in the house. Although, beginning in 1811 she was often ill and in great pain, she carried out her duties cheerfully and faithfully, being known for her strict observance of the rule. During this time, she sometimes had ecstasies in church, in her cell or at work. When the convent was suppressed by the King of Westphalia in 1812, she took refuge in the house of a poor widow.

When the sick and the poor went to visit the "bright little sister", Anne Catherine was blessed with a mysterious knowledge which enabled her to know their diseases and to suggest remedies that always helped them. She was quick and lively and easily moved to great sympathy for the sufferings of others. She prayed and suffered much for the souls in purgatory, whom she often saw, and for the salvation of sinners, whose miseries were known to her even when far away. She had numerous revelations of the life of Our Lord and Our Lady.

Early in 1813 she became ill and bedridden. She began to have the marks of the stigmata, the wounds of Christ, on her body, including the marks of the thorns. She also had a cross on her breastbone. The stigmata became widely known and many people sought to visit her. Although she tried to hide the stigmata, the local bishop ordered an investigation into them. It was conducted by the Vicar General and three physicians, and was very thorough in order to avoid any pretext for ridicule on the part of the enemies of the Church. In the end, the investigators were convinced of the sanctity of Anne Catherine and of the genuineness of the stigmata.

At the end of 1818, God granted her earnest prayer to be relieved of the stigmata. The periodic bleeding of her hands and feet stopped and the wounds closed, although other wounds remained. On Good Friday each year they would all reopen.

When the famous poet Clemens Brentano went to visit her in 1819, she recognised him and told him he had been pointed out to her as the one who would fulfil God's command to write down for the good of souls the revelations she had received. Over the next five years he filled many notebooks with the main points, and later read out to her what he had written, changing it until she was completely satisfied. In 1833, he published the first volume, *The Dolorous Passion of Our Lord Jesus Christ*. He prepared for publication *The Life of the Blessed Virgin Mary*, but he died in 1842 and the book was published posthumously in 1852.

During the summer of 1823 Anne Catherine began to grow ever weaker and she finally passed away on 9 February 1824 at the age of 49. In February 1975 her remains were transferred to a beautiful marble tomb in the Holy Cross Church in Dülmen. Her cause of beatification was presented to the Vatican in 1892, and she was beatified by Pope St John Paul II in 2004.

It was made clear at the time that the beatification was based on the sanctity of her life, not on the authenticity of her writings. Nonetheless, some of the revelations in them, like those which led to the discovery of the house of Our Lady in Ephesus and the description of Mary's wedding ring in Perugia, are truly extraordinary. As always, we should not read these private revelations as if they were historical fact, as we do the scriptures. But they are at least plausible descriptions of the events they narrate. And clearly, many people have benefitted from reading them.

889 St Dominic Savio

Some time ago you wrote about some young saints. A friend recently mentioned St Dominic Savio, another young saint. Can you tell me when he lived and what he is known for?

When it comes to young saints, St Dominic Savio must certainly be ranked among them, for he died at the age of only fourteen. Dominic was born in 1842 in the Italian village of Riva in the Piedmont region of northern Italy, one of ten children of Carlo and Brigitta Savio. His father was a blacksmith and his mother a seamstress. They were poor, hardworking and pious, and they gave their children a good Christian upbringing. When he was only four, Dominic was able to pray by himself. He attended Mass regularly with his mother and, if he arrived for Mass before the church was opened in the morning, he would kneel on the ground, even in the mud or snow, to pray.

In school, Dominic was known for being very intelligent and hardworking. At the age of five he began to serve Mass and he endeavoured to attend Mass everyday as well as to go to confession regularly. Even though at that time the customary age for children to receive their first Communion was twelve, the parish priest allowed Dominic to do so when he was only seven, since he knew the catechism and he understood the significance of the Eucharist. Later he would say of that day that it was "the happiest and most wonderful day of my life."

On the day of his first Communion Dominic made some promises, which he wrote down in a little book and re-read many times. His promises were: to go to confession often and to go to Holy Communion as often as his confessor allowed, to sanctify Sundays and feast days in a special way, to have Jesus and Mary as his friends, and to choose death rather than sin.

For secondary education Dominic went to the County School at Castelnuovo d'Asti, five kilometres from his home at Murialdo, where his parents moved when he was two. There he caught the attention of Fr Giuseppe Cugliero, one of his teachers, who introduced him to St John Bosco in October 1854. Don Bosco found Dominic eager to go to Turin with him, as he wanted to study for the priesthood.

In Turin, at the Oratory of St Francis de Sales, Dominic placed himself under the guidance of Don Bosco. He studied hard and would happily listen to talks and sermons, asking for clarification of any points that were not clear to him. When the dogma of the Immaculate

Conception was defined by Pope Pius IX in 1854, Dominic renewed his First Communion promises at the altar of Mary in the Oratory. Don Bosco says that from that moment on, Dominic's efforts to seek holiness were so obvious that Don Bosco recorded them for future reference.

In his effort to grow in holiness Dominic made his bed uncomfortable with little stones and pieces of wood, he slept with a thin blanket in winter, wore a hair shirt and fasted on bread and water. His superiors forbade him to do some of these penances, as they would affect his health. Don Bosco told him that the best penance would be to perform his daily duties with perfection and humility, and that obedience was the greatest sacrifice.

Moved by the declaration of the dogma of the Immaculate Conception, Dominic with some friends started the Sodality of Mary Immaculate, to obtain the help of Mary during life and at the time of death. Moreover, all the students under Don Bosco observed a monthly Exercise of a Happy Death, during which they went to confession and Communion as though they were the last ones of their life. At this time, Dominic already knew that he would die soon.

In the early months of 1857, Dominic developed a severe cough and Don Bosco thought it best that he go home to be treated there. On the morning of his departure, March 1, Dominic made the Exercise of a Happy Death with great devotion, saying that this would be the last time he did it. At home, his cough worsened, despite medical treatment. Certain that he was dying, Dominic asked for Confession, Communion and the Anointing of the Sick. He died on March 9, probably from pleurisy.

Don Bosco's biography of the saint was instrumental in spreading devotion to him. Dominic was beatified by Pope Pius XII in 1950 and canonised by him in 1954. At the time he was the youngest canonised saint who was not a martyr.

890 St Maria Goretti

I was interested to read your accounts of Saints Tarcisius and Dominic Savio, who were very young. Could you tell me something about St Maria Goretti, who was also very young? For example, is it true that her killer attended her canonisation ceremony?

Most people know the basic facts about St Maria Goretti – that she was killed at the age of eleven defending her purity – but a more thorough study reveals many fascinating details, including what happened to her killer in later life.

Maria Teresa Goretti was born on 16 October 1890, the third of seven children of Luigi and Assunta Goretti, a farming family from Corinaldo, in the Italian province of Ancona. When Maria was five, the family became so poor that they had to give up their farm and move away to work for other farmers. In 1896 they moved to Colle Gianturco, some eighty kilometres outside Rome, and in 1899 they moved again to Le Ferriere, near Latina in the province of Lazio. There they shared a house with the family of Giovanni Serenelli and their son Alessandro.

When Maria was just nine, her father became sick with malaria and died. While her mother and siblings worked in the fields, Maria would cook, sew, clean the house and look after her younger sister Teresa. On 5 July 1902, Maria was sitting on the outside steps of the house, sewing one of Alessandro's shirts and watching Teresa, while Alessandro was threshing beans in the barnyard. Knowing she was alone, Alessandro returned to the house and threatened to stab her with an awl if she did not give in to his sexual desires. She would not give in, and told him that what he wanted to do was a mortal sin and he would go to hell.

When he attacked her, she resisted bravely, screaming "No, it is a sin! God does not want it!" Alessandro first choked her but when she insisted she would rather die than give in to him, he stabbed her eleven times. She tried to reach the door, but he stopped her and stabbed her three more times before running away.

Teresa awoke with the commotion and started crying, and when her mother and Giovanni Serenelli came to check on her, they found Maria on the floor bleeding. She was taken to the hospital in Nettuno, where she underwent surgery without anaesthesia, but her injuries were very severe. When she woke up halfway through the surgery, one of those in the theatre said to her, "Maria, think of me in paradise." She looked at him and said, "Well, who knows which of us is going to be there first?" "You, Maria", he replied. "Then I will gladly think of you", she said.

In the presence of the Chief of Police, Maria told her mother that Alessandro had harassed her before, and had made two attempts to violate her. She had been afraid to reveal this earlier since he had threatened to kill her if she did. The following day, July 6, after forgiving Alessandro and saying that she wanted to have him with her in heaven, she died of her injuries.

Alessandro was arrested shortly after the attack, and was later tried and sentenced to thirty years in prison. He remained unrepentant until he had a dream in which Maria appeared to him and gave him some lilies, which burned in his hands. After that he was a changed man.

After his release, Alessandro visited Assunta, Maria's mother, and begged her forgiveness. Assunta forgave him and they attended Mass together the next day, receiving Holy Communion side by side. Alessandro reportedly prayed to Maria every day and called her "my little saint". He attended Maria's canonisation ceremony in St Peter's Square in 1950, along with Assunta and her four remaining children. Some 500,000 people attended the ceremony.

Alessandro later became a lay brother in the Order of Friars Minor Capuchin, working as a receptionist and gardener in the monastery until his death in 1970 at the age of 87.

St Maria's feast day is July 6, the day of her death, and her body lies in the Passionist Basilica of Nostra Signora delle Grazie e Santa Maria Goretti in Nettuno, south of Rome.

After she died, three of Maria's brothers reported that they had heard Maria speaking to them and giving them messages. Particularly interesting is the account of Mariano, who heard Maria telling him to remain in his trench when the rest of his unit charged the Germans in World War I. He did so and was the only survivor of the charge. He died in 1975 after raising a large family.

891 Pope St Paul VI

I know that Pope Paul VI was canonised in 2018. I was born during the pontificate of St John Paul II and don't know much about Paul VI. For what should he be remembered?

Before answering your question, let me give you a brief overview of his life.

Pope Paul VI was born Giovanni Battista Montini in 1897 in Concesio in the province of Brescia, Italy. His father Giorgio was a lawyer, journalist, director of Catholic Action and a member of the Italian parliament. His mother Giudetta was from a family of rural nobility. He had two brothers, one of whom was a physician and the other a lawyer and politician.

Giovanni Battista was ordained priest in 1920 in Brescia and in the same year completed his studies in Milan for a doctorate in Canon Law. He did further studies in Rome and in 1922, at the age of twenty-five, he began work in the Vatican's Secretariat of State. After a posting in the nunciature in Poland beginning in 1923, he returned to Rome where he held several positions in the Vatican, especially in the Secretariat of State, where he also served as a personal assistant to Pope Pius XII. During the Second World War he coordinated assistance to thousands of refugees.

In 1954 Pope Pius XII appointed him Archbishop of Milan and in 1958 Pope John XXIII made him a cardinal. Following the death from cancer of Pope John XXIII early in June 1963, Cardinal Montini was elected Pope later that month, taking the name Paul VI.

Pope Paul VI will be remembered for a number of very important acts that had great repercussions on the universal Church. The first was his decision to continue the Second Vatican Council, which had begun in 1962 under Pope John XXIII. When a Pope dies during an Ecumenical Council, his successor must decide whether to continue the Council or declare it concluded. Pope Paul VI chose the former and the result was the collection of documents produced by the Council, many of which have had great significance for the life of the Church. Pope Paul closed the Council on 8 December 1965.

After the Council ended, Pope Paul VI set in train the mechanism for the revision of the *Code of Canon Law*, which had been announced by Pope John XXIII. The previous Code was promulgated in 1917 and the new one would be based in great measure on the documents of the Council. The revision was completed after Pope Paul's death and came into effect in 1983.

In July 1968 Pope Paul VI gave the Church what was undoubtedly his most important and controversial document: the encyclical *Humanae vitae*. Echoing the constant tradition of the Church, as articulated by Pope Pius XI in the encyclical *Casti connubii* (1930), he declared that no form of contraception was acceptable as a means of avoiding pregnancy. He knew the encyclical would meet with a negative response from many but, after much prayer and with considerable courage, he repeated the traditional teaching of the Church. As expected, the encyclical was applauded by many but also criticised by many, both within and outside the Church.

In addition to *Humanae vitae* Pope Paul VI wrote six other encyclicals, the most important of which were *Ecclesiam suam* (1964) on the Church, *Mysterium fidei* (1965) on the Eucharist, *Populorum progressio* (1967) on social development and *Sacerdotalis caelibatus* (1967) on priestly celibacy.

Another important contribution of Paul VI was the establishment of the Synod of Bishops as a permanent advisory body to the Pope. The Synod is a periodic gathering of bishops from around the world to discuss issues proposed by the Pope. Several meetings of the Synod were held under Paul VI, including one on evangelisation which led to his Apostolic Exhortation *Evangelii nuntiandi* in 1975.

The reform of the Roman Curia was another of Pope Paul VI's accomplishments. Having worked in the Curia for more than thirty years, he understood it well and, in a number of stages, he reduced its bureaucracy, streamlined the existing congregations and other bodies, and brought about a broader representation of non-Italians in it.

The reform of the liturgy was still another very important contribution of Pope Paul VI. A new Roman Missal was introduced in 1969, with four Eucharistic Prayers instead of the former one. This was followed by a new Lectionary, with a much broader selection of readings from Scripture.

Paul VI was the first Pope to make pastoral visits to other countries, including the Philippines and Australia in 1970 and the Holy Land in 1974.

Pope St Paul VI died on 6 August 1978, the feast of the Transfiguration. He was canonised by Pope Francis on 14 October 2018 and his feast day is 29 May, the day of his priestly ordination.

892 Blessed Alexandrina da Costa

A friend recently told me about a Portuguese mystic, Blessed Alexandrina da Costa, who supposedly survived only on the Eucharist for some years. Is this true?

It is true, surprising though it may seem. We should always remember that events like this are miraculous, since the human body needs more than the Eucharist to obtain all the nutrients it needs to survive and be healthy. But who was this mystic?

Alexandrina Maria was born on 30 March 1904 in Balasar, Portugal. She received a solid Christian education from her mother and her sister, Deolinda, her father having left when she was very young. Her lively nature made her likeable to everyone and her unusual physical strength enabled her to do long hours of heavy farm work in the fields.

When she was twelve, Alexandrina became sick with an infection and nearly died. The consequences of this infection would remain with her as she grew up and would become the first sign of what God was asking of her: to suffer as a "victim soul".

When Alexandrina was fourteen, while she sewing one day with her sister Deolinda and a young apprentice, three men broke into their home and attempted to sexually assault them. To preserve her purity, Alexandrina jumped from a window, falling four metres to the ground and breaking her spine, leading to paralysis. For the next five years Alexandrina had to drag herself to church where, hunched over, she would remain in prayer, to the great amazement of everyone. With her paralysis and pain worsening, however, from 14 April 1925 until her death thirty years later she had to remain bedridden, completely paralysed.

Alexandrina prayed to Our Lady for the grace of a miraculous healing, promising to become a missionary if she were healed. Little by little, however, God helped her to see that suffering was to be her vocation and that she had a special call to be the Lord's "victim". The more she understood that this was her mission, the more willingly she embraced it. She said: "Our Lady has given me an even greater grace: first, abandonment; then, complete conformity to God's will; finally, the thirst for suffering". She understood that she was called to open the eyes of others to the effects of sin, inviting them to conversion, and to be a living witness of Christ's passion, contributing to the redemption of humanity.

From 3 October 1938 until 24 March 1942, Alexandrina lived the three-hour "passion" of Jesus every Friday, experiencing in body and soul Christ's suffering in his final hours. During these hours, her paralysis was in some way overcome, and she would relive the Stations of the Cross, her movements and gestures accompanied by excruciating pain. She was also assaulted by the devil, tormented with temptations against the faith and with physical injuries. Added to her physical suffering was the misunderstanding of priests, including her spiritual director and the Archbishop of Braga. Finally, in 1944, a Salesian priest, Fr Umberto Pasquale, came to her aid.

After December 1938, Alexandrina corresponded regularly with Sr Lucia Santos, then a Carmelite nun who, together with her cousins Francisco and Jacinta Marto, had seen Our Lady at Fatima in 1917. In 1944, she joined the "Union of Salesian Cooperators", offering her suffering for the salvation of souls and for the sanctification of young people.

From 27 March 1942 until her death thirteen years later, Alexandrina received no nourishment of any kind except the Holy Eucharist. Her weight dropped to as little as 33 kilos. The medical doctors who examined her, did so in a cold and hostile way, only increasing her suffering. But she was consoled by Jesus telling her: "You will very rarely receive consolation... I want that while your heart is filled with suffering, on your lips there is a smile". As a result, in spite of her physical suffering, she was always outwardly joyful and smiling, radiating peace to all who visited her.

Alexandrina died on 13 October 1955. Her last words were: "I am happy, because I am going to heaven". She was beatified on 25 April 2004 in St Peter's Square by St John Paul II.

893 Blessed Franz Jägerstätter

I recently saw the inspiring film A Hidden Life *about Franz Jägerstätter, an Austrian who refused to take the oath of allegiance to Hitler during the Second World War and was put to death for it. Can you tell me more about this man?*

Franz Jägerstätter was born on 20 May 1907 in St Radegund in Upper Austria. His mother was unmarried at the time and he was given the name Franz, after his father. After his father was killed in the First World War, his mother married Heinrich Jägerstätter, who adopted Franz as his son.

Franz received a basic education in his village's one-room schoolhouse. After school he worked as a farmhand and also as a miner. He was somewhat unruly in his younger years and in 1933 he fathered an out-of-wedlock daughter. In that year he inherited the farmstead of his foster-father. He was generally known as an ordinary Catholic who did not draw attention to himself.

In 1936 Franz married his wife Franziska, a deeply religious woman, and their marriage produced three daughters. In addition to working on his farm, Franz was the sacristan of the parish. Inspired by Franziska, he studied the Bible and the lives of the saints, and he began to attend Mass and receive Holy Communion daily.

When German troops moved into Austria in March 1938, Franz was offered the position of mayor of St Radegund, but he declined it. The following month he was the only person in the village to vote against the Anschluss, the annexation of Austria by Germany, choosing to follow his conscience rather than go along with the majority. He became ever more anchored in his Catholic faith and put his complete trust in God. In 1940 he joined the Third Order of St Francis.

Although he was not involved with any political or resistance organisation, he remained openly anti-Nazi. He had a brief period of military training but was not immediately called into active service, his service being deferred four times. He knew that if he was called up he would, in conscience, have to refuse to take the oath of loyalty to Hitler. Finally, in October 1940, he was conscripted into the German Wehrmacht. He did his training in the garrison at Enns but was able to return home in 1941 with an exemption as a farmer.

With his experience in the military, the attacks on the Church and reports of the Nazi euthanasia program, he seriously questioned the morality of the war. He went to Linz to discuss this with his bishop but was saddened by the bishop's reluctance to confront the issues.

After many delays, he was finally called to active duty in February 1943. At that time the oldest of his three daughters was just six. Once again in the garrison of Enns, he declared his conscientious objection to fighting in the war and he offered to serve as a paramedic. The offer was turned down. He was immediately arrested and placed in custody, first in Linz and then, in early May, in Berlin-Tegel. A priest from St Radegund visited him in jail and tried to talk him into serving, but Franz had made up his mind and refused to do so. When he heard the fate of the Austrian priest Fr Franz Reinisch, who had been executed for refusing to take the Hitler oath, he was determined to follow his example.

In a military trial, on July 6 Franz was found guilty of sedition and was sentenced to death. On 9 August 1943 he was executed by guillotine in the Brandenburg-Görden prison at the age of 36. Shortly before his death he wrote: "If I must write ... with my hands in chains, I find that much better than if my will were in chains. Neither prison nor chains nor sentence of death can rob a man of the faith and his free will. God gives so much strength that it is possible to bear any suffering.... People worry about the obligations of conscience as they concern my wife and children. But I cannot believe that, just because one has a wife and children, a man is free to offend God". After the war, in 1946, his ashes were buried in the St Radegund cemetery.

In June 2007 Pope Benedict XVI declared Franz Jägerstätter a martyr and on 26 October of that year he was beatified by Cardinal José Saraiva Martins in the cathedral of Linz. His wife and daughters were present for the ceremony. Franziska died in 2013, two weeks after turning one hundred.

Franz's feast day is 21 May, the day of his Baptism.

894 Venerable Jérôme Lejeune

My doctor, who is a Catholic, has named his practice after Jérôme Lejeune, who, I believe, has been declared Venerable by the Church. Who was he?

Jérôme Lejeune was a French paediatrician and geneticist who was a champion of human life at all ages and who, among other things, was famous for discovering the cause of Down Syndrome. He visited Australia several times and I had the joy of hearing him speak at Warrane College at the University of New South Wales in the 1970s. His daughter Clara has written a biography of him, titled Life is a Blessing, published by Ignatius Press in 2000.

Lejeune was born on 13 June 1926 in Paris, into a middle-class family. He studied medicine, graduating in 1951. He then took up work with Professor Raymond Turpin at the National Centre of Scientific Research, doing research into the cause of Down Syndrome.

In 1952 he married Birthe Bringsted, a Danish lady who had gone to work in Paris as an au paire. Brought up a Lutheran, Birthe became a Catholic shortly before their wedding. They had five children together and Lejeune was ever a devoted father to them and a loving husband, writing to Birthe every day he was away.

In 1958, using a photomicroscope which he had invented to photograph cells, he discovered that the cause of Down Syndrome was a third chromosome 21, a condition known thereafter as Trisomy 21. He liked to say that people with Down Syndrome had something more, not less.

After that discovery, Lejeune was awarded numerous prizes and membership in international academies and institutions. Among the prizes was the Kennedy Prize, which he received directly from President John F. Kennedy in Washington.

In 1964 Dr Lejeune was made the first ever Professor of Fundamental Genetics in the Faculty of Medicine in Paris. In 1965 he became Head of the Cytogenetics Unit at the Necker Children's Hospital in Paris, where he investigated with his team over 30,000 chromosome cases and treated more than 9000 people with intellectual disorders.

In 1969 the American Society of Human Genetics awarded Lejeune its highest distinction, the William Allen Memorial Award. In his acceptance speech in San Francisco, he challenged his audience to consider whether a mass of cells in the womb of its mother was a human being or not, and whether it should be rejected if it did not meet our expectations, or rather it should be protected in all possible ways. He said that it troubled him that his discovery would lead to many of these embryos being aborted. Some of the audience applauded politely while others stood up and booed.

Thereafter Lejeune became an enemy of the left, and of many others in the medical and scientific communities, for his defence of life and his opposition to abortion and contraception. His daughter Clara wrote in her book: "Here is a man who, because of his convictions ... was banned from society, dropped by his friends, humiliated, crucified by the press, prevented from working for lack of funding ... He lived his faith ... and from it he drew courage, kindness, attentiveness to others, and above all, what was most striking: the absence of fear."

In 1974 Pope St Paul VI named Lejeune a member of the Pontifical Academy of Sciences, a title which he regarded as one of his most important. In 1981, Lejeune and his wife Birthe had lunch with Pope St John Paul II on 13 May, the day on which just a few hours later the Pope survived an assassination attempt. And in 1993 Pope John Paul II asked Dr Lejeune to draft the statutes for the new Pontifical Academy for Life. The Academy was founded on 11 February 1994, and on 26 February Dr Lejeune became its first President. He knew he was suffering from advanced cancer and less than two months later, on Easter Sunday, 3 April, he died.

His cause of beatification and canonisation was opened in Paris in 2007 and, on 21 January 2021, Pope Francis approved the decree of his heroic virtues, making him the Venerable Jérôme Lejeune.

Among his sayings was: "The enemies of life know that to destroy a civilisation, they must first destroy the family at its weakest point – the child". He was truly a remarkable man.

895 Blessed Carlo Acutis

I was happy to hear of Carlo Acutis' recent beatification, especially since he was so young. To have his holiness recognised by the Church, he must have done much in his short life. Can you tell me something about what he did?

The whole Church, and especially millennials, rejoiced at the beatification of this young man, who died in 2006 at the age of only 15. Although of Italian background, Carlo was born in London in May, 1991, to wealthy parents Andrea and Antonia. In September of that year the family settled in Milan, where Carlo grew up.

Although his parents were not very religious, Carlo showed a great interest in the faith from an early age, asking many questions, which were answered by the family's Polish baby-sitter. At the age of seven he asked to make his First Communion and was allowed to do so. After that he went to Mass every day and he prayed before the tabernacle either before or after Mass.

He said the rosary every day and he went to confession every week. His great passion was for the Eucharist, which he called his "highway to heaven." This led to his mother's conversion, from someone who had gone to Mass only a few times in her life to one who went regularly. Carlo wrote: "Someone who goes out in the sun becomes tanned, but when he goes before Jesus in the Eucharist he becomes holy." At the age of seven he wrote: "To be always united with Jesus, this is the program of my life."

Carlo was a very normal boy, handsome and popular, a natural jokester who enjoyed making his classmates and teachers laugh. He wrote in his notebook: "Sadness is looking at oneself, happiness is looking at God." He loved to play soccer, he played the saxophone, and he liked films, comic editing and playing PlayStation. Like many other young people, he was fond of Nutella and ice cream but he learned to dominate his desire for them through the virtue of temperance. He would say: "What's the use of winning a thousand battles if you can't beat your own passions?" Not wanting to give his family's cleaners extra work, he would rise early to make his bed and tidy up his room. Raejsh, a Hindu who did the cleaning, was impressed that someone "as handsome, young and rich" wanted to live such a simple life. Through Carlo's example, Raejsh became a Catholic.

As he grew older, Carlo became worried about his friends whose parents were divorcing and he invited them home to support them. He defended children with disabilities at school who were being bullied, and he did voluntary work with the homeless and destitute. He used his first savings to buy a sleeping bag for a homeless man he often saw on the way to Mass. His funeral was packed with many poor people whom Carlo had helped during his short life.

The virtue of chastity was very important for Carlo. He used to say: "Each person reflects the light of God" and it hurt him when his classmates did not live according to Christian morals. He would encourage them to live this virtue by helping them understand that the human body is a gift from God and that sexuality has to be lived as God intended.

He was considered a "computer geek" by those around him on account of his great skill with computers and the internet. At the age of eleven he began creating a website of Eucharistic miracles from around the world, completing it in 2005, a year before his death. On the website he wrote: "The more often we receive the Eucharist, the more we become like Jesus, so that on this earth we will have a foretaste of heaven."

In the autumn of 2006 Carlo was diagnosed with Acute Myeloid Leukemia, one of the worst types of the disease. When told of his illness, he said: "I offer to the Lord the sufferings that I will have to undergo for the Pope and for the Church, so as not to have to be in purgatory and be able to go directly to heaven." He also commented: "I'm happy to die because I've lived my life without wasting even a minute of it doing things that wouldn't have pleased God". One of his famous sayings was: "Everyone is born an original but many die like photocopies". Carlo died an original, on 12 October 2006. The call for his beatification began a short time later and he was beatified on 10 October 2020. Remarkably, his mother prayed to him to have more children and she gave birth to twins at the age of 44, exactly four years to the day after his death.

896 St José Sánchez del Río

I was fascinated by your account of the life of the young Blessed Carlo Acutis. Are there any other young people who have been beatified or canonised in recent times?

While the beatification of Carlo Acutis received a lot of publicity, another young saint who managed to slip largely under the radar is José

Sánchez del Río, a Mexican boy who was martyred in 1928 at the age of only fourteen and was canonised in 2016 by Pope Francis.

José was born on 28 March 1913 in Sahuayo in the state of Michoacán, the third of four children. He loved his faith and had a strong devotion to Our Lady of Guadalupe (cf. J. Flader, *Question Time 4*, q. 596).

When he was only twelve the Mexican government, in accordance with the anti-clerical laws written into the Mexican Constitution, began eliminating Church privileges and seizing Church property throughout the country. They closed religious schools and convents and exiled or killed many priests. This led to the so-called Cristero War, when Catholics rose up to defend their rights. When the war broke out in 1926, José's brothers joined the Cristeros but his mother would not let him take part. The Cristero general, Prudencio Mendoza, also refused to let such a young boy enlist. José insisted that he wanted the chance to give his life for Jesus Christ and go to heaven.

The general finally gave in and allowed José to be the flagbearer of the troops. The soldiers nicknamed him Tarcisius, after the early Christian saint who gave his life in order to protect the Blessed Eucharist from profanation (cf. q. 876). During heavy fighting on 25 January 1928, General Mendoza's horse was killed and José gave him his own horse so that he could go on fighting. José then sought cover and fired at the enemy troops until he ran out of ammunition. He was captured by the government troops and imprisoned in the sacristy of the local church.

The troops ordered him to renounce his Catholic faith under threat of death, but he refused. To break his resolve the soldiers made him watch the hanging of another Cristero, but José only encouraged the man, saying that they would soon meet up again in heaven. In prison José prayed the rosary every day and wrote an emotional letter to his mother, telling her that he was ready to fulfil the will of God, to whom he had dedicated himself. His father attempted to raise a ransom to save him, but he was not able to appease the government in time to save José's life.

According to two childhood friends, who witnessed José's death, on the night of 10 February 1928 the soldiers cut the bottom of his feet and obliged him to walk through the town toward the cemetery. They also cut him with a machete until he was bleeding from several wounds. He moaned with pain, but did not give in. It was his own Way of the Cross and the cemetery would be his Calvary. He shared in Christ's passion and death, offering himself for the good of others and the love of God. As he walked, he recited the rosary, prayed for his enemies and sang songs to Our Lady of Guadalupe. Several times they told him, "If you shout, 'Death to Christ the King' we will spare your life" but José answered, "I will never give in. Long live Christ the King and Our Lady of Guadalupe!"

At the cemetery the soldiers stabbed him repeatedly with their bayonets, but their commander spared José an agonising death and shot him. Just before dying José traced a cross in the dirt and kissed it. He was only fourteen. His remains are enshrined above a side altar in the church of St James the Apostle in his home town of Sahuayo.

José was declared Venerable by St John Paul II in 2004 and was beatified by order of Pope Benedict XVI in Guadalajara, Mexico, in 2005. A miracle attributed to his intercession involved the inexplicable recovery of a Mexican baby who doctors had said had no hope of survival. This paved the way for his canonisation in Rome by Pope Francis on 16 October 2016.

José's feast day is 10 February, the day of his death. He is a great model for young people in standing up for the faith in spite of opposition.

José is one of the characters portrayed in the film *For Greater Glory*, which depicts the story of the Cristero War.

897 Saints Francisco and Jacinta Marto

With your accounts of young saints, what can you tell me about the two young children who saw Our Lady at Fátima and died shortly afterwards?

The children were Francisco and Jacinta Marto who, along with their cousin Lúcia dos Santos, saw Our Lady at Fátima, Portugal, in 1917.

Francisco and his younger sister Jacinta were just nine and seven years of age when Our Lady appeared to them. Lúcia, their cousin, was ten. All three were from Aljustrel, a little village near Fátima. Like other children growing up in the country at that time, Francisco and Jacinta could not read or write. Much of their time was spent minding the family's sheep on the hillsides near their home. At the same time, they had a deep faith and love for God, and they prayed the rosary every day.

Francisco had a placid disposition and liked to be by himself to think. After seeing Our Lady, he especially preferred to pray on his own, saying this would "console Jesus for the sins of the world." He prayed for hours on end. Jacinta was more outgoing, with a sweet singing voice and a gift for dancing. Deeply affected by the vision of hell which the children saw in the third apparition, she was convinced of the need to do all she could to save sinners through penance.

All three children wore a rough rope around their waist inside their clothing as a form of penance so they could offer this sacrifice for sinners. They wore it day and night until Our Lady told them Jesus did not want them to wear it at night. The Congregation for the Causes of Saints, in the report that confirmed Jacinta's beatification, said she seemed to have an "insatiable hunger for immolation."

The children were also very generous with the poor, even though they were poor themselves. When they were out in the fields, if they came across children who were poorer than they were, they would give them their own lunches. This caused them to experience considerable hunger and Francisco often had severe headaches as a result. But he would offer his headaches for the conversion of sinners.

In one of the apparitions Our Lady said that she would take Francisco and Jacinta to heaven soon, but that Lúcia would remain on earth. In fact, those two became victims of the influenza epidemic that swept through Europe in 1918. Even though they were very sick they insisted on walking to church for Eucharistic devotions. They would kneel with their heads on the ground, as they said the angel had instructed them to do.

When he seemed to be close to death, Francisco refused to go to hospital and he died at home the next day, 4 April 1919. When Jacinta's state worsened dramatically, she was taken to hospital in the nearby town of Ourém in an effort to save her life, even though she insisted that this was futile. When her condition worsened, her parents wanted to take her to the children's hospital in Lisbon, which at that time admitted only children from the city, so they took her first to the small orphanage of Our Lady of Miracles in Lisbon.

There she developed purulent pleurisy and underwent an operation in which two of her ribs were removed. Because of the weakened condition of her heart, she could not be fully anaesthetised and she suffered terrible pain, which she offered for the conversion of sinners. On 19 February 1920 she asked the chaplain to bring her Holy Communion and give her the Anointing of the Sick because she was going to die that night. He told her she was not that ill and he would return the next day. By the next morning she had died, alone as she said she would.

The two young saints were beatified together by Pope St John Paul II on 13 May 2000, the anniversary of the first apparition of Our Lady. Pope Francis canonised them in Fátima on the centenary of the first apparition, 13 May 2017. They are the youngest saints not to have died as martyrs.

898 A new pathway to canonisation

I understand that Pope Francis has approved a new pathway to canonisation. Can you tell me what it is?

In 2017 Pope Francis introduced a new pathway to beatification and canonisation, complementing the three traditional ones. The traditional pathways are martyrdom, a life of heroic virtues and a less commonly used one of widespread fame of sanctity such that the Pope can waive the usual lengthy formal investigation and authorise veneration of the person as a saint.

The new pathway amounts to the offering of one's life in service to others. It was proclaimed by Pope Francis on 11 July 2017 in the Apostolic Letter *Maiorem hac dilectionem*. The title comes from Our Lord's words "Greater love has no man than this, that a man lay down his life for his friends" (Jn 15:13).

On introducing the document, Archbishop Marcello Bartolucci, secretary of the Vatican's Congregation for the Causes of Saints, said the new pathway was meant "to promote heroic Christian testimony, up to now without a specific process, precisely because it did not completely fit within the case of martyrdom or heroic virtues."

The Pope's Apostolic Letter establishes that, for the offering of one's life to be effective for beatification, five criteria must be met.

First, there must be a free and voluntary offering of life and heroic acceptance propter caritatem, moved by charity, of a certain and untimely death.

Second, there must be a connection between the offering of life and premature death.

Third, there must be the exercise, at least as far as ordinarily possible, of Christian virtues before the offering of life, and then until death.

Fourth, there must be a reputation of holiness and of signs of holiness, at least after death.

Fifth, a miracle is required for beatification, occurring after the death of the Servant of God and through his or her intercession.

The document does not speak of a second miracle being required for canonisation, as is the case when a person is canonised for having lived heroic virtues. Thus the new pathway is seen as a middle ground between the cause of martyrs, where a miracle is required only for canonisation, and that of those who lived heroic virtues, where two miracles are required, one each for beatification and canonisation.

Commentators have suggested the names of two persons whose causes might proceed following the new pathway.

One is the Venerable Edel Quinn, whose heroic virtues have already been recognised. She was born in Ireland in 1907 and, in spite of having contracted tuberculosis, joined the Legion of Mary at the age of 20, dedicating herself to helping the poor in the slums of Dublin. In 1936 and very ill with tuberculosis, she went as a Legion Envoy to Kenya, where she settled and did missionary work all over East and Central Africa, establishing Legion branches in Kenya, Tanzania, Uganda, Malawi and Mauritius. She died of tuberculosis in Nairobi in May 1944 and was declared Venerable by Pope John Paul II in December 1994.

Another is the Irish Jesuit Fr Willie Doyle. The youngest of seven children, Fr Doyle was ordained a Jesuit priest in 1907 and served as a military chaplain with the Royal Dublin Fusiliers during the First World War. He was killed on 16 August 1917 in the battle of Langemarck while rescuing wounded soldiers and his body was never recovered. His cause of beatification and canonisation was proposed in 1938 but was not followed through.

Having offered to serve as a military chaplain, Fr Doyle wrote in November 1914: "My offering myself as war chaplain to the Provincial has had a wonderful effect on me. I long to go and shed my blood for Jesus, and, if He wills it, to die a martyr of charity. The thought that at any moment I may be called to the Front, perhaps to die, has roused a great desire to do all I can while I have life. I feel great strength to make any sacrifice and little difficulty in doing so. I may not have long now to prove my love for Jesus."

There can be no doubt of Fr Doyle's willingness to accept death for the sake of charity.

Apparitions of Our Lady

899 Apparitions of Mary in the Ukraine

With the present war going on in the Ukraine, I was happy to hear from a friend that Our Lady has appeared several times in that country. If this is true, can you tell me when she appeared and what, if any, were her messages?

Our Lady did appear in the Ukraine, on several occasions. But first, it is interesting to note that Ukraine, or Kyivan Rus as it was at the time, was the first European nation to be dedicated to Our Lady, by Prince Yaroslav the Wise in 1037.

On 12 May 1914, Our Lady appeared in the village of Hrushiv, some eighty-five kilometres northwest of Lviv near the Polish border. She was seen near the local church of the Blessed Trinity by twenty-two people who were mowing the fields at the time. People gathered from the entire area to see the apparition, which lasted into the next day.

The people of Hrushiv had planted a weeping willow tree at the site many years before to commemorate an appearance of Our Lady some 350 years earlier. Later, a spring suddenly appeared beneath the tree. During the severe cholera epidemic of 1855, one of the villagers dreamed that the Blessed Virgin had instructed the residents to clear and reclaim the ancient spring and hold Mass there. The Mass was celebrated and not one cholera death was reported afterwards.

In the 1914 apparition Our Lady told the people: "There will be a war. Russia will become a godless country. The Ukraine, as a nation, will suffer terribly for eighty years and will have to live through the world wars, but it will be free afterwards." All of this came to pass.

The First World War began two months later, on 28 July. Russia became a godless country following the Bolshevik Revolution of 1917 and the atheist, communist, leaders of Russia inflicted terrible suffering on the people of Ukraine. There was the Holodomor in 1922-23, during which some 3.5 million mainly ethnic Ukrainians were starved to death when the Soviet authorities confiscated all their household foodstuffs and prevented them from moving. Between the 1930s and 1950s millions more were arrested, sentenced and deported to the hard labour camps of the Gulag. There were also purges, the destruction of Ukrainian churches, both Orthodox and Catholic, and the devastation and suffering inflicted during the Second World War by both the Nazi and the Soviet armies. To this was added the Chernobyl nuclear power plant explosion on 26 April 1986. The prophecy that Ukraine would become free was borne out seventy-seven years after the apparition, when the country gained its independence from Moscow on 24 August 1991.

Then, on 26 April 1987, seventy-three years after the 1914 apparition and exactly one year to the day after the Chernobyl disaster, Our Lady appeared again in Hrushiv. She was seen in a bright light floating above the cupola of the church, and a television program was able to record part of the phenomenon.

Our Lady was first seen by 12-year-old Marina Kizyn. She immediately called her mother and a few neighbours, who all went and saw Mary. Soon, hundreds and then thousands came from all over Russia to see the apparitions, which continued every day until August 15. It is estimated that as many as 500,000 people saw her by the time the apparitions ended.

Amongst the many documented messages of Our Lady were the following: "I have come on purpose to thank the Ukrainian people because you have suffered most for the Church of Christ in the last seventy years. I have come to comfort you and to tell you that your suffering will soon come to an end. Ukraine will become an independent state." "Forgive your enemies. Through you and the blood of the martyrs will come the conversion of Russia. Repent and love one another.

"Say the rosary. It is the weapon against Satan. He fears the rosary. Recite the rosary at any gathering of people." "The Eternal God is calling you. This is why I have been sent to you. Throughout your long persecution you have not lost faith, hope, or love. I always pray for you, my dear children, wherever you are."

These words can bring hope and consolation to the people of the Ukraine in their present terrible suffering, and we can join them in praying to Our Lady for peace in that troubled land.

900 A recent apparition of Mary in the Ukraine

I have a friend from the Ukraine who said Our Lady appeared in that country in 2002. Is this true and, if so, can you tell me anything about it?

According to the reports, on 27 August 2002 two girls from the village of Nyzhne Bolotne, in western Ukraine, went to a grove to get some water from a spring. Olenka Kuruts was ten years old and her friend Mar'yanka Kobal was nine. Olenka looked up to see what she described as a "beautiful lady" standing some distance behind Mar'yanka. Mar'yanka also saw her. Because the lady did not say anything, they became frightened, thinking she might be a witch. The lady was standing on a small cloud adorned with flowers, just above the ground. She was wearing a white dress with a blue belt and a white headscarf. When the girls arrived home they told their parents.

Olenka's parents did not believe her story and they scolded her for wasting time on such foolishness. But Mar'yanka's father Petro was a Greek Catholic priest, and he cautioned the girls to be careful and always make the sign of the cross. Later that day, the girls went to pick up Olenka's sister from kindergarten and they saw the lady again. When they made the sign of the cross to protect themselves, the lady was pleased and smiled, making the sign of the cross too. The girls asked her who she was, and she told them she was "the most pure Virgin."

In later apparitions Our Lady said that she came to promote the authority of the priests among the people, to unite the Church, to bring together the Ukrainian people who were separated, and to promote more prayer. Mary asked that the priest inform the local Church authorities, particularly "the old Bishop Marhitych", who was the auxiliary bishop of Mukachevo.

The bishop was informed and he immediately went to the village to question the girls. He wanted to know if the lady could confirm her identity in some way, and the girls replied that when people started praying at the spring, confirmation would be given. On August 31 Bishop Marhitych held a religious service at the spring. He then supported and promoted the visions.

Word spread and soon many pilgrims from all over the Ukraine were going to the site in the hope of seeing a miracle. A chapel was built and people reported seeing Our Lady, some saying she was weeping and others also seeing the Holy Family. The cross standing in front of the chapel lost its gilding and blood appeared on it instead. A sample was sent to a laboratory, and tests revealed that it was truly blood. Many people said that they could look directly at the sun without damage to their eyes. Miracles were reported at the spring and some people smelled incense or roses, despite neither being visibly present.

Several weeks after the apparitions began, Olenka said she saw a man appear next to the priest during a Mass. She whispered to Mar'yanka, who also saw him. They described him as tall, with shoulder-length hair and a beard. There were wounds on his hands and he was very good looking. The girls both reported that he seemed to be conducting the service along with the priest, making the same gestures. Wondering if this was Jesus, they asked Our Lady at her next appearance, and she confirmed that it was Jesus.

Many people thought the girls must be making up a story, but the girls were healthy and normal, active in typical activities for their age, and they had no history of lying or telling tales.

On one occasion when Olenka kissed the feet of Jesus who appeared before her, she suddenly felt a sharp pain in her hands, feet, heart and head. She collapsed on the ground, spreading her arms out in the position of someone being crucified. She could not be lifted from the ground. A boy ran back to the village for help, returning with Father Atanasy Chiypesh and a watchman. They eventually got her home after sprinkling water on her face. Unable to speak, she wrote that she would not be able to attend school during Lent due to her inability to walk. Father Atanasy questioned her carefully, and she told him she had accepted an offer to suffer along with Jesus. The pains of the stigmata lasted for some time, but then ceased.

At present there is a monastery of the Holy Family on the site, as requested by Our Lady. On the 27th of each month busloads of pilgrims arrive, and each year on August 27 the anniversary is celebrated with fireworks. Clearly, belief in the apparitions is well established.

INDEX

abortion 78, 164-5, 188-90, 217, 225, 240, 311
Acutis, Blessed Carlo 311-3
Alexander the Great 64-5
Alexandrina da Costa, Blessed 305-7
Ambrose St 29, 73
Amoris laetitia 196-8
angels 18, 24, 72-3, 86, 104, 106, 113, 139, 258-61, 265
    Guardian 94-6
    hierarchy of 90-2
    knowledge of 92-4
Aquinas, St Thomas 4, 8, 24, 42, 91-2, 111, 113, 117, 155, 162, 168, 260
Athanasius, St 73, 269
Augustine, St 4-5, 25, 73, 110-1, 117, 125, 162

Baptism 42, 44-5, 84, 163, 165, 176
    changing the formula of 116-8
    consequences of invalid 118-20
Basil the Great, St 269
Benedict XII 113
Benedict XV, Pope 2
Benedict XVI, Pope 38, 74, 76, 78, 87, 136, 145-6, 269, 272-3, 294, 309, 315
Bernadine of Siena, St 108
Bonaventure, St 96

Calasanz, St Joseph 286-8

Calloway, Fr Donald 253
Camillus de Lellis, St 282-4
canonisation, new pathway 317-9
Champions of the Rosary 253
Chrysostom, St John 29, 73
Christ, Jesus
    Ascension 85, 109, 112-4
    Messiah 20-1, 83
    Redemption 24-5
Christadelphians 82-4
Christus vivit 182-3
Claver, St Peter 288-90
Communion, Holy 128, 138-40, 142, 174-5, 181, 196, 299, 302, 308, 317
    age for First Communion 152
    divorced receiving 160-2
    mentally impaired receiving 162-3
    under both species 156
    President Biden and 164-6
    Protestants receiving 158-9
    Spiritual Communion 166-8
Constantine 29-31, 33, 37, 68, 70-1, 264, 267
Corona, St 170-1
Covid-19 139, 164
    bright side of isolation 222-3
    restrictions 139
    vaccinations 216-20
Cupertino, St Joseph of 290-2
Cyril of Jerusalem, St 29, 134

Damascene, St John 104-5

deacons, women 175-7
Dei verbum 1, 7-8
Desert Fathers 268-70
Desiderio desideravi 128, 130-1
dying
    attending the 226-8
    pastoral care of 244-6

Ecclesia Dei 144
Ecclesia de Eucharistia 166
Emmerich, Blessed Anne Catherine 296-8
Escrivá, St Josemaría 16, 124, 128, 167, 187, 258
Eucharistic miracle, Legnica 168-70
eugenics 78-80
euthanasia 79-80, 224ff, 308
    advanced directives and 242-4
    cooperation in 240-2
    defending Church teaching on 224-5
    financial pressure and 238-40
    legal in which countries 230-2
    medical care at end of life 232-4
    why the call for 228-30
Evangelii gaudium 75, 131
Evangelium vitae 231
excommunication 160, 165, 188-90

Fatima 307
forgiveness 36, 119, 138, 172, 174, 184-6, 293, 302
Francis, Pope 69, 74-5, 89, 116, 128, 130-1, 141, 143-6, 159, 164, 171, 173, 181-3, 192, 194-7, 228, 230, 263-5, 268, 275, 305, 311, 314-5, 317-8
Francis de Sales, St 108, 255, 299
Freemasons 80-1

Gaudete et Exsultate 181
gender transition 208
    children, assisting the transition of 207-8
    Church and 205-6
    conversion therapy legislation 209-10
    conversion therapy testimony 211-12
    gender dysphoria, treating 203-4
    gender terminology 213-5
General Instruction of the Roman Missal 134, 142
Goretti, St Maria 301-3
Gravissimum educationis 199
Gregory of Tours, St 104, 106
Gregory the Great, St 31, 265, 267

Helena, St 28-31, 33, 264, 267
Herod
    Agrippa I 59-61, 63
    Agrippa II 61
    Antipas 57-8
    Archelaus 55-6
    Herod the Great 53-4
    Philip the Tetrarch 61-2
holiness, call to 180-2
Holy Hour 249
    Archbishop Fulton Sheen and 248-50
    priests and 250-2

INDEX

Imitation of Christ, The 277-9
inspiration, of Scripture 1-2

Jägerstätter, Blessed Franz 307-9
Januarius, St 274-5
Jerome, St 4, 110-1
John Cassian, St 269
John Chrysostom, St 29, 73
John Paul II, Pope St 38, 71, 136, 144-6, 166, 1173-4, 180-1, 195, 231-2, 237, 294, 298, 303, 307, 311, 315, 317, 319
John XIII, Pope St 109, 144-6, 296, 303-4
Joseph, St
   Assumption into heaven 107-9
   betrothal 97-9
   Seven Sundays of 261-3
   wedding 99-100
Josephus, Flavius 56, 62

Kateri Tekakwitha, St 292-4
Kempis, Thomas à 277-9
kinesiology 190-2

Lejeune, Venerable Jérôme 309-11
Lydwine of Schiedam, St 275-7

Marto, Saints Francisco and Jacinta 315-7
Mary, Blessed Virgin
   apparitions in Uktaine 320-4
   Assumption 103-7
   betrothal 97-9
   devotion to 255, 276, 291
   icon of 263-5

Immaculate Conception 103, 109, 300
Our Lady of the Snows 266-7
wedding 99-100
wedding ring 101-3
Mass, Holy
   as sacrifice 121-2
   care in 131-2
   changing words of Consecration 135-6
   centre of all activity 127-8
   fragments of host in 133-4
   intentions 125-6
   Latin Mass 143-6
   Martin Luther on 147-51
   offering for intentions 123-4
   on-line Masses 139-40
   priest in 129-30
   Supper of the Lamb 137-8
   women acolytes and lectors 141-2
Memorare 254-7
Ministeria quaedam 142
Mormons 84-6

Neri, St Philip 284-6
Nicholas of Flüe, St 279-81

Ott, Ludwig 112

patience 186-8
Paul VI, Pope St 69, 75, 142, 144-5, 157, 173, 296, 303-5, 311
Pell, Cardinal George 87-8
Penance, sacrament of 152, 245
   repentance and absolution 171-3
   Third Rite 173-5

Pius IX, Pope 261, 275 300
Pius V, Pope St 70, 105, 144, 258, 267, 285
Pius XII, Pope 30, 37-8, 44-5, 103, 248, 281, 288, 300, 303
Plenary Council 2020 173
Pontifical Biblical Commission 4, 6, 9
Providentissimus Deus 2, 4-6
Pseudo-Dionysius 91

redemption 24-5, 27, 112, 121, 237, 249, 306
Redemptionis sacramentum 136-7
Rosary 105, 124, 164, 184, 222, 250, 252-4, 267, 280, 312, 314-6, 321

Sacrosanctum concilium 117, 157
Salvation is from the Jews 20, 26, 43, 45, 67, 76
Samaritanus bonus 224, 226, 228, 232, 235, 241, 243-4
same-sex attraction
    children with 192-4
        Pope Francis and civil unions 194-6
Sanchez del Rio, St José 313-5
Savio, St Dominic 298-300
Schneider, Bishop Athanasius 81
Scripture, Sacred 1-6, 90, 295
    inspiration 1-2

interpretation 5-6
literary forms 7-8
translations 11-12
truthfulness 3-4
Second Vatican Council 7-8, 118, 113, 117, 135-6, 142, 144-6, 157, 180, 199, 304
Seton, St Elizabeth Ann 294-6
Sheen, Archbishop Fulton 248-51
Schoeman, Roy 20, 26, 43-5, 47, 76
Shroud, of Turin 36
Spiritus Domini 141
Spiritus Paraclitus 2
suffering
    sharing suffering with others 234-6
    finding meaning in 236-8
Summorum Pontificum 145-6
synagogue 39, 45, 51-3, 64, 139

Talmud 27
Tarcisius, St 272-3
Traditionis custodes 143-6
Trent, Council of 111, 122-3, 144, 149, 152, 156-7, 172

vaccinations 215
    Covid-19 morality of vaccinations 216-8
    mandatory 218-20
vocation, discerning 182-4

www.ingramcontent.com/pod-product-compliance
Lightning Source LLC
Chambersburg PA
CBHW050201240426
43671CB00013B/2200